W9-CPD-424

Anger Management and Violence Prevention

A Group Activities Manual for Middle and High School Students

Teresa Schmidt, LCSW, BCD

JOHNSON INSTITUTE®

HAZELDEN®

ANGER MANAGEMENT AND VIOLENCE PREVENTION
A Group Activities Manual for Middle and High School Students

Copyright © 1993 Hazelden Foundation. Previously published 1993 by the
Johnson Institute-QVS, Inc. First published 1998 by Hazelden. All rights reserved.
No portion of this book, except designated student materials and teacher visual aids,
may be reproduced mechanically, electronically, or by any other means, including
photocopying, without written permission of the publisher:

Hazelden
15251 Pleasant Valley Road
Center City, MN 55012
651-213-4000 or 800-328-9000
www.hazelden.org
Library of Congress Cataloging-in-Publication Data

Schmidt, Teresa M.
     Anger management and violence prevention: a group activities manual for middle
and high school students / by Teresa M. Schmidt.
          p.   cm.
     Includes bibliographical references (p. 000).
     ISBN 1-56246-084-6
     1. School violence — United States — Prevention. 2. Anger in adolescence —
United States. 3. Anger — Study and teaching (Secondary) — United States. 4. Activity
programs in education — United States. I. Title.
     LB3013.3.S35 1993
     371.5'8—dc20

                                                                                93-33424
                                                                                CIP

Cover and text design: Lindberg Design
Printed in the United States of America
99 / 5 4 3

C O N T E N T S

Acknowledgments

I would like to thank Thelma Spencer, Ed.D., with whom I collaborated to write *Peter the Puppy Talks About Chemical Dependence in the Family*, one of the books in the *Building Trust, Making Friends* series. *Anger Management and Violence Prevention* uses the format that Thelma and I developed in my living room over Christmas vacation in 1988, although the current work is solely my responsibility.

The middle school counselors of York County, Virginia, participated in the field testing of the first draft. Dr. Leslie Kaplan, who was at that time director of guidance of York County Public Schools, made that training possible. The administration, SAP staff, and guidance counselors of Avon High School and Avon Middle School, Avon, Indiana, also graciously provided opportunities for field testing the first draft.

I am grateful for the help and support of my family. My sons, Matthew and Thomas Schmidt, are always ready to provide consultation and support, and they have managed to reach adolescence at a time when the experience of mothering teenage boys became very useful. They have shown supreme patience over the past five years during which I wrote several structured support-group manuals. My husband, Wiltz Wagner, has inspired me to maintain high standards for these books, has taken me on the motorcycle rides which have kept everything in perspective, and has given much love and affection which have enhanced the current writing.

ABOUT THE AUTHOR

Teresa M. Schmidt, LCSW, BCD, has been a clinical social worker since 1970. A graduate of the College of William and Mary and the Smith College School for Social Work, Ms. Schmidt has had extensive experience in outpatient settings. Bringing her clinical experience in mental health to Newport News Public Schools, Newport News, Virginia, in 1987, she worked with Dr. Thelma Spencer to develop and implement in a school setting a prevention/intervention group program for children from chemically dependent families. Ms. Schmidt is co-author with Dr. Spencer of the *Building Trust, Making Friends* series: *Peter the Puppy Talks About Chemical Dependence in the Family; Tanya Talks About Chemical Dependence in the Family; Thomas Barker Talks About Divorce and Separation;* and *Della the Dinosaur Talks About Violence and Anger Management*. Ms. Schmidt currently lives in the cornfields of Indiana, where she maintains a private practice, consults with local school systems on leading support groups, and conducts training workshops for mental health and school professionals on the local, state, and national level.

Introduction

Adolescents live in an important transitional stage. They move from the sheltered home into an arena where peers and outsiders are increasingly more important than their family. They must deal with a number of developmental issues: they need to accept physical changes initiated by puberty, learn how to regulate their emotions, and deal with increasing advances in cognitive ability. Furthermore, they need to confront the growing importance of peer relationships and the reworking of family relationships, and they need to start creating an individual identity.

Imagine a group of adolescents who face these developmental issues in the best of all possible worlds. They have what current theorists call protective factors, factors that help them through these developmental issues. And, since they live in the best of all possible worlds, they have these protective factors on four levels. Theorists describe these levels in an ecological-integration framework: the personal, family, social, and societal levels. These students have pluses on the personal level: they are bright, attractive, and able to manage their emotions. They have good interpersonal skills and a sense of their ability to impact positively what happens to them. On the family level, they have parents who are stable role models and good economic providers. Their parents are able to provide the structure and nurturing that children need, without being either too permissive or too autocratic. They have not had to deal with the stresses of parental divorce, chemical dependence, or family violence. On the social level, these adolescents have good peer relationships, get along well with their grandparents, and are active in school, church, or community organizations. They live in clean, crime-free suburban or rural neighborhoods. Finally, on the societal level, these mythical adolescents live in a world that does not condone violence, either in the family or on the street. This world has solved the issues of racism, sexism, unemployment, and educational and economic inequality. It provides adequate medical and health care for all segments of society and supports families in their parenting responsibilities.

Unfortunately, average adolescents are far from these mythical teens. Typical adolescents are more likely to have encountered risk factors, in addition to protective factors, on all four levels of the ecological framework. On the personal level, adolescents may be victims of parental maltreatment; they may have low IQs and learning disabilities; they may be physically unattractive; they may be aggressive and violent in their interpersonal relationships. On the family level, they may experience parental divorce, chemical dependence, or violence. Their parents may be unemployed and unable to provide adequately for them. On the social level, they may be isolated and uninvolved in any school, church, or community activities; they may have no extended family or social network. Or they may live in a poor urban area near illegal markets like prostitution and drug dealing and look for their sense of community in a gang that thrives on violence. Or they may come from families where men beat their wives and have done so for several generations. And, on the societal level, they live in the United States in the 1990s, a time marked by cultural acceptance of family violence, ranging from parents disciplining children by spanking to wife beating; a time when a violent crime is committed every 17 seconds, according to the FBI's crime clock for 1991; a time when violence is seen daily on TV and in movies; and a time when many children and families experience social and economic inequalities, poverty, and inadequate health care.

As a helping professional—guidance counselor, school psychologist, school social worker, Student Assistance Program (SAP) worker, Core Team member, school nurse, teacher, or probation officer—you want to increase the protective factors, the positive tools for living that adolescents possess. You want to increase the protective buffers that adolescents have in their environment, as they face the developmental issues of their middle and high school years. You want to help them develop skills to deal with their anger in positive ways, as well as to deal with the stresses of their families. You want them to be part of the social support system that you provide for teens. You may also want to help change cultural values so that violence will not be condoned in society and individual responsibility and interpersonal support will be rewarded.

Anger Management and Violence Prevention: A Group Activities Manual for Middle and High

*School Students** has been developed to help caring professionals like you to intervene with at-risk adolescents. You will reach them on the social level, within the context of a group. Through the group, you will provide them with a social support system as they learn personal skills to manage their own emotions and to deal with the stresses and possible traumas they witness in their families.

This group activity manual is targeted for the adolescent who has risk factors on any of the four ecological levels—the personal, family, social, and societal levels. Appropriate members for the *Anger Management and Violence Prevention* group are the teen who is a frequent visitor to the office for aggressive behavior; the student who confides that her father slaps and chokes her mother; or the boy who wonders whether he will be considered a wimp if he practices nonviolence in his daily life.

Anger Management and Violence Prevention uses the same group model as the Building Trust, Making Friends series, *Peter the Puppy Talks About Chemical Dependence in the Family, Tanya Talks About Chemical Dependence in the Family, Thomas Barker Talks About Divorce and Separation,* and *Della the Dinosaur Talks About Violence and Anger Management.* That 11-session group model uses both clinical and educational theory to help elementary students from chemically dependent, divorced, or violent families, and middle school students from chemically dependent families.

This complete and easy-to-use manual contains all you need to lead a group of middle or high school students through *Anger Management and Violence Prevention.*

Part One provides guidelines and materials to help you initiate and implement a support-

---

* A companion manual called *Changing Families: A Group Activities Manual for Middle and High School Students* written by Teresa Schmidt, is also available from Johnson Institute (see page 218). *Changing Families* is designed to help students develop coping strategies for dealing with the stresses and issues in their changing home life due to divorce, separation, death, or remarriage.

Now available from Hazelden. Call us at 1-800-328-9000.

group program in your school or agency.

Part Two contains materials to help you understand current theories on adolescent development, facts and theories about violence and family violence, and the effects of family violence on children, especially adolescents.

Part Three contains the complete group guide for leading an *Anger Management and Violence Prevention* group. The group guide includes the objectives, necessary preparations, background information and guidelines, handouts, and detailed step-by-step plans for each of the 11 sessions.

Part Four contains support materials, a list of references and supplementary readings, and a list of important resources. This section will further help group leaders and other staff make the group process successful and rewarding for everyone involved.

Overall, this manual provides practical and creative ways to help adolescents clarify their views on violence and look at their own protective and risk factors on each level of the ecological framework. In theoretically correct and clinically sound ways, it teaches adolescents concrete problem-solving skills to use in anger situations and provides age-appropriate and relevant scenarios in which they can practice these skills. Females practice setting limits when faced with control, force, or unwanted sexual activity in dating relationships. Males practice saying no to peers who are encouraging them to engage in destructive activity. The manual also helps teens to correct their misconceptions about family violence and to solve problems that come up in peer and family relationships. Most importantly, the teens are encouraged to adopt the value that violence is not acceptable and to assume the personal responsibility never to use violence in their own lives.

Part One

Establishing
A Support-Group Program
for At-risk Students

A comprehensive support-group program offers groups for at-risk adolescents from separated, divorced, or stepfamilies, as well as from families experiencing chemical dependence or violence. This section provides information on implementing a group program—including a structured support group like *Anger Management and Violence Prevention*—in your school, agency, or other counseling setting. The section includes information on acquiring administrative support, recruiting and training staff, developing a referral network, screening candidates, and forming and scheduling groups. You will also find information on informed consent, confidentiality, and self-disclosure on the part of group leaders. The section will also point out effective ways to follow up on the individual, group, and system level.

Perhaps the most effective and practical setting to offer support groups for adolescents is in the school. This is the case for a variety of reasons. First, the families of many at-risk adolescents may be experiencing extreme stress: the stress of family violence, chemical dependence, separation or divorce, or the stress of being a stepfamily. Many families undergoing such stress are in a state of denial and don't seek professional help. Second, even families who aren't in denial often lack the ability or means to make use of professional help. Third, many professional helping facilities, such as treatment centers for chemical dependence or battered women's shelters, aren't equipped to work with children or adolescents. Fourth, the organizational structure of some helping facilities may not allow the professionals who do have the skills and training to deal with teens' access to them. Finally, the adolescents themselves may not be able to put their distress into words, may not know that help is available, or may not want to betray their families by admitting there is a problem and asking for help. Better than any other setting, schools are in a position to offer prevention services to the large number of at-risk adolescents who would otherwise never receive them.

Although schools may be able to reach the largest numbers of adolescents, a group program may be used in a variety of other settings as well: in mental health centers, in private practices, in battered women's shelters, in chemical dependence treatment centers that provide family services, and in agencies that serve troubled teenagers. After deciding where it will best fit in your school's (or agency's) situation, you must undertake the task of getting it started. The first step in doing that is gaining administrative support.

Gaining Administrative Support

If a school is to support a group program, the principal's backing is necessary. If principals establish student support groups as a priority, they will direct teachers to allow students to leave the classroom in order to participate. Likewise, principals will also be prepared to answer questions from hostile, resistant, or concerned parents, although such calls are rare. Principals, however, may feel that they're taking unnecessary risks by supporting groups for at-risk students, especially those from chemically dependent or violent families, and may not see any benefits for their school.

Offer an in-service for building administrators, teachers, and other staff. Increase their awareness of the needs and characteristics of at-risk adolescents. Describe how offering support groups will benefit the students, their families, the school, and the community. Describe the misconceptions that adolescents from at-risk families often have. Explain how the group will correct students' misconceptions, while allowing them to remain loyal to their families. Recount how adolescents who learn that they haven't caused, and can't be responsible for fixing, their family's problems will feel better about themselves, will perform better at school, and will be less likely to get into serious trouble either in school or in the community. Explain that learning coping strategies will help adolescents take better care of themselves. Point out that support groups generally help students develop more positive attitudes about themselves and, thus, about learning. School staff members will feel good about referring students to groups that really work. Good groups will give both administrators and classroom teachers more free time to do their jobs.

An in-service for the *Anger Management and Violence Prevention* group can serve several additional purposes. First, it will give a comprehensive look at the protective and risk factors on four ecological levels that influence a person to choose violent behavior. Second, it will help the audience become aware of six styles of expressing anger, and of the anger management steps and problem-solving skills to use in anger situations. It will take time for group members to change aggressive behavior. Their efforts will be enhanced if the entire school faculty and administrative team understand the importance of using anger management steps and problem-solving skills and can help the students apply them in actual anger situations. Third, many adults, even professionals, will benefit on a personal level and may use the steps and skills themselves.

If you're blessed with wholehearted administrative approval, it's still a good idea to provide in-service sessions for school personnel to acquaint them with the issues for at-risk adolescents. Design a simple presentation describing the purposes of offering a support-group program, the role of the group, and the dynamics of the group model. The better school staff understand the purposes of a group program, the better will be their acceptance and support.

Staffing and Training

The authorization to provide prevention and intervention services for at-risk adolescents can come from the superintendent or school board, in the form of drop-out prevention, substance abuse prevention, violence prevention, or services to at-risk children. A support-group program will be enhanced if implemented by and with trained personnel. Effective staff may include members of Student Assistance Programs and CORE Teams, social workers, psychologists, guidance counselors, chemical dependence counselors, nurses, Drug and Alcohol Resistance Education (DARE) officers, and teachers—all of whom can be trained to lead groups to help at-risk adolescents. Although you'll have to depend on the staffing patterns of your school or agency, keep in mind that the needs of the students will be better met if personnel from various helping professions work together—not engage in territorial battles—to provide services.

The better trained your personnel, the better they'll be able to meet the needs of at-risk adolescents. Training should include the following:

- information about the goals of the group program

- education on specific issues to be dealt with in the groups (chemical dependence, divorce and separation, or family violence)

- instruction on how to lead groups

- ongoing supervision

One training model for leading student support groups might require a three-hour graduate level course alcohol and other drugs or family violence, 20 hours of in-service, and 10 hours of supervised experience leading groups. Another model might consist of 15 hours of experiential in-service, during which staff members take turns leading and participating in the entire group program together. After this experience, they would be ready to co-lead a group with a certified worker. A third model might have a trainer provide staff development for new group leaders and in-services for school faculty at the beginning of the school year. The trainer then can assist new group leaders in developing referrals and screening potential group members. The trainer then leads a group, with a new leader observing. When the group is repeated during the second half of the school year, the new leader facilitates the group, with the trainer observing and providing supervision.

A fourth model meets the needs of professionals who are implementing this program by themselves. This model combines the expertise of different professionals as group co-leaders: for example, a teacher can co-lead a group with a chemical dependence counselor. The complementarity of skills, training, and experience will again better serve the needs of adolescents.

Finally, you can also check your local resources for facilities that provide training. These may include chemical dependence treatment facilities, state and local health organizations, colleges and universities, state departments of education, and social welfare agencies. You can also find help by turning to a national organization, such as the Johnson Institute, which specializes in training. (See Resources for Help on page 220.)

Developing Referrals

Once you've gained administrative support and have begun training leaders to lead groups, begin to develop a list of at-risk adolescents who could benefit from being part of a group. You can build this list by looking to a number of referral sources, including the following:

- school counseling/social work case histories
- other school staff
- parents
- students themselves
- broader community

School Counseling/Social Work Case Histories. Ask school counselors or social workers to recommend potential group members from their caseloads.

Other School Staff. Look for referrals from any and all members of the school staff: building administrators, teachers, maintenance personnel, secretaries, DARE officers, CORE Teams, school nurses, bus drivers. With the help of your in-services, all school staff members can learn to identify students who may be at-risk. By understanding how the support-group program oper-

ates and the services it provides, staff can refer students appropriately.

Parents. Some referrals will come directly from parents who might disclose during an interview or conference their stress over a family difficulty such as divorce, family violence, or chemical dependence. As leaders become more experienced in facilitating these groups, they gain confidence in asking about the presence of these problems in a family conference or history interview. Many parents will welcome the chance to have their children learn skills for healthy living. Introduce the group as an educational and preventive service. To allay parents' fears that the group might be intended to discover pathologies in their families, stress that the group is clearly designed to educate and inform teenagers, to correct their misconceptions, and to teach coping skills. Describe, too, the instructional process. This will help parents recognize that the group experience will be a positive one for their child, not a negative or judgmental one.

Students Themselves. Another referral source is your school's student body. Self-referrals are likely to begin as soon as students become aware that you are offering support groups. Offer classroom presentations on the various groups available. Once the students understand what the groups are about, they'll find it easier to self-refer.

Begin your presentation by announcing that you will be offering some groups during the school year, and that you want the students to know about them. Give the students an idea of what happens in group. For instance, if you're offering an *Anger Management and Violence Prevention* group, lead the students in a centering exercise. Discuss a scenario involving an adolescent who lives in a violent family. Describe styles of expressing anger and have the students act out one of the problem-solving skills to use in an anger situation. Repeat the process for the other groups you plan to offer.

Be assured that adolescents enjoy hearing about anonymous teens and how they might react to various stresses. Adolescents are more likely to sign up for groups if presented in this way. After your presentation, have the students fill out a self-referral form. (See the Self-referral Group Survey Form on page 215.)

Broader Community. Sharing information about the support-group program with parents, professionals, and other concerned adults at a community forum will lead to referrals from the broader community. For example, once therapists and social workers from treatment centers and mental health agencies know that you are offering groups, they will be able to refer clients to it.

When it comes to referrals, the rule of thumb is "the broader the referral network, the better." The broader the referral network, the better the chance at-risk adolescents will be reached and helped.

Screening Candidates

N o matter how students are referred for membership in a group, each candidate should be screened individually before you grant membership. The screening process consists of a brief interview that details demographic factors, the student's adjustment and attitude toward school, and the family or living situation. (See the Screening Interview Outline on page 214.) If the student is self-referred, and if you have no knowledge of the particular family stress, screening will help gather specific information about it.

During the screening interview, make the young person as comfortable as possible, acknowledge loyalty to the family, stress confidentiality, and reassure him or her that such questioning will not take place in front of other group members. Ask respectfully for specific information about the family stress. Listen carefully to the student's reason for self-referral, and then use your best judgment about whether or not to include the student in the group.

If you know about the family stress of a particular candidate, and the adolescent is in denial

(therefore, generally not self-referred), there's no need to break that denial during the screening interview. Simply help the student see that being part of the group is a way to learn about issues like divorce, chemical dependence, anger management, or violence prevention.

If you feel that the student belongs in a group, discuss the group process, including group format and session topics. Describing the format will prepare the student for what will happen in group and will reassure him or her about the safety of the group. Explain the rules and tell the student that to be in the group he or she must make a commitment to attend every group session and to keep all the rules. Explaining the rules during the screening interview sets the stage for good behavior during the group sessions.

At this point in the screening interview, ask the students if they want to participate in the group, and if they are willing to follow the rules. This is important so that the group members will have a sense of ownership and investment in the group. Experience has shown that students who are coerced to join a group may remain resistant throughout all the sessions.

The prospect of screening every group candidate individually may seem a bit daunting, but such screening isn't just for your sake. It's also a valuable experience for the student. The screening may also serve as a case-finding procedure, during which cases of alcohol and other drug experimentation or sexual or physical abuse may come to light and can be dealt with properly. Naturally, cases of sexual and physical abuse should be reported immediately to appropriate authorities.

Acquiring Informed Parental Consent

T o ensure a group's integrity and success, you need to acquire consent from the parents whose children are candidates for group membership. Procedures for acquiring parental consent must consider the children's needs, the parents' rights to privacy, the school's desire to help its students, and the provisions of the law so as to avoid any legal action being taken against the school.

The simplest way to get informed consent is to have the school mail a letter to the parents of all prospective group members. (See the sample Parental Consent Letter on page 210.) The letter clearly but simply:

- describes the group process

- encourages parents to allow their child to receive the services the group can provide

- informs parents that they must contact the school if they do not want their child to participate

If you feel that parents will be resistant, call or visit with them personally to talk about the group. Explain that you're not looking for family pathology or problems, but rather are hoping to correct misconceptions and to teach coping skills. Once the group program is explained well to parents, few are likely to refuse permission for their child to take part.

If you've clearly explained the purpose and format of the group to the parents and they still don't want their child involved, there are still two ways you can help the adolescent. First, make sure that the student is present for any in-school presentation about the group, either one you offer as a recruitment tool or one that students themselves might provide. An at-risk adolescent can begin to integrate facts, concepts, and specific skills even when the presentation is brief. Second, you can refer the student to the school counseling services for individual assistance. Some counselors modify support groups to use with students individually. Finally, remember, these groups are not the only help available to at-risk adolescents.

Forming and Scheduling the Groups

You know from your own experience that the best groups—of any kind—are made up of different individuals with varying temperaments and personalities. The same is true for support groups. To the best of your ability, see to it that a group is a mix of adolescents who are outgoing, shy, talkative, quiet, boys, girls, and so on. Because of the wide variation in development among early adolescents, you should not have more than a two-year spread for middle school students in a group. However, high school groups seem to work even with a four-year spread.

For rich group dynamics and useful interactions, eight seems to be the maximum number of participants for structured groups. When the group size extends beyond eight, the level of individual attention and sharing diminishes. If you find that more students want to participate, offer more groups as it becomes possible to do so.

The location, size, and atmosphere of a group's meeting room are important in establishing a safe, welcoming space for students to open up and take risks. Generally, classrooms aren't the most satisfactory places for group meetings; they're almost always too large and are filled with too many distractions. Ideally, the meeting room is small, comfortable, and quiet, a place where interruptions and potential distractions are minimal. Privacy is essential so teenagers won't be afraid that others outside the room can see or overhear them. Sitting together at a table will help promote group cohesion and simplify discussion.

Survey your school facility for a good place for group meetings. Obviously, such a space is often at a premium in a school setting, so remember that your most important considerations are privacy, quiet, and regular availability.

Besides matters of space, scheduling must also deal with matters of time. Plan to hold group sessions on a weekly basis so that the adolescents have time to integrate the insight and support gained from each session. Weekly sessions are also less likely to interfere with the students' studies and other activities. Although you'll want to make the meeting place and day consistent, you may rotate meeting times so that the students won't miss instruction in the same subject each week. For example, for the first week, schedule the group meeting during the first instructional hour; for the second week, schedule it during the second instructional hour, and so on.

In all matters of scheduling, administrative support is an invaluable aid to help foster teacher cooperation in releasing students from regular classes. Remember, however, that cooperation is a two-way street. Let teachers know that students participate in the group on the condition that they make up all missed work. Likewise, give teachers a schedule of group meetings so that they'll know in advance what class a student will miss, won't plan field trips or tests for those times, and can make arrangements for the student to make up missed schoolwork.

Assuring Group Confidentiality

Confidentiality is the cornerstone of safe and supportive groups. To share problems and deep feelings, group members must know that what they say will be kept in confidence. Experts have pointed out that at-risk children are very reluctant to reveal family problems. For example, there are unspoken rules in many at-risk families: "Don't talk; don't trust; don't feel" (Black, 1981). It's important to realize that the adolescents will not open up if they think that what they share will become common knowledge around school.

In setting up a group, therefore, take extra care to assure and protect confidentiality. The stu-

dents must realize that outside of the group sessions they may not discuss who else is in their group or what they say. The group members can, however, discuss the facts and information they learn during group. The group leader has responsibilities as well. Except in cases where the law requires such revelation (for example, where a group leader suspects that a child is being physically or sexually abused), it is inappropriate for a group leader to reveal to others anything a student may share. It's a good idea, therefore, to inform the students of this at the very first session.

But what about teachers in the school? Don't they have a right to know when a student will miss class because of his or her participation in a group? Yes, they do. But isn't this a breach of confidentiality? No, not at all. To help maintain confidentiality, you need only inform teachers that the group is part of the school counseling program and that the students in it are going to learn basic facts about alcohol and other drugs, anger management, family violence, or divorce. For even further confidentiality, you might give the group a simple generic name. That way, neither school staff nor anyone else (except specific group members) will know what kind of group a student is in or what the student's specific problem(s) might be. Teachers will only know that one or more of their students are taking part in a group.

In a support group, the students have opportunities to share feelings and to self-disclose as they choose, all the while remaining loyal to their families. Although they have many opportunities to take an active part in every group session, if they choose to pass, they may, and the group leader respects their decision. Meanwhile, through warm acceptance and a nonjudgmental attitude, the leader builds an atmosphere of trust. As the students grow more secure, they feel safe to self-disclose and identify and share feelings, which the group leader helps them express in appropriate ways. Self-disclosure, however, is not the goal of the group. Group members who never say a word in group can still benefit.

Self-disclosing by Leaders

Since the group members aren't required or asked to self-disclose, should group leaders self-disclose? If used correctly, self-disclosure can be a useful group technique with middle and high school students. Even so, leaders should be very cautious and think carefully before self-disclosing. Sharing facts about one's personal life is appropriate if it's positive role modeling or if it will help illustrate a point effectively. However, leaders should never employ self-disclosure for purposes of eliciting the same from students, nor should they use the group for personal therapy. For example, leaders must not express feelings or share experiences that they haven't adequately resolved or dealt with themselves.

Role Modeling by Leaders

Although group leaders should make their own decisions regarding self-disclosure, they should be prepared to share of themselves several times during each group session. In *Anger Management and Violence Prevention,* leaders act as role models for important components. They begin the go-arounds for the feelings check-in, the affirmation, and the closing activity of each session. During the feelings check-in, for example, leaders act as role models by sharing appropriate feelings and facts, such as "I'm glad to see you" or "I'm feeling sad because my dog died." However, leaders should never share a feeling or issue that has not been dealt with or resolved adequately. Doing so would be poor role modeling.

Following Up Group Participation

Some adolescents who participate in a group will require further services. If, for instance, students have severe behavior problems, it's unlikely that one group experience will enable them to deal much differently or much more effectively with the stress in their lives. Realizing this, be sure to make further help available. That help can come in the form of individual, group, or system follow-up.

Individual Follow-up. A counselor can continue to see students individually. Follow-up counseling sessions can help them learn to integrate the concepts and skills the group presented and to use them in their own lives.

Group Follow-up. For students with serious behavior problems, participating in other group experiences can be very beneficial. Students are often eager to participate in another group, since they enjoy the familiarity, consistency, and predictability of the group format, as well as the ability to discuss problems openly in a safe place with peers they trust. Students should not, however, participate in more than one group at a time. Instead, encourage them to spread their participation over one or two years.

System Follow-up. Students with particularly intense behavior problems may require the services of a schoolwide helping plan as follow-up to their participation in a group. Such services can include any or all of the following: (1) individual counseling; (2) successive group experiences; (3) a schoolwide plan for anger management; (4) participation in a peer counseling program; and (5) frequent consultation between counselor and teachers and administrators in charge of discipline. Of course, an adolescent or family may be referred for outside therapy.

Part Two

THEORETICAL BASES
FOR ANGER MANAGEMENT AND
VIOLENCE PREVENTION

Violence, Family Violence, and Prevention

K evin, a freshman in high school, is frequently sent to the office for fighting with other students. Kevin's peers think that walking away from a fight would mean they are wimps. Kevin believes that when he gets angry, he should get rid of the anger by hitting someone. He says that he once broke the arm of someone who made him angry, and that on another occasion he broke every bone in a boy's face. Although those statements were never verified, it *was* known to school administrators that Kevin's stepfather shot his mother and his half sister to death. Although Kevin speaks of his violent behavior without remorse, he does acknowledge that he will end up in jail if he continues to act in such violent ways.

S chools today, as well as other agencies that serve adolescents, are frequently faced with students like Kevin, and with the problems they present. On the personal and family level, Kevin has experienced the severest kind of family violence, the murder of his mother by his stepfather. On the social level, his peers, who are developmentally dealing with issues of gender identification, believe that to be violent is to prove manhood. Kevin also lives in a society where guns are readily available and where violence is glorified in the mass media.

Although you, as a helping professional who works with adolescents, may intervene on the individual level with students like Kevin, you will be more effective if you are aware of the current findings on violence and family violence, and the recommendations that experts have made for prevention of violence. You will also be empowered to help students like Kevin if you learn the theoretical bases for the interventions that have been designed for *Anger Management and Violence Prevention*. Chapter 1 gives this overview.

Chapter 2 provides an overview of the issues in adolescent development; a review of the developmental tasks of early childhood, which can affect the tasks of adolescence; and the impact that maltreatment has on achieving these tasks with competence and success.

Violence

I n a 1993 interdisciplinary report commissioned by the federal government, *Understanding and Preventing Violence* (Reiss and Roth), a panel chosen by the National Academy of Sciences defined "violence" as "behaviors by individuals that intentionally threaten, attempt, or inflict physical harm on others" (p. 2). The panel, known as the Panel on the Understanding and Control of Violent Behavior, looked at the statistics regarding violent crimes compiled by the FBI, including murder, forcible rape, robbery, and aggravated assault. The panel also considered school fights, violence among inmates, and violence in homes to be violent behavior. The panel did not include a third level—violence by large collectives, such as wars, state violence, riots, and organized crime—in their study.

The panel found that the United States tends to be more violent than other societies, with higher rates for homicide and other violent crimes. In spite of popular belief, the United States is not becoming more violent, the homicide rate having peaked twice in this century, with a decline following each peak. Among the consequences of violent crime are death and injury; financial losses; psychological damage; reduced quality of life; the destruction of families and neighborhoods; the fortification of schools, homes, and businesses; and the abandonment of community resources such as parks and playgrounds.

FACTORS THAT INFLUENCE VIOLENT BEHAVIOR

The panel studied many aspects of violent behavior, including factors that occur on four ecological levels—personal, family, social, and societal.

Risk Factors and Protective Factors

Of the risk factors that influence violent behavior, none directly cause violent behavior. *It may take several factors, on several levels, to interact in a way that leads a person to develop violent behavior.* For instance, factors that have to do with pregnancy complications—like birth trauma, low birthweight, and birth-related central nervous system problems—are correlated with later violence, but only if the person who experiences the

trauma is also raised in an unstable, nonintact family. Temperament is another example of a risk factor that interacts with other factors. Some psychological studies introduce toddlers to new situations; shy and restrained toddlers are said to have an "inhibited" temperament, while some are relatively fearless and are described as "uninhibited." Fearless behavior has been found to be a risk factor for children with low socio-economic status, whereas fearfulness may act as a protective factor against aggression. Temperament may explain why only a proportion of children from high-risk homes and neighborhoods develops antisocial or violent behavior.

On the **personal level,** researchers have found the following early childhood antecedents for violent and aggressive behaviors:

- *in infancy:* pregnancy and birth complications, low birthweight, and an uninhibited, fearless temperament

- *in the preschool years:* fearless behavior, hyperactivity-impulsivity-attention deficit, restless behavior, and poor concentration

- *in the early school years:* daring and risk-taking behavior, poor ability to defer gratification, low IQ, low empathy, and abnormally frequent viewing of violence on television; school failure and interactions involving bullying and peer rejection

Brain dysfunctions are also associated with violent behavior. Brain dysfunctions that interfere with language processing or cognition are especially common in conduct-disordered children, early school failures, delinquents, criminals, and diagnosed psychopaths—populations with elevated risks of committing violent acts.

Predictors of violent behavior on the **family level** include:

- harsh and erratic discipline, lack of parental nurturance, physical abuse and neglect, poor supervision, and early separation of children from parents, as well as violent or criminal behavior by family members

On the **social level,** predictors include:

- peer rejection, early school failure, low income in large families, poor housing, and growing up in a high crime neighborhood

On the **societal level,** risk factors include:

- violence condoned in society; violence glorified in the mass media; easy accessibility of firearms; and economic inequalities

Researchers are also identifying *protective,* or *compensatory, factors* that reduce childhood aggressive behavior. On the personal level, these include a shy temperament, high IQ, and being firstborn. On the family level, protective factors include living in a small, stable family characterized by low discord, by affectionate caregivers, and by high income, which reduce the risk of perinatal complications that might cause brain dysfunctions. On the social level, protective factors include having good peer relationships and school success, living in a low crime area, and having adequate housing.

Returning to the **personal level,** the panel emphasized that aggressive and violent behaviors are (1) learned responses to frustration, and (2) instruments for achieving goals. This learning occurs by observing models of such behavior in the family, among peers, in the neighborhood, and in the mass media.

In looking more closely at the correlations with violent behavior on the **social level,** the panel found that violent crime is greater in geographic areas that have concentrations of poor families and greater income differences between poor and nonpoor. It is also greater in areas with differential social organization, such as high population turnover and community transition, greater family disruption, and high housing/population density—all of which affect a community's capacity to supervise young males. There is also likely to be a breakdown in *social capital,* the capacity to transmit positive values to younger generations. Violent crime is also greater where there are opportunities associated with violence, such as illegal markets in drugs and firearms.

Circumstances of Violence

The circumstances of crime also include risk factors. Violence depends in part on whether judgment and communication have been impaired by use of alcohol or other drugs and on the presence of firearms. Violent events are also likely in interactions that include threats and counter-threats, the exercise of coercive authority, insults, and weapons displays.

Alcohol and Violence

The panel's exploration of the relation of alcohol and other drug use to violent behavior found that alcohol and drug use may not cause violent behavior, but may potentiate it. Using alcohol and other drugs can increase irritability, lower internal controls, affect judgment, and impair communication skills. Studies have found that adult problem drinkers are more likely to have behaved violently, but alcoholics are not more prevalent among violent offenders than among other offenders.

Family Violence

The panel's review of family violence included spouse assault, physical and sexual assault of children, sibling assault, and physical and sexual assault of other relatives who live in the household. Unlike violence between strangers, family violence occurs between people who are in a continuing relationship and interact daily. Therefore, repeated violations by the offender are common; the victim is generally relatively powerless and vulnerable to the aggression of the more powerful offender. The victimizer often uses threat of further violence to prevent disclosure.

Family violence can range from verbally to physically aggressive acts. In studies done by national telephone surveys, Gelles and Straus (1988) found that 16 out of every 100 couples reported at least one incident of physical aggression during the year before the survey, with four out of 100 couples reporting severe violence. Other surveys of select populations, such as divorce filings or batterers, made higher estimates of prevalence of family violence (Reiss and Roth, p. 227).

In discussing child abuse, the panel reported that children under age 4 are more vulnerable to homicide than older children (Reiss and Roth, p. 234). Socioeconomic status is highly related to rates of child maltreatment. In one study, the rate of physical abuse was three and one-half times greater and the rate of sexual abuse six times greater for children from families with incomes less than $15,000 (Reiss and Roth, p. 235).

Family violence issues should be seen in the context of changes in the family structure in the United States:

- In 1970, 40 percent of households were two-parent families; in 1990, the figure was 26 percent.

- In 1990, 19 percent of white, 62 percent of black, and 30 percent of Hispanic children under age 18 lived with only one parent (Reiss and Roth, p. 222).

One major theory explaining family violence is an unequal distribution of power. Men use both their physical power and their social power to maintain a dominant position over women, and both women and men exercise power over children. However, this theory does not account for the fact that the majority of men and women do not engage in family violence.

Theories of Violence

Several theories attempt to explain the development of aggression and violence.

Instinct, Drive Theory. This theory postulates that aggression is an instinctive drive in people, and a biological necessity for survival in a hostile environment.

Frustration-Aggression Theory. The premise of this theory is that when people get frustrated, they get aggressive, for instance, when they cannot achieve their goals.

Social Learning Theory. Albert Bandura's theory (Bailey, 1976) holds that aggressive behavior is learned and maintained through environmen-

tal experiences. It can be learned vicariously, that is, by watching or modeling someone else's aggressive behavior.

Cognitive-Behavioral Theories. These theories postulate that aggressive behavior is the product of angry, aggressive thoughts. L. R. Huesmann and L. D. Eron's theory (Reiss and Roth) is that during early childhood, children learn "scripts," which suggest what events are about to occur, how the person should react to these events, and what the outcome will be. The parents' cognitive processes influence those of the children. Therefore, aggressive behavior in these children and adults is stable due to the process of repeated rehearsal, whether through fantasizing, observation, or actual behavior, which lead to aggressive scripts.

K. A. Dodge's cognitive-behavioral theory (Reiss and Roth) is a social information processing model of aggression. This model describes five cognitive operations that occur sequentially in the development of aggressive behavior: encoding, interpretation, response search, response decision, and enactment. Aggressive children tend to interpret the behaviors of peers as more hostile and are less capable of generating potential responses to conflict situations.

Theorists have also described two kinds of aggression: *emotional* or *reactive*, where people react in an angry, volatile manner, and *instrumental* or *proactive*, where aggression is used to meet goals. This correlates with physiologists' findings of "affective aggression," which has a high degree of autonomic arousal, and "instrumental aggression," which has a low degree of autonomic arousal and is a cold-blooded, reward-seeking form of aggression.

Violence Prevention

The panel recommended improved measurement systems for violence and crime and continued research to aid in creating social policies for violence prevention. It also recommended problem-solving initiatives in six areas, including the psychosocial level, maximizing police interventions in illegal markets, and a comprehensive initiative to reduce partner assault.

To prevent violence on the psychosocial level, the panel recommended intervention "in the biological and psychosocial development of individuals' potentials for violent behavior, with special attention to preventing brain damage associated with low birthweight and childhood head trauma, *cognitive-behavioral techniques for preventing aggressive and violent behavior and inculcating prosocial behavior, and the learning of attitudes that discourage violent sexual behavior*" (Reiss and Roth, p. 22, emphasis added). The panel described interventions that have shown some success in reducing childhood aggressive behavior: (1) "social learning and cognitive-behavioral interventions with elements that emphasize the undesirability of aggression, nonaggressive methods of solving interpersonal problems, social skills training, and watching television programs that emphasize prosocial behavior" and (2) "interventions such as tutoring by peers or specially-trained high school students to reduce early-grade school failure" (Reiss and Roth, p. 8, emphasis added).

Cognitive-Behavioral Interventions. The panel found that programs combining cognitive and behavioral approaches proved to be the most effective forms of intervention, provided that they emphasize the *undesirability of aggressive behavior* and provide the child, or adult, with *alternative problem-solving behavior.*

Social Skills Training. Some social-skills training programs are effective in changing aggressive behavior in children, particularly those that include social relations training, prohibition of aggression, anger control, and cognitive-behavioral problem solving.

Other Findings. Gelles and Straus (1988), who researched family violence at the University of New Hampshire for almost 20 years, analyzed the various steps women take to stop their violent victimization. They found that a woman who "firmly negotiates an end to the violence and indicates that she will not tolerate being hit has the greatest chance of ending her partner's violent behavior" (p.159). This firm, emphatic,

and rational approach is also much more effective if taken after the first incident of the most minor violence. Gelles and Straus recommend two goals for prevention of family violence:

- eliminate cultural norms and values that accept violence as a means of resolving conflict and problems in families

- develop programs and policies that support families and reduce internal and external stresses and inequalities (p. 194)

Neidig and Friedman (1984) and Stordeur and Stille (1989) describe their intervention programs for men who batter. The goal of both programs is an immediate and complete end to the violence; and, while individual, family, and societal dynamics are acknowledged, the hallmark of these programs is holding the individual responsible for his violent behavior.

Jaffe et al. (1990), who have studied the children of battered women, call for schools to make a major commitment to end family violence, realizing that schools can help to change the underlying societal values that condone violence. Their recommendations include teacher education, curriculum development, and student involvement. One curriculum they describe challenges existing sex-role stereotypes and the view that violence relates to power and control, and teaches alternative conflict-resolution strategies.

This material was drawn from the following sources:

Bailey, R. H., ed. 1976. *Violence and Aggression.* New York: Time-Life Books.

Crime in the United States, 1991: Uniform Crime Reports. Federal Bureau of Investigation, U.S. Department of Justice, Washington, D.C. 20535.

Gelles, R. J., and M. A. Straus. 1988. *Intimate Violence.* New York: Simon & Schuster.

Jaffe, P. G., D. A. Wolfe, and S. K. Wilson. 1990. *Children of Battered Women.* Newbury Park, CA: Sage Publications.

Neidig, P. H., and D.H. Friedman. 1984. *Spouse Abuse: A Treatment Program for Couples.* Champaign, IL: Research Press.

Reiss, A. J., and J. A. Roth, eds. 1993. *Understanding and Preventing Violence.* Washington, D.C.: National Academy Press.

Stordeur, R. A., and R. Stille. 1989. *Ending Men's Violence Against Their Partners.* Newbury Park, CA: Sage Publications.

CHAPTER • 2

Adolescent Development and Intervention Models

C hapter 1 explored current theories on violence, family violence, and recommendations experts have made for prevention on a psychosocial level. Chapter 2 will review issues in
adolescent development, look at the effects of
maltreatment on the developmental tasks of
childhood and adolescence, and describe the
theoretical bases for the concepts, methods, and
techniques in this manual.

Adolescent Development

T he theory of lifespan developmental psy-
chology looks at child and adolescent development in a comprehensive way (Coleman and
Hendry, 1990). While psychoanalytic theory
examines adolescent development as a time of
turmoil in the individual, and sociological theory looks at roles and role changes, the lifespan
approach posits that there is a human ecology:
individuals live in families, and both individuals
and families develop in the context of their geo-
graphical, historical, social, and political settings. Both individuals and families grow and

develop and change, and they reciprocally influence each other as they do so. Theorists are
increasingly looking at individuals as being pro-
ducers of their own development: they are active
agents in shaping or determining their lives.

The ecological framework used by many
researchers consists of four levels: the personal
(ontogenetic) level, the family (microsystem)
level, the social (exosystem) level, and the societal (macrosystem) level. Adolescence is a time
of enormous change in at least three of the four
levels of this framework; the changes on the personal level will be reviewed here.

ADOLESCENT CHANGES ON THE PERSONAL LEVEL
Physical Development

E arly adolescence is marked by impressive
physical changes beginning at puberty. The
word *puberty* comes from Latin and means the
age of manhood. During the growth spurt,
height and weight increase; the weight of the
heart nearly doubles; there is accelerated growth

of the lungs and a marked increase in physical strength and endurance, especially in boys. There is extreme variation in this growth spurt, as it starts at different ages for males and females. In girls, the growth spurt can begin at 7 or 8, or not start until 12, 13, or 14. The average age of rapid growth for girls starts at 11 and peaks at 12. For boys, the average age of rapid growth starts at 13 and peaks at 14. Sexual maturation also differs from boys to girls. For boys, the first sign of the approach of puberty is an increase in the rate of growth of the genitals, followed by the appearance of pubic hair; the appearance of facial hair accompanies the beginning of the growth spurt. In girls, the menarche usually occurs after the peak velocity of the growth spurt.

The enormous growth and the body changes affect the identity and self-concept of the early adolescent. The variations of growth can have an impact on these teens. For boys, early maturation has social advantages. Early maturing boys have been found to be more relaxed, more popular, less dependent, and more attractive to both adults and peers. The situation is less clear for early maturing girls. Some studies have shown that they are less popular and more likely to show signs of inner turmoil; others report enhanced self-confidence and social prestige. In addition to the social significance of their growth, children in puberty must also adjust to the physical effects of their growth. Early adolescents are frequently clumsy as their coordination catches up to their bodies. Their focus is on their bodies as indicated by studies in which early adolescents describe themselves using physical characteristics, whereas older adolescents describe themselves by their intellectual or social aspects.

Thinking and Reasoning: Formal Operational Thinking

The development of thinking and reasoning in adolescents moves them from thinking like children, in concrete ways, to thinking like adults, in abstract ways. Coleman and Hendry describe

Jean Piaget's stage of *concrete operations,* ages 7 through 11, when children's thought is relational. Children begin to master notions of classes, relations, and quantities. Conservation and seriation are possible, enabling children to formulate hypotheses and explanations about concrete events. Children formulate a hypothesis originating from the concrete data, rather than from internal resources. And, once the hypothesis is formulated, children in concrete operations are reluctant to change the hypothesis, tending instead to alter the data.

As adolescents move into the stage of *formal operations,* they are able to utilize a number of important capabilities: one of these is the "contrary-to-fact" proposition, which has been described as a shift in thinking from the real to the possible, which facilitates a hypothetico-deductive approach to problem solving and to the understanding of propositional logic. Adolescents develop the ability to think about mental constructs as objects that can be manipulated, and they can master concepts such as probability and belief.

Coleman and Hendry (1990) describe a study of concept-formation where children of 8 to 9 years and adolescents between 13 and 14 were shown pictures of wheeled and nonwheeled tools and vehicles. Shown pairs of a wheeled and nonwheeled object, the child was asked to choose one item. A light went on when the wheeled object was chosen. Only half of the younger children came to the conclusion that choosing a wheeled object made the light go on, and it took them nearly all of the 72 trials. By comparison, all the adolescents solved the problem, and many did so in as few as 10 trials. The adolescents thought of hypotheses, tested them, and discarded them if they did not work. The younger children came to a hypothesis based on the data (tool versus nontool or vehicle versus nonvehicle) and were unable to give up the hypothesis even though they failed on most trials. These children were unable to differentiate the hypothesis from reality.

Coleman and Hendry point out that the change

from concrete to formal operations occurs slowly in adolescents, and there may be shifting back and forth. And some adolescents may develop formal modes of thinking in one area, such as a verbal area, and later in other areas, such as mathematic and scientific areas.

Social Cognition

Social cognition theorists look at the child's concrete thinking and egocentrism, and compare them to the adolescent's formal operational thinking, which allows the adolescent to think about the thought of other people. Coleman and Hendry describe Robert Selman's stage theory of social cognition, which involves role taking, perspective taking, empathy, moral reasoning, interpersonal problem solving, and self-knowledge. Selman's stages describe early adolescence (ages 10 - 15) as a time when the teen has the capacity for a more complex type of social cognition. The teen moves beyond simply taking the other person's perspective (in a back-and-forth manner) and is able to see all parties from a more generalized third-person perspective. By age 15, the adolescent may move to a still higher and more abstract level of interpersonal perspective taking that involves coordinating the perspectives of society with those of the individual and the group.

Self-concept Development

Adolescents experience great change in self-concept as a result of (1) the major physical changes of puberty, which affect body image; (2) the intellectual growth, which allows for a more complex and sophisticated self-concept; (3) the increasing emotional independence from parents, and the need to make important choices about values, friendships, sexual behavior, alcohol and other drug use, and occupation. Adolescent self-concept involves issues about *gender identification* and *sex role*. Studies show children generally have distinct ideas about these issues; there is much more ambiguity in early adolescents; and older adolescents, approaching adulthood, again have a stronger perceived gender identity.

Researchers have looked at *self-esteem*, an aspect of self-concept, as rising from:

1. *competence,* or success in meeting achievement demands

2. *social acceptance,* or attention, worthiness, and positive reinforcement received from significant others

3. *control,* or feelings of internal responsibility for outcomes

4. *virtue,* or adherence to moral and ethical standards

Some adolescents will value competence in sports, while others will value popularity. Studies show that early adolescents have the most difficulty with self-esteem, with girls worrying more about body image and same-sex popularity. There seems to be a general rise in self-esteem during adolescence.

The self-concept literature also discusses the concepts of *locus of control* and *self-agency.* These concepts see individuals as having the capacity to engage in purposive, goal-oriented, if rule-bound action, rather than as passive products of socialization. People who have an external locus of control have a passive worldview, regarding important events as being essentially independent of their actions. They tend to have outer self-esteem, based on the perceived opinion of others derived from the occupation of a particular position in the social structure. In contrast, people who have a sense of self-agency, an internal locus of control, believe that they have some control over their lives, and that their fate is in their own hands. They tend to have inner self-esteem, deriving directly from the experience of themselves as agents who can make things happen in the world and attain their goals, regardless of obstacles.

Erikson's (1968) description of forming an idea of identity as a major task of adolescence is another aspect of self-concept, pertaining especially to older adolescents. Erikson describes four states of identity. Adolescents in the state of *identity diffusion* have no commitment to a vocation or set of beliefs and are not actively trying to make a commitment. Teens who have not experienced their own identity crisis and are committed in goals and beliefs, but largely as a result of choices made by others, are in the state of *identity foreclosure*. Young people in a state of crisis, who are actively searching among alternatives in an attempt to arrive at the choice of identity, are in the state of *moratorium*. Finally, teens who have had a crisis, who have resolved it on their own terms, and who have a firm commitment to an occupation, an ideology, and social roles are in the state of identity *achievement*.

EFFECTS OF FAMILY MALTREATMENT ON DEVELOPMENTAL TASKS

Teens and their families must cope with two major developmental tasks during the adolescent years. First, the family must adjust to the adolescent's physical and cognitive growth; and, second, the family must prepare the adolescent to leave the home and enter the adult world of work and love.

Cicchetti and Howes (1991) provide a framework for looking at how families can help adolescents master their developmental tasks. They see development as a series of tasks which are age and stage appropriate, but which remain critical to the child's continual adaptation. For instance, attachment, the major task of infancy, continues to be relevant as children reach the tasks of later years, such as emotional regulation, autonomy, peer relations, and school adjustment. Cicchetti and Howes believe that some families provide *potentiating*, or *risk, factors*, increasing the likelihood of the child developing incompetence, while other families provide *compensatory*, or *protective, factors*, which increase the probability of competence in the child's developmental tasks. Cicchetti and Howes describe the effects of maltreating parents on the developmental achievements of young children in five

areas: attachment, emotion regulation, autonomous self, peer relations, and school adjustment. The adolescent's behavior and adjustment will be affected by how competently he or she mastered these early developmental tasks.

Task 1: Attachment

The task of infancy, to form secure attachment relationships with the primary caregiver, is especially affected by the characteristics of the caregiver. An adequate caregiver will be sensitive and responsive to the infant's needs. Mothers who are inconsistent in their accessibility and responsiveness to their infants tend to have babies who are both anxious and angry. Mothers who tend to withhold close bodily contact, especially at times of high infant intensity, have babies who are anxious and avoidant of the mother. Children who have insecurity and fear in these initial relationships may expect maltreatment in later relationships and may continue to express their own anger or avoidant behavior in later childhood and adult relationships (Crittenden and Ainsworth, in Cicchetti and Carlson, 1989).

Task 2: Emotion Regulation

Emotional self-regulation, the ability to modulate and initiate both positive and negative affect, is another early childhood task that continues to be an important task throughout the rest of the lifespan. Cicchetti and Howes believe "that the use of emotional language helps one control nonverbal emotional expressions, which in turn enhances regulation of the emotions themselves" (Cicchetti and Howes, 1991). Parents who use emotional language by putting feelings into words help their children learn to organize and control their emotional expressions. Maltreated children are overly aware of aggressive stimuli, an adaptive coping mechanism to alert them to signs of immediate danger. However, such awareness of aggressive stimuli is not adaptive when children are in nonthreatening situations.

Task 3: Autonomous Self

The toddler develops a sense of being a separate individual with personal thoughts, feelings, and behaviors, a foreshadowing of the adolescent move to independence. Maltreated toddlers show evidence of low self-esteem, not smiling when they see themselves in the mirror and talking less about themselves. In a tool-use/problem-solving situation, maltreated 2-year-olds show increased anger, frustration with their mother, and noncompliance, revealing a difficulty in making a smooth transition to autonomy. Maltreated children in grades 1-3 see themselves as more competent and accepted than comparison children, and more competent than their teachers perceive them to be. Such inflated self-perception may reflect unrealistic coping strategies that help them gain a sense of personal competence and control in chaotic home settings, but may eventually cause them to feel like failures. By grades 4-6, maltreated children view themselves as less competent and accepted, and more in accordance with teacher ratings, showing a lower self-worth.

Task 4: Peer Relations

Positive peer relationships can be buffering factors in the lives of maltreated children. However, maltreated children tend to display more disturbed patterns of interaction with peers, showing higher levels of physical and verbal aggression in interaction with peers and a higher degree of withdrawal from interaction. Both patterns lead to increasing isolation and peer rejection.

Task 5: Adaptation to School

This final task of childhood involves integration into the peer group, acceptable performance in the classroom, and appropriate motivational orientations for achievement. Maltreated children may have unmet physical needs and concerns over safety and may tend to search for acceptance. They may show dependence on teachers, score low on tests of cognitive maturity, and show less readiness to learn in school. In contrast, the optimum state for the child is a secure readiness to learn: a dynamic balance between establishing secure relationships with adults and feeling free to explore the environment in ways that will promote cognitive competence.

Obviously, an ambivalent attachment relationship, an inability to regulate emotion, a failure to develop a sense of autonomous self, poor peer relationships, and poor adaptation to school in early childhood will make chances for a successful, competent, or even adequate, adjustment in adolescence more difficult. Adolescents who had problems in the earlier developmental tasks may have problems negotiating the pubertal changes and the movement to independence. The next section addresses the impact of families on the achievement of adolescent developmental tasks.

Task 6: Adjustment to Physical, Social, and Cognitive Changes

Gabarino (in Cicchetti and Carlson, 1989) describes how the family structure can affect how families deal with adolescent changes. *Authoritarian families* are paternalistic and harsh, and use rigid and domineering styles of child-rearing. Parents tend to avoid feelings and use high levels of force. Authoritarian parents tend to allow their adolescent little freedom, and there is increased conflict over spending money, friends, social life, and activities outside the home. If the parental discipline has been severe without much love and affection, teens may become overtly aggressive and may seek peer acceptance from membership in a delinquent gang.

Permissive families tend to be overindulgent, making few demands upon children, setting few limits, and demanding a high level of emotional gratification from children. Some permissive parents tend to be too protective and overinvolved, hampering the drive for emotional independence.

In contrast, *authoritative families* (which are different than authoritarian families) grant just enough autonomy so the adolescent can develop a sense of self-governship and control; they also provide enough structure so that the teen is not overwhelmed by responsibility or lost with no direction. Authoritative parents use negotiation techniques, are flexible, and are able to adapt general principles and techniques ("set rules," "offer encouragement") to their particular adolescents.

Taking into account that development is an interactive process between children and families, Gabarino points out that it is more difficult to parent teenagers than to parent children. Many adolescents have attained adult size, and some are larger and stronger than their parents; this presents a problem for parents who have used physical force to control their children. Adolescents are also more likely to be able to reason like adults and are less willing to accept parental decisions without questioning them. Both size and reasoning ability are problematic for authoritarian families. Teens are more likely to have significant relationships outside the family, with teachers, coaches, and peers. These outside influences, especially the development of a love interest, can be very threatening to some parents, especially overcontrolling parents who have tried to control by intrusion. Gabarino reports that it is far more expensive to raise teenagers than to raise children, causing stress for families in a marginal economic status or for permissive families who have tried to control through indulgence.

In comparing maltreatment in children and adolescents, Gabarino reports that adolescent maltreatment equals or exceeds the incidence of child maltreatment. It includes all forms of abuse and neglect, but psychological abuse and sexual abuse are prevalent. Females are more likely to be abused in adolescence than in childhood, whereas the risk for males peaks early and generally declines through adolescence. Adolescents at high risk for maltreatment are less socially competent and exhibit more developmental problems than their peers. On the family level, some adolescent maltreatment is a continuation of child abuse; but some is a dete-

rioration of unwise patterns of childrearing or the inability of the family to deal with new challenges in adolescence. Families at high risk for maltreatment in adolescence are more likely to contain stepparents, but there are fewer socioeconomic class differences than for child maltreatment.

Finally, Gabarino cites studies showing that families at high risk for adolescent maltreatment tend to be multiproblem families, with high rates of divorce and separation, financial stresses, and family conflict. They are authoritarian families with paternalistic, harsh, rigid, and domineering styles of childrearing. Parents deny their feelings to each other or to the children. They use high levels of force. Overindulgent families are also at high risk for adolescent maltreatment. As mentioned, these families place few demands upon children, set few limits, and demand a high level of emotional gratification from the children. When teens seek to form primary attachments outside the home and to act impulsively, overindulgent parents react with excessive force. Maltreated adolescents describe their parents as being more punishing. Abusive families are chaotic and enmeshed, whereas nonabusive families are flexible and connected.

Task 7: Independence

In addition to the task of adjusting to the physical, emotional, social, and mental changes of adolescence, families must prepare the adolescent to leave the home and enter the adult world of work and love. Their study of children of battered women led Jaffe et al. (1990) to describe effects of family violence on this task of adolescent development.

Some adolescents move straight from parents who are violent to violence in their own relationships in dating and early courtship. As Jaffe et al. say, "For adolescent girls it is a crucial turning point in which they may start to accept threats and violence from boyfriends who control them through this behavior" (p. 28). Some teens run away to avoid the violence; some act out in delinquent behavior; some adolescent boys imitate behavior that has been modeled for them by assaulting their mother or siblings. Still other adolescents, especially older adolescents, may adopt parenting responsibilities and try to protect members of the household from the violence. Adolescents, and all children, are affected by "what behaviors are modeled, by the trauma that they are experiencing, and by the distress of their parents" (p. 31). They thus are impaired in their move to leave home, leaving without preparation to avoid violence or staying longer than they should to help.

Breaking the Cycle of Violence

An important point that Gabarino makes is that, contrary to the popular belief that adolescence is a time of turmoil and family chaos, studies and surveys show that a majority of adolescents are neither crazy nor rebellious and do not show overt signs of disorder. Repeated studies show that only 20 percent of adolescents experience extreme turmoil. Although adolescent maltreatment does exist, adolescent abuse is less likely to be transmitted intergenerationally than is child abuse. Much research attention is being given to the protective factors that buffer children and adolescents from the effects of maltreatment.

In their study of child abuse, delinquency, and violent criminality, Lewis et al. (in Cicchetti and Carlson, 1989) point out that most physically abused children do not become violent delinquents. However, a high proportion of delinquents, particularly violent delinquents, and of violent adult criminals, suffered extreme abuse in childhood. Studies show that childhood abuse itself does not predict violent behavior in adulthood. A combination of three factors—including *neuropsychiatric factors,* such as perinatal difficulties or childhood head trauma (often from abuse), a *family history of violence,* and *child abuse*—seems to engender violence. Often, the severe abuse was interspersed with times of

indifference or complete abandonment. The family history of violence is particularly significant: violent criminals who were not victims of violence themselves commonly were witnesses to extreme physical violence or the threat of such violence between parents.

Kaufman and Zigler in an important article, "The Intergenerational Transmission of Child Abuse" (in Cicchetti and Carlson, 1989), also question the relation between childhood abuse and adult behavior. Their review of the literature finds a transmission rate of 30 percent, plus or minus 5 percent. While this rate is not insignificant, it is much less than popularly believed. Kaufman and Zigler go on to describe compensatory, or protective, factors which lessen the transmission of abuse. *On a personal level, these include a high IQ, an awareness of early abusive experiences, a resolve not to repeat the abuse, a history of a positive relationship with one caregiver, special talents, physical attractiveness, and good interpersonal skills. On the family level, compensatory factors are healthy children, a supportive spouse, and economic security. On the social level, compensatory factors include good social supports, few stressful events, a strong, supportive religious affiliation, positive school experiences and peer relations as a child, and therapeutic interventions. On the societal level, compensatory factors include a culture opposed to violence and economic prosperity.*

INTERVENTIONS WITH MALE BATTERERS

Interventions with male batterers generally include cognitive-behavioral techniques that emphasize anger control. These interventions usually include three components: relaxation and stress reduction; accurate identification of emotions and cognitive restructuring; and interpersonal skills development (Stordeur and Stille, 1989).

In their group program for male batterers, Neidig and Friedman (1984) use all three components. They describe attribution theory, the basis of the anger-control techniques in their program: an individual's perceptions—appraisal, expectations, and cognitions (internal sentences)—of an external event will determine his arousal to anger. Neidig and Friedman try to teach their group members to make internal beliefs and automatic thoughts conscious as a first step so that they can substitute less inflammatory rhetoric. They teach group members to identify the cues that signify rising anger, including physiologic changes (breathing, pulse rate), cognitive processes (self-statements such as labeling, mind reading, catastrophizing, and vengeance), and specific behaviors (pacing, shouting). They encourage their clients to replace "hot" escalating thoughts with "cool," rational thoughts. Neidig and Friedman go on to teach the differences between passive, assertive, and aggressive behaviors. A passive person will withdraw and do nothing when angry; an aggressive person may have outbursts of poorly controlled rage. In contrast, an assertive person will be active, clarifying personal rights and developing verbal skills to communicate and compromise. They also teach stress reduction, including relaxation; communication skills; and conflict containment and constructive, noncoercive problem-solving skills.

INTERVENTIONS WITH WOMEN: *THE DANCE OF ANGER*

In her book to help women deal with their anger, Harriet Lerner (1985) focuses on how frequently a woman's anger is a signal that something is wrong in a relationship. She points out that many women turn their anger inward and become depressed; others rant and rave, perhaps venting anger, but continuing the imbalance in the relationship. Lerner recommends that women move slowly in their effort to see their anger as a tool for change in relationships. First, she suggests that women look at the real issues underlying their anger and clarify where they stand on the issues. She suggests that women then learn communication skills to improve problem solving and conflict resolution. Next, she encourages women to observe and interrupt nonproductive patterns of interaction, which is

much easier to do after an intense anger has calmed. Finally, Lerner warns women who change their part in a relationship pattern to anticipate and deal with countermoves or "Change back!" reactions from others. Although her book is directed at women, many of her techniques and principles apply to men as well.

Theoretical Bases for Anger Management and Violence Prevention

This section will pull together the findings on violence, the theories of violence, and the recommendations for prevention reported in the last chapter, and the findings on adolescent development and tasks and the effects of maltreatment reported in this chapter.

This manual is based on the cognitive-behavioral theory that aggressive behavior is the result of angry, aggressive thoughts. The social learning theory also applies, since aggressive behavior is frequently learned by watching someone else's aggressive behavior. The concept of emotion regulation is a major theoretical basis for this manual: putting emotions into language helps to organize and control expression of emotion. Group members identify and describe their feelings on a weekly basis.

This manual will focus on helping adolescents learn how to change their emotional, or reactive, aggressive behavior. Just as the most effective intervention programs for male batterers acknowledge individual, family, and societal dynamics, yet hold the batterers accountable for their violent behavior, this group model will hold each person responsible for how he or she expresses anger. The basic tenet of the book will be the value judgment that it is unacceptable to use violent behavior to express anger, and that violent behavior can only be justified if used as an instrument to protect one's life, family, or country. The firm belief in this value presented in the group model should help to counteract the loss of social capital, the capacity to transmit positive values to younger generations.

The first half of the manual focuses on teaching nonaggressive methods to solve interpersonal problems and on giving the students practice in using these methods. Since adolescents can think abstractly and can take an idea or belief and imagine where it would lead, scenarios (short scenes depicting adolescents in real-life situations) and role-playing techniques are used extensively to teach the students.

The scenarios address two issues that are common problems for teens. First is the issue of gender identification: many men believe that to be violent is to prove manhood. Several scenarios encourage adolescent males to consider that acting responsibly instead of nonviolently is a sign of a mature male. Second is the issue of setting limits: many adolescent girls believe they must yield to sexual advances or violence in a relationship. Several scenarios coach adolescent girls to set limits firmly and with determination.

The second half of the group model focuses on family violence, the effects of family violence on adolescents, and how teens can cope with the stresses that family violence creates for them. The group model enables students to put into words that violence has occurred in their families and encourages them to resolve not to repeat violence in their own lives. Through their relationship with the group leader students will be empowered to learn anger management steps and problem-solving skills to use in anger situations, to describe family violence for themselves, and to resolve not to repeat violent behavior. Several of the protective factors described by Kaufman and Zigler to prevent the intergenerational transmission of abuse can occur through participating in an *Anger Management and Violence Prevention* group: an awareness of family stress, a resolve not to repeat the abuse, a relationship with a caring adult, improved interpersonal skills, a social support system, an improved school experience, and a therapeutic intervention.

The Role of the Group in Anger Management and Violence Prevention

This material is presented in a group model for a number of reasons:

1. Group experiences reduce the isolating belief that the adolescent is the only one who gets angry or whose family has been violent.

2. Group experiences help adolescents learn to identify, validate, tolerate, and express their feelings appropriately.

3. Group experiences help adolescents become aware of their self-talk and also help them learn what other adolescents are thinking.

4. Group experiences help adolescents become aware of their patterns in relationships and in expressing anger.

5. Group experiences help adolescents practice changing their behavior in relationships and in expressing anger.

6. Group experiences help adolescents correct their misconceptions, such as their belief that they have caused the family violence or they are bad if they get angry.

7. Group experiences help adolescents develop empathy by learning that others have problems too.

8. Group experiences help adolescents learn and practice coping strategies to get along with peers and family members.

9. Group experiences help adolescents learn that they can ask for help and can take care of themselves.

The material in this manual is geared to the adolescent who is having trouble controlling his or her own angry and aggressive behavior; an overview of violence and cognitive-behavioral techniques helps the adolescent take responsibility for behavior. The material is also geared to the adolescent who has experienced family violence; again, the focus is on giving the adolescent the facts about family violence, and on encouraging the adolescent to develop his or her own protective factors, coping strategies, and resiliencies to cope with family stress in a healthy way.

As students learn to deal effectively with their anger and the stresses of family violence, their sense of competence and control should increase. They should have a more powerful sense that they can influence what happens in their lives.

This material was drawn from the following sources:

Cicchetti, D., and V. Carlson, eds. 1989. *Child Maltreatment: Theory and Research on the Causes and Consequences of Child Abuse and Neglect.* New York: Cambridge University Press.

Cicchetti, D., and P. W. Howes. 1991. "Developmental psychopathology in the context of the family: Illustrations from the study of child maltreatment." *Canadian Journal of Behavioral Science.* 23: 257-81.

Coleman, J. C., and L. Hendry. 1990. *The Nature of Adolescence.* New York: Routledge.

Crittenden, P. M., and M. D. S. Ainsworth. 1989. "Child maltreatment and attachment theory," in Cicchetti and Carlson, eds., *Child Maltreatment: Theory and Research on the Causes and Consequences of Child Abuse and Neglect.* New York: Cambridge University Press (pp. 432-63).

Erikson, E. H. 1968. *Identity: Youth and Crisis.* New York: W. W. Norton.

Gabarino, J. 1989. "Troubled youth, troubled families: The dynamics of adolescent maltreatment," in Cicchetti and Carlson, eds., *Child Maltreatment: Theory and Research on the Causes and Consequences of Child Abuse and Neglect.* New York: Cambridge University Press (pp. 685-706).

Jaffe, P. G., D. A. Wolfe, and S. K. Wilson. 1990. *Children of Battered Women.* Newbury Park, CA: Sage Publications.

Kaufman, J., and E. Zigler. 1989. "The intergenerational transmission of child abuse," in Cicchetti and Carlson, eds., *Child Maltreatment: Theory and Research on the Causes and Consequences of Child Abuse and Neglect.* New York: Cambridge University Press (pp. 129-50).

Lerner, H. 1985. *The Dance of Anger.* New York: Harper & Row.

Lewis, D. O., C. Mallouh, and V. Webb. 1989. "Child abuse, delinquency, and violent criminality," in Cicchetti and Carlson, eds., *Child Maltreatment: Theory and Research on the Causes and Consequences of Child Abuse and Neglect.* New York: Cambridge University Press (pp. 707-21).

Neidig, P. H., and D. H. Friedman. 1984. *Spouse Abuse: A Treatment Program for Couples.* Champaign, IL: Research Press.

Stordeur, R. A., and R. Stille. 1989. *Ending Men's Violence Against Their Partners.* Newbury Park, CA: Sage Publications.

Part Three

GROUP GUIDE FOR ANGER MANAGEMENT AND VIOLENCE PREVENTION

*A*nger Management and Violence Prevention educates and empowers students in grades 6-12 to deal effectively with their anger, to use anger management and problem-solving skills, and to discover the coping skills they need to survive and remain healthy in situations of family violence. This section of the manual describes the characteristics of the *Anger Management and Violence Prevention* group model: a specific and definite progression of themes, a structured format that remains the same for all group sessions, and the use of "displacement communication." It outlines the benefits of using this group model in schools and suggests how the group model might be adapted for guidance counseling and family therapy. Thereafter, follow the complete session plans for leading an *Anger Management and Violence Prevention* support group.

Progression of Themes

This manual contains 11 group session plans for facilitating a support group for middle school and high school students. The sessions follow a specific thematic progression.

SESSION 1 : Violence Prevention

SESSION 2 : Feelings

SESSION 3 : Six Different Styles of Expressing Anger

SESSION 4 : Skills to Problem-Solve Anger Situations

SESSION 5 : Anger Management Steps

SESSION 6 : Family Violence

SESSION 7 : The Effects of Violence on Families: Family Sculptures

SESSION 8 : Coping Strategies

SESSION 9 : Setting Personal Goals

SESSION 10: Group Presentation (optional)

SESSION 11: Developing a Support System

In Session 1, the group manual provides material about the incidence of violence, theories about the causes of violence on four ecological levels, and a description of the risk factors and protective factors that influence an individual to choose violent behavior. The group members are asked to become aware of their own values regarding violence.

In Session 2, anger is presented as a normal feeling. The group participants learn to put thinking between their feelings and their behavior, and to see how negative and positive thinking can influence both feelings and behavior.

In Session 3, the group manual introduces six styles of expressing anger: stuffing, withdrawing, blaming, triangling, exploding, and problem solving. The descriptions of these styles enable the students to observe how they and their acquaintances deal with anger, and to put those patterns into words.

Sessions 4 and 5 present cognitive-behavioral techniques to help the students handle their anger in positive ways. The students learn and practice five problem-solving skills to use in anger situations. They also learn the anger management steps, which help them put thinking between their feeling and their behavior. The practice situations are age appropriate and relevant: one coaches adolescent girls to set sexual limits in a dating relationship; another coaches girls to set firm limits regarding violent behavior after the first, most minor incident. Adolescent males look at scenarios where they are taunted to prove their manhood; they, too, are coached to set firm limits.

Sessions 6, 7, and 8 introduce the issue of family violence and the effect family violence has on teens and other family members. The material helps to correct misconceptions common to adolescents in violent families. The teens also learn coping strategies to deal with problems that come up in their families; they learn to keep themselves safe, to avoid assuming responsibility for someone else's feelings or behavior, and to do good things for themselves.

The objective of Session 9 is to help the students learn how to set personal goals. Group members identify ways they can take good care of their bodies, minds, feelings, and choices.

Session 10 involves an educational presentation by the group members. Audiences can range from a principal or an administrator, to a class, to an entire grade level. Successfully teaching their peers the basic facts reinforces the students' learning and increases their self-esteem. It helps give the group a sense of cohesiveness and closure. It also raises the education and awareness level of the audience and provides an opportunity for future referrals.

In Session 11, the students celebrate their learning and growth. They create their own support system that will help them know where to go and to whom to turn for help when they need it in the future.

GROUP FORMAT

The group model presented in this manual follows a structured format for each group session that is both educationally and clinically sound.

Each plan begins with the **Objectives** section. The section sets a clear direction for the group session.

The section **Session at a Glance** outlines the session and includes suggested times for each of the plan's components. If you carefully go over the plan in advance, this section can serve as a quick reference as you move through the session.

The **Preparation** section, which follows, lists materials needed and gives directions for getting ready for the session. When directions in this section call for copies of various materials, most may be found in blackline master form at the end of the session. Other support materials are found in Part Four of this manual.

The **Background and Guidelines** section will enrich your understanding of the session's focus and key concepts, as well as guide you through the plan itself.

Thereafter, the session unfolds in three stages: **Beginning the Session, Exploring the Material,** and **Wrapping Up.** The three-part format includes the same components from session to session.

1. Beginning the Session

   • Review of group rules
   • Centering exercise
   • Feelings check-in
   • Review of basic facts (beginning with Session 2)
   •Review of assignment (beginning with Session 2)

2. Exploring the Material

   • Mini-lecture (the heart of the session)
   • Group discussion
   • Activity (in most sessions)
   • Basic facts
   • Homework assignment to practice skills

3. Wrapping Up

   • Repetition of centering exercise
   • Affirmation
   • Closing activity

Since the format and its components remain constant through all 11 sessions, these components deserve a closer look.

Rules and Rules Contract. Creating an atmosphere in which a group of teenagers (some of whom might not know each other) feel secure and willing to share thoughts and feelings is a major undertaking. Many students will have never participated in a group process before, so they'll be unaccustomed to the expectations and the boundaries of a group. Group rules ensure that all group members will be treated with the dignity and respect they deserve. Group rules also establish a standard of behavior for the adolescents. They establish the expectation that students can be responsible for their behavior.

As group leader, you should initially present the Group Rules Contract (see page 66) in the screening interview and explain that all members of the group will be asked to sign the contract. In the initial session, you will again go over the rules with the group, and explain the consequences for not following the rules. You can decide on your own consequences, but it often works well to give misbehaving students one warning, and then ask them to leave if they cannot follow the rules a second time. Explain that the student can return the following week and will again receive one warning; but, if asked to leave a second time, the student will not be able to attend the rest of the group meetings. Group members show that they agree to follow the rules by signing the contract. Rules are displayed in the group meeting room.

After a review of the rules in Session 2, teens are usually able to follow the rules easily. However, if student behavior deteriorates, review the rules at the beginning of the next group session, making sure that the students understand them all. For the sake of group morale, it is important to enforce the consequences if a student cannot follow the rules. As difficult as it is to remove students from the group, allowing them to misbehave amounts to enabling. Consistency in enforcing consequences reminds the adolescents that they're safe in group and that all group members will behave as they promised.

Centering Exercise. This exercise sets the stage for group work in a positive way. The techniques learned in the centering exercise, which include deep breathing and tensing and relaxing muscles, are not limited to group work only. Once mastered, teens can use them in "real-life" situations. Repeated toward the end of a group session, the centering exercise not only reinforces learning but also enables the adolescents to calm down—especially if intense feelings arose during the session—and get ready to return to their classroom.

Feelings Check-in. During the feelings check-in, the group members learn to identify, own, and express feelings in appropriate ways. As group leader, you will validate, accept, and tolerate the students' feelings. For example, a teen might say he wants to kill his father because of a fight his parents had. In response you might say, "It sounds like you're feeling very angry and

upset! Can you tell us what you're so angry about?" After the student responds, you could continue, "Many teens feel angry when that happens in their families. But in this group we're teaching nonviolent ways to express anger, and we're teaching teens how to cope with violence in their families. We'll learn more about how to handle these kinds of problems in later sessions."

By accepting and validating feelings and by helping the students identify helpful ways to express feelings, you will consistently teach that feelings aren't bad or dangerous, that they can be felt and expressed, and that they will pass. Thus, the feelings check-in functions both as a corrective and therapeutic experience for the group members.

Review of Basic Facts. Beginning in Session 2, the basic facts learned in previous sessions are reviewed for understanding. This weekly repetition and clarification is an effective technique to change misconceptions that adolescents may have, especially about the acceptability of violent behavior and about codependence.

Leaders of groups of high school students can consider this weekly review optional, although for impact, the basic facts should be reviewed at least every other week. You can use your own judgment on the best way to present the basic facts. It is strongly recommended, however, that you or the students make a poster for each basic fact. The posters will then be ready for the presentation of basic facts in Session 10. An alternative is to have the students look at the List of Basic Facts (see page 209), which you can staple to the inside of their folders, on the left side for easy accessibility. A third alternative is to write each basic fact on an index card and pass the cards out to the students.

Assignment. In each session, you will give the students a homework assignment, which is designed to help them practice what they have learned. The assignments are based on cognitive-behavioral theory and the principle of starting behavioral change by observing current behavior. Some assignments require group members simply to observe themselves, their friends, and their families to see what anger styles they use, and to think about what problem-solving skills they could use. The assignment is given at the end of each session, and it is reviewed at the beginning of the next session. The review, a go-around where the students report what they have observed, is an important component of this group. Being expected to put what they see into words will force the group members to be more observant. And hearing how other group members are trying to use their new skills provides encouragement and motivation for all. Be sure to be nonjudgmental as you conduct the go-around. Remember that behavioral change starts with the smallest, concrete steps. Be sure to reinforce the students' ability to observe their current style of expressing anger, even if you think it is harmful.

Mini-lecture. In this component, you will present basic facts about violence prevention, anger management, and family violence. The session plan provides all the information you will need. In most sessions, you will integrate your "lecture" with questions, brainstorming, reading, discussion, and role-playing scenarios. The group manual provides various handouts to help convey and reinforce the basic information. In using the handouts, be aware that some group members may have difficulty reading them. In this case, you may want to read the handouts to the group or call on able readers to do the reading.

Discussion. Each session's lecture is usually followed by questions you may use to initiate group discussion. In the discussion, the students have the chance to process the basic facts, and, you have the chance to make sure they understand the concepts and issues presented.

Activity. The activity is generally a brief written exercise that reinforces the material presented in the lecture. In a nonthreatening way, the activity is designed to engage the students in active understanding of the material. The activities in some sessions enable the students to express their perceptions of their situations, but only to the degree they can and want to share them.

Basic Facts. The basic facts summarize the essential message of the material in a way that is easily understood and remembered. New basic facts are introduced by having the students look at the List of Basic Facts.

Affirmation. In the affirmation, the students tell something they liked about the session or something they learned in the session. This gives them a chance to end the group on a positive note, even if intense feelings have arisen during the group. The affirmation reinforces the content presented and helps the adolescents learn to choose a positive attitude.

Closing. The closing exercise helps the group develop a sense of bonding, cohesiveness, acceptance, and sharing. It allows for physical touch in a safe, nonthreatening atmosphere, which may be a new experience for many of the adolescents. The same closing exercise concludes each session. Older students who feel uncomfortable holding hands may pass the wish in any appropriate way, such as through a pat on the elbow or shoulder.

The *Anger Management and Violence Prevention* format provides the students with a total experience that is structured as well as welcoming and accepting, instructional as well as creative and enjoyable, challenging as well as affirming and fun. Since the format remains the same for each session, it meets the needs at-risk adolescents have for consistency and predictability.

The format encourages the students to participate as fully as possible in the group process. Go-arounds, where everybody gets a chance to describe feelings and experiences, are used extensively to make it easy for students to share in a safe, nonthreatening way. Although the students are never forced to take part and are given the right to "pass," the format allows each group member at least three opportunities per session to speak and other, nonverbal, opportunities to participate as well.

If you are a new group leader, you should follow up each session by filling out a copy of the Process and Progress Form (see page 211). This form enables you to evaluate the session's effectiveness and to track the students' progress. It also serves as a useful tool when training new group leaders. If you are an experienced leader, you may follow up each session by filling out the Progress Notes (see page 212). No matter what your experience is, it is a good idea to keep some form of notes on each session.

Each group session is designed to take approximately 45 minutes, but can be shortened or extended to meet local circumstances. You may feel that some sessions contain enough information to be scheduled over two meeting times. If you have the time, you may simply follow the session plan as given, but only present half of the plan during one session time.

Session 10 is an optional session. Its structure varies from the other sessions in that group members will present facts they've learned to an invited audience. You may or may not choose to involve the students in this session. For this session to be successful, you should schedule two meeting times to present it. Use the first time period as a practice session to help the students decide on the type and content of their presentation, to make all necessary preparations, and to practice their presentation. Use the second time period to conduct the actual session. To guarantee success, plan ahead for Session 10. Read the Background and Guidelines material for Session 10 now to help you decide if you want your group to do a presentation or to develop a unique project.

Displacement Communication

In its progression of themes, the group model uses a therapeutic technique called displacement communication (Kalter, 1990) to help adolescents deal with family stress, while allowing them to save face or to remain loyal to their families. Lacking knowledge and perspective, young children are not often verbal or articulate in describing family problems or their reactions to those problems. While adolescents may have greater knowledge and perspective, they still might not want to discuss the problems, both in an effort to avoid or deny their own distress and to preserve their families' good name. Some adolescents are often unaware of their specific feelings and are unable to name them. They're also unaware of their internal conflicts and end up acting them out by fighting, misbehaving, somatizing, overeating, or trying to be perfect.

Recognizing that many adolescents don't communicate directly, the group model combines a direct and an indirect method of communication through lecture material, scenarios, and role plays.

The displacement communication model developed by Kalter contains the following six steps:

1. Represent in the displacement material (lecture or scenario; stuffed animals for younger children) the behaviors that signify emotional distress (fighting, crying, chemical use, sexual acting out).

2. Acknowledge how upsetting such behavior is to the displacement figure (character in scenario).

3. Address the displacement figure's underlying conflict or emotional pain.

4. Correct any misconceptions in the displacement.

5. Accept conflicted feelings.

6. Present alternative ways of expressing and coping with conflict.

These steps are incorporated in the group model's sessions. The sessions' lectures, in a nonjudgmental way, educate the students about family violence. Family stress and behavior are described. The lecture identifies the underlying conflict and the emotional pain common to adolescents in the family situation. The lecture then corrects their misconceptions and misperceptions by teaching them the three Cs: children don't cause and can't control or change parental violence. The sessions teach the students how to identify, accept, and express their feelings in appropriate ways. Finally, the sessions teach alternative coping strategies to enable the students to deal more successfully with their stress.

Adolescents easily identify with the family examples provided in the scenarios. Without having to describe family situations, the group members can compare themselves to the behavior and situation described. Due to the material's non-threatening and nonjudgmental nature, the students are able to use new ideas without feeling pressured. They are able to save face and get help without feeling disloyal to their families.

Benefits of Use

Using this group model for at-risk adolescents can benefit your school on a number of levels, including the logistics level, the individual level, and the system level.

The Logistics Level. Logistically, the model provides structure for new and untrained group leaders. This manual provides complete guidelines for each session. In addition, considerable background material is provided to explain the theoretical purpose of each session. The structure of the group format considerably reduces behavior problems during group sessions. Generally, adolescents enjoy participating in these groups and eagerly recommend them to their friends.

The Individual Level. Adolescents who have participated in *Anger Management and Violence Prevention* support groups have benefited in a variety of ways, including the following: (1) the behavior of group members in school improved, even the behavior of aggressive high school males; (2) group members increased their attachment to school, which has proved to be effective drop-out prevention; (3) middle school

students were helped to abstain from alcohol, marijuana, and other drugs; and (4) students integrated concepts taught in the group into other situations.

The System Level. This group model recommends in-service programs for administrators and teachers about issues facing adolescents from at-risk families. In-services raise the awareness and education levels of teachers and administrators about the issue of family violence. In-services may also help some participants to identify for the first time that they are children from such families and to understand problems they have had or are still having in their own lives. Many who share in the in-service may have friends or relatives affected by someone else's violence. Participants may be encouraged to gain further education about these particular issues; to offer informed help to students or acquaintances who come from violent families; and to seek any professional help they may need themselves. Thus, the in-service plants the seeds of recovery for many.

USING THE GROUP MODEL IN GUIDANCE COUNSELING

Guidance counselors and other professionals have found the group model's centering exercises, anger management plan, problem-solving skills, and basic facts useful not only when working with adolescents in groups but also when working with them individually. Because the group's concepts—including the basic education about the issues and the correction of typical misconceptions—are clear and easily identifiable, they enhance assessment skills. They also empower counselors to be more effective in individual counseling with students. Instead of just discussing feelings with the students, counselors can impart information and correct misconceptions. Also, the skills presented in the group are effective techniques that adolescents learn, master, and use.

Guidance counselors who have led *Anger Management and Violence Prevention* groups have been able to use the centering exercises, anger management plans, basic facts, and coping-strategy scenarios in classroom guidance. They report that students who have participated in these groups are usually actively involved in the classroom discussion, which reveals that adolescents truly do integrate crucial concepts presented by the group (for example, "It is never acceptable to use violence to express anger"). Counselors generally report that leading these groups gives them a sense of greater competence, effectiveness, and empowerment.

USING THE GROUP MODEL IN FAMILY THERAPY

This group model works not only in schools, mental health facilities, and treatment centers. It also works well in therapy with families experiencing violence or with families in which children exhibit aggressive behavior.

By using the group's format and materials, therapists can help family members become aware of and learn the facts about anger and violence. The family members can see the impact the issue has made on their family and their feelings about it. The group model can help the family with anger management, coping strategies, setting personal goals, and developing a support system. During family sessions, the helping professional serves as a role model for parents.

Just as *Anger Management and Violence Prevention* corrects misconceptions for teenagers, it also corrects them for parents. For instance, a mother engaged in long-term conflict with an ex-spouse may come to see that it's important for her children to be friendly with both parents, and she will then lessen her part in the conflict. Likewise, parents who express anger by yelling or who try to control through physical force can learn to use—and benefit from—the group's centering exercises, anger management steps, and problem-solving skills. Finally, all parents can benefit by learning to put thinking between feeling and behavior.

This group model was developed for caring professionals like you who are concerned about at-risk adolescents. It will help you enhance the emotional growth, safety, and self-esteem of these young people. Living healthfully and well is a risky business. All children, especially at-risk children, deserve the chance to take that risk.

Violence Prevention

Objectives

To help the students:

- recognize the difference between emotional or expressive aggression and instrumental aggression

- realize that many factors contribute to an individual's choice to act in violent ways, but each individual is ultimately responsible for his or her behavior

- begin to identify factors that apply to their decisions to act aggressively, whether in an expressive or an instrumental way

- become aware of the value judgment that expressive aggression is never acceptable

Session at a Glance

1. Welcome and Group Rules (Group Rules Contract)—3 minutes

2. Centering Exercise: "White Water Rafting"—4 minutes

3. Ice-breaker—6 minutes

4. Mini-lecture and Discussion—15 minutes

5. Activity: identify your own risk factors and protective factors for violence—5 minutes

6. Basic Facts: read Basic Facts 1, 2, and 3; discuss—3 minutes

7. Assignment—2 minutes

8. Centering Exercise: "Breathing Through Your Feet"—4 minutes

9. Affirmation: share something you liked about the group—3 minutes

10. Closing: pass a silent wish—1 minute

Preparation

- Make a copy of the Group Rules Contract (see page 66) for each student. To save time at the copy machine, also make copies of the Feeling Wheel (page 83), the handouts for each session, and the List of Basic Facts (page 209).

- Copy the group rules onto a large sheet of posterboard that you can display in the group meeting space during this and future sessions.

- Have a large manila folder for each student; print the student's name on the folder.

- Include in each student's folder:

  —a 3" x 5" lined index card

  —the Group Rules Contract

  —Handout 1A ("Violence and Aggression")

  —Handout 1B ("Scenarios")

  —Handout 1C ("Risk Factors and Protective Factors for Aggressive Behavior")

  —Handout 1D ("Protective Factors for Child Abuse")

  —Handout 1E ("My Risk Factors and Protective Factors")

  —Assignment 1

  —the List of Basic Facts stapled to the inside of the folder, on the left side, for easy reference

- Have the folder, a pencil and crayons or markers at each student's place.

- Make a poster to use during the session's ice-breaker. On newsprint, list the following questions:

  —What is your name?

  —Your age?

  —Your year in school?

  —Who lives in your house?

  —If you could be anywhere, where would you like to be?

  —What do you want to do after high school?

  —What three words ending in "-ing" describe you?

- Read through the session plan before meeting.

Background and Guidelines

This session introduces the students to a group setting. During the screening interview, you prepared the students for the group by explaining the structure and format of the group and the progression of themes. You explained the group rules and secured their agreement to follow the rules. Your comfort and confidence during this session will ensure the students that group is a safe, nonthreatening place to learn about anger management and violence prevention.

This session provides general information about violence. It clearly establishes the group standard that expressing anger through violence is not acceptable. This section reviews current theory about violence and aggression and basic statistics about violent crime and juvenile violence. More information will be presented in this section than you will present to the students. You can also use this background information to enhance your own understanding and to help you explain the material you do present.

VIOLENCE AND AGGRESSION

Violence is a form of human aggression. It is behavior with the intent to harm someone or something. Aggression can be verbal; words can be vicious weapons.

Aggression is categorized as *emotional* or as *instrumental*. Emotional or expressive aggression is *reactive*, occurring in response to a particular provocation, pain, threat, or frustration; it is used to express anger. In emotional anger, whatever provokes the anger causes the brain and hormones to order the heart to pump faster and to send more blood with food and oxygen to the muscles. The palms sweat; the face flushes red with anger. *Instrumental* or *proactive* aggression is used to attain a goal or an award; no anger need be involved. An act of violence to attain membership in a gang is an act of instrumental aggression; so is the violence involved in wars.

Four Factors in Aggression

Researchers name four factors that are usually present in acts of human aggression: arousal, trigger, weapon, and target.

Arousal. Arousal refers to a physiological state that is a reaction to stress, getting the body ready for some kind of action. There are involuntary symptoms in a person in a state of arousal: the heart beats faster, the rate of breathing increases; the face flushes; and hands shake or sweat. Arousal can be a reaction to fear, joy, sexual activity, or physical exercise. Arousal to anger generally occurs when individuals perceive pain, frustration, or aggression against themselves. Emotional arousal caused by *pain*, such as a physical injury, is likely to result in violent behavior. Discomfort caused by very hot and oppressive *weather* can also be a factor in violent behavior. (The FBI's 1991 crime statistics indicate that more violent crimes are committed in the summer than in the winter.) The *threat of aggression*, such as a person staring at another person, can also be an emotional arouser.

Crowding is also seen as a serious threat by some people: some people are uncomfortable when other people invade their psychological elbowroom. Again, the FBI crime statistics reveal that more violent crime occurs in large cities than in rural areas. A 1969 report estimated that a resident of Chicago living in the area of greatest population density faced a one in 77 risk of being assaulted. In the less dense, "better" areas of the city, the risk was only one in 2,000. The risk decreased to one in 10,000 for individuals living in the rich suburbs (Moyer, 1987).

Frustration can be another cause of emotional arousal. Frustration is the emotion generated by interference with a person's progress toward a goal. The nearer the goal, the more violent is the aggressive response when the goal is made unobtainable.

Trigger. Researchers have called the event that

releases emotional arousal a trigger. Sometimes a trigger is just the last straw in a long series of events that have caused pain, discomfort, or frustration.

Weapon. Every act of violence requires a weapon. Weapons used in violence range from a sharp tongue, to hands used in a beating, to a knife, to guns. Even cars have been used as weapons in aggressive behavior. Some people attribute the high murder rate in the United States to the easy accessibility of guns. The FBI statistics for 1991 indicate firearms were used in 70 percent of the murders committed in the United States that year.

Target. The last factor in aggression is the target. Sometimes a target can serve as the trigger that sets off the aggression. Sometimes a target can be displaced, as in the classic example of the man whose boss reprimands him. The man goes home and yells at his son, who then kicks the dog. Another example of displacement occurred in the South. A study showed that lynchings of blacks were more prevalent during periods of economic distress, when cotton prices went down and many people were out of work. Since the lynch mobs were unable to attack the causes of falling cotton prices, they targeted blacks.

Group Violence

Research shows that people are more violent in groups than when acting alone. Groups allow individuals to remain anonymous and to share in the responsibility for what they do. Group membership often allows people to rationalize violence since they believe that it serves a higher cause. Finally, groups such as a military hierarchy are based on the concept of obedience to authority. Individual soldiers are absolved from responsibility for their violent behavior because they are just following orders.

Researchers have looked at the causes of group aggression. First, *prejudice* legitimizes making people outside the group victims of aggression or discrimination. Second, *economic or political competition for limited resources* can cause group aggression. Third is the practice of *dehumaniz-*

ing the victims. For example, in the popular novel and movie *Silence of the Lambs,* the serial killer dehumanizes his victims by calling them "it," rather than their names. Hitler dehumanized the Jews by treating them like animals, taking their clothes away, tattooing them with identifying numbers, and spraying them with insecticide. This paradox of group violence—rationalizing acts of aggression and blaming the victims rather than the aggressor—is common even in some theories of family violence.

STATISTICS ABOUT VIOLENCE IN THE UNITED STATES

*T*he Uniform Crime Reports for the United States, a reference document compiled annually by the FBI, documents the numbers and kinds of crimes reported to law enforcement agencies nationwide. The FBI lists four kinds of violent crime: murder, forcible rape, robbery, and aggravated assault. All violent crimes involve force or threat of force.

Murder is the willful killing of one human being by another. The FBI does not include deaths caused by negligence, attempts to kill, assaults to kill, suicides, accidental deaths, or justifiable homicide in this category. Justifiable homicides are limited to the killing of a felon by a law enforcement officer in the line of duty, and the killing of a felon by a private citizen.

Forcible rape is the carnal knowledge of a female forcibly and against her will.

Robbery is the taking or attempting to take anything of value from the care, custody, or control of a person or persons by force or threat of force or violence and/or by putting the victim in fear.

Aggravated assault is the unlawful attack by one person upon another for the purpose of inflicting severe aggravated bodily injury. This type of assault usually is accompanied by the use of a weapon or by means likely to produce death or great bodily harm. In comparison, a simple assault is one where no weapon is used and which does not result in serious or aggravated injury to the victim.

CRIME CLOCK

The FBI reports that in 1991 one violent crime was committed every 17 seconds: one murder every 21 minutes, one forcible rape every 5 minutes, one robbery every 46 seconds, and one aggravated assault every 29 seconds. Violent crimes reported to law enforcement during 1991 exceeded 1.9 million offenses. This annual total was the highest ever recorded, up 5 percent over 1990, 29 percent over 1987, and 45 percent over 1982.

From 1990 to 1991 the nation's cities collectively recorded a 5 percent rise, while rural and suburban counties recorded increases of 6 and 4 percent, respectively.

Thirty-six percent of all violent crimes reported in 1991 were committed in the South; 24 percent were committed in the West; and 20 percent were committed in both the Northeast and Midwest. (The FBI considers the South to be the area from the District of Columbia down to Florida and west to Texas.)

Violent crimes occur more frequently in the summer months, while the lowest totals are experienced during the winter. Aggravated assaults accounted for 57 percent of the violent crimes reported to law enforcement in 1991; robberies comprised 36 percent; forcible rapes, 6 percent; and murders, 1 percent. Firearms were the weapons used in 31 percent of all murders, robberies, and aggravated assaults, collectively, in 1991.

Ninety-three percent of black murder victims were slain by black offenders, and 85 percent of white murder victims were killed by white offenders. Males were most often slain by males (87 percent in single-victim/single-offender situations); nine of every 10 female victims were murdered by males. Firearms were the weapons used in approximately seven out of every 10 murders committed in the United States.

Almost half of the murder victims in 1991 were either related to (12 percent) or acquainted with (34 percent) their assailants. Among all female murder victims in 1991, 28 percent were slain by husbands or boyfriends. Four percent of the male victims were killed by wives or girlfriends. Arguments resulted in 32 percent of the murders during the year.

Juvenile Violence

In a report studying juvenile violence between 1965 and 1990, the FBI states that the nation experienced its highest juvenile (ages 10-17) violent crime arrest rate, 430 per 100,000 juveniles, in 1990. This rate was 27 percent higher than the 1980 rate. In the 25-year-period from 1965 to 1990, the overall murder arrest rate for juveniles increased 332 percent, from 2.8 per 100,000 to 12.1 per 100,000. During the past decade, there has been a 79 percent increase in the number of juveniles who commit murders with guns. The aggravated assault rate has risen steadily, and it has the highest number of arrests. This would suggest that today's youth are more inclined to settle a dispute by engaging in a physical altercation.

The FBI statistics make extremely clear that violent behavior is a problem in the United States and an increasing problem for adolescents.

CAUSES OF AGGRESSION

Researchers have studied the causes of aggression, and their theories range from the personal level to the societal level. The newest theories on the causes of aggression use the most comprehensive models possible. These models involve looking at risk factors (factors that increase the likelihood of the problem, such as child abuse) and compensatory, or protective, factors (factors that decrease the likelihood of the problem). Risk factors and protective factors are described on four ecological levels: personal (ontogenetic), family (microsystem), social (exosystem), and societal (macrosystem). An ecological model of theories of violence would look at factors on all levels.

ON THE SPECIES LEVEL

Biological necessity for survival of the fittest. Charles Darwin and other theorists believed that violence enabled the strongest to survive, thereby ensuring the survival of the species.

ON THE PERSONAL LEVEL

An innate instinct. Sigmund Freud postulated two basic drives: one was the life force, and the second was an unconscious death wish. Turned inward, the unconscious death wish results in masochism; when turned outward, in aggression. Konrad Lorenz named three reasons why vertebrates fight animals of their own kind: sex, territory, and dominance. The fact that aggression is much more common in males than in females supports this theory.

Brain activity. This model proposes that neural systems in the brains of animals and humans produce aggressive or destructive behavior when activated by the target. Although these neural systems exist and are innately organized, aggression is not necessarily inevitable, nor is it uncontrollable. Moyer (1987) quotes studies that show that brain stimulation can cause specific kinds of aggression: *intermale aggression*, an anger reaction associated with *anxiety*, and intense *rage* accompanied by *pain*. Aversive stimulation, particularly pain and a variety of deprivation states, such as food and sleep deprivation, increases the tendency for irritable aggression. Some extreme violence has been associated with a brain tumor.

ON THE FAMILY LEVEL

Learned behavior. Some learned behavior is mere *imitation*. Albert Bandura, who studied nursery school children, found that children imitated aggressive behavior in a model, especially if the model was someone they knew, and someone in authority. Rewards make the learning stronger. Children also learn aggressive behavior from their parents: aggressive children tend to come from homes where the parents are rejecting and punitive, inconsistent in their guidance, and constantly fighting between themselves and undermining each other's values. Mothers and fathers may encourage their children to fight in self-defense: spanking is used in 90 percent of American homes.

ON THE SOCIAL LEVEL

On the next ecological level, aggressive behavior can be motivated by the attitudes of *peers*. Adolescent gangs often require acts of aggression for membership. *Peer rejection* and *early school failures* are also associated with adult violence. Growing up in a *low income family*, *living in poor housing*, and *living in a high crime neighborhood*, with illegal markets such as drugs and prostitution, are risk factors for violence.

ON THE SOCIETAL LEVEL

Finally, on the cultural level, violence is often vividly displayed and glorified on *television* and in *books*. Studies show that children who watch violence on television are more aggressive in their play and may lack empathy for victims of violence. Some researchers blame the *heritage of the American frontier*—where violence was necessary for survival—for the cultural tradition of violence in America. The easy *availability of firearms* in the United States is an important factor in the high rate of violent crimes. Studies have shown that having a weapon available makes aggressive behavior more likely. *Political* and *economic inequality* is also blamed for the high rate of violence.

Causes of Juvenile Violence

Some social scientists believe that juvenile violence reflects a *breakdown of families, schools, and other societal institutions*, reflecting several ecological levels. They point to the fact that 70 percent of juvenile offenders come from single-parent homes, and that the percentage of single-parent families in the United States has tripled since 1950. The unprecedented rise in juvenile violence has also coincided with an increase in juvenile heroin/cocaine arrests and an increase in illegal use of weapons by young people.

RISK FACTORS AND PROTECTIVE FACTORS FOR AGGRESSIVE BEHAVIOR

Handout 1C ("Risk Factors and Protective Factors for Aggressive Behavior") is an easy-to-read chart describing risk factors and protective factors that have been identified for aggressive behavior. (See page 69.)

Studies show that aggressive children tend to become violent teenagers and adults. However, not all aggressive children grow up to be violent, and not all children who experience risk factors become violent. It is important when looking at risk factors and protective factors to realize that there is not a direct cause-and-effect relationship. It may take several factors, on several levels, to interact in a way that leads a person to develop violent behavior. The following examples demonstrate some interactions that have been identified.

Personal Level

PRENATAL FACTORS

Some birth traumas, like low birthweight and birth-related central nervous system problems, correlate with later violence, but only if the person who experiences the trauma is also raised in an unstable, nonintact family.

TEMPERAMENT

When toddlers encounter unfamiliar children and adults, some are shy, vigilant, and restrained ("inhibited"); others are sociable, spontaneous, and relatively fearless ("uninhibited"): fearless behavior may be a risk factor for children with low socioeconomic status, whereas fearfulness may act as a protective factor against aggression. Temperament may explain why only a proportion of children from high-risk homes and neighborhoods develops antisocial or violent behavior.

Family Level

A small, stable, intact family with high income and nonviolent parents may be an important protective factor for a child who has below average IQ and who has attention deficit and hyperactivity.

Social Level

PEER AND SCHOOL FACTORS

Peer rejection often correlates with childhood aggression, but the relationship may be that childhood aggression causes peer rejection. Teaching aggressive children how to get along with others may improve their acceptance by peers. The intervention of teaching social skills would be a protective factor.

Societal Level

Studies show that exposure to television violence encourages aggressive behavior by children and adults; however, not all people who see violence on television become violent. Abnormally frequent watching of television violence is the risk factor.

Protective factors can be important and effective in helping people choose not to be violent. It's important to understand that while a high proportion of delinquents, particularly violent delinquents, and of violent adult criminals, suffered extreme abuse in childhood, most physically abused children do not go on to become violent. And, only a third of people who were abused in childhood become abusers themselves. Researchers are identifying protective factors that help a person choose not to be aggressive or violent, or to abuse their children as they were abused. Handout 1D ("Protective Factors for Child Abuse") lists these factors on the personal, family, social, and societal levels. (See page 70.)

Two factors on the personal level—an awareness of early abusive experiences and a resolve not to repeat the abuse—are especially relevant for the *Anger Management and Violence Prevention* group. Wolin and Wolin (1993) describe seven resiliencies that some people develop to help them rise above their experiences in troubled families. The resiliencies are insight, independence, relationships, initiative, creativity, humor, and morality. The Wolins found that being able to describe the problems of their families in words helped the survivors not to repeat the troubled patterns. Helping children develop their own resiliencies moves them away from the "Damage Model"—the model that suggests children are bound to have problems if they come from families experiencing divorce, chemical dependence, violence, mental illness, or other dysfunctions. Instead, the Wolins use the "Challenge Model," which acknowledges the danger presented by the troubled family, but which also sees growing up in a troubled family as an opportunity to develop resiliencies that promote growth and well-being. A resolve not to use violent behavior is a resiliency that this group fosters in group members.

WHAT TO DO WITH AGGRESSION

Some studies show that the act of catharsis—letting all the anger out—may not be effective: verbal aggression increases anger; physical activity and watching violence on TV may not decrease aggression.

Prevention and control are shown to be more effective. On a societal level, some theorists recommend (1) removing political and economic injustices that breed frustration and (2) changing cultural values to turn people away from violence.

On a personal level, most theorists recommend using cognitive-behavioral techniques to help individuals learn alternatives to aggressive and violent behavior and to help them develop prosocial skills. These interventions should emphasize the undesirability of aggression and should teach nonaggressive methods of solving interpersonal problems.

The following factors have been found to be important in helping people choose alternatives to aggressive behavior:

• allow time for angry persons to cool off

• distract them

• offer explanations for the action that angered them

The role of the mind is critical in controlling aggression: how people respond to a triggering event depends on the way they think, their interpretation of an event, their motivation, and their previous experience.

People are more likely to engage in nonaggressive behavior if they are rewarded. The nonviolence movement in India led by Gandhi was rewarded by social changes. Positive reinforcement for positive behavior is much more effective at restraining violence than is negative reinforcement for negative conduct. Punishing misbehavior is not as effective as rewarding nonaggressive behavior.

WHEN VIOLENCE IS JUSTIFIED

The Semai tribe in Malaya may provide a model of when violence is appropriate. This is a society that does not condone violence.

The Semai tribe is so nonviolent that not a single murder has ever been recorded among them; they have no need for a police force. However, when their country was threatened in World War II, they fought against the Communists, very violently, to protect their home. After the war, they went back to gentle, nonviolent ways.

This support group model focuses on prevention and control of violence, especially on the personal level. You can hope that there will be some improvement on the societal level so that political and economic injustices that breed frustration will be eliminated. You can also hope that cultural values will shift so that violence is not glorified on television and in movies, and parents will begin to teach their children to be nonviolent. On the social level, you can hope for an improvement in housing in the inner city, decreasing overcrowding.

Anger Management and Violence Prevention attempts to change the system by starting with a group of teenagers. In this group, you will adopt the value that violence to express anger is not acceptable, and that violence is only acceptable if necessary for self-defense, as for the Semai tribe in Malaya. You will teach cognitive-behavioral techniques that have proven effective in dealing with emotional aggression: to take time to cool off, to look at what has caused an angry action, to put thinking between feeling and behavior, and to use behaviors other than hurting someone or something. We will also look at ways to express anger that may not be violent, but are still harmful, in order to learn more helpful ways to express anger. By trying to help the students develop their own protective factors on a personal level, the group itself is an intervention that is a protective factor on the social or neighborhood level.

This material was drawn from the following sources:

Crime in the United States, 1991: Uniform Crime Reports. Federal Bureau of Investigation, U.S. Department of Justice, Washington, D.C. 20535.

Bailey, R. H., ed. 1976. *Violence and Aggression.* New York: Time-Life Books.

Moyer, K. E. 1987. *Violence and Aggression: A Physiological Perspective.* New York: Paragon House Publishers.

Reiss, A. J., and J. A. Roth, eds. 1993. *Understanding and Preventing Violence.* Washington, D.C.: National Academy Press.

Wolin, S., and S. Wolin. 1993. *The Resilient Self.* New York: Villard Books.

Zevin, J. 1973. *Violence in America: What Is the Alternative?* Englewood Cliffs, NJ: Prentice-Hall.

Beginning the Session

INTRODUCTION

Welcome the students and have them sit at a table. Explain that this group is about anger management and violence prevention. Describe how you will start with an overview of violence and the factors that put a person at risk for violent behavior. Explain that you will make the value judgment that the use of violence to express anger is unacceptable, and that each individual has the responsibility to choose not to use violence in his or her own life. In following sessions, you will help the students see how putting thinking between feelings and behavior helps them avoid aggressive behavior. You will teach them some techniques for anger management and problem solving so that they can be more aware of how they express anger and learn to make better choices in expressing anger. Then, you will move on to look at family violence and the effects of family violence on adolescents. Finally, you will teach them some coping strategies to deal with family violence, or with the violence that can occur in dating relationships. Stress that this is not a class and there will be no grades. You expect everyone in the group to have fun as you learn alternatives to aggressive and violent behavior.

GROUP RULES

Pass out the folders. Explain that the students will use their folders every time they meet and that everything they need will be in these folders. Ask the group members to take their copy of the Group Rules Contract out of their folders. Meanwhile, display the poster you made listing the group rules. Tell the students that like every group—use examples of groups like band, sports teams, and yearbook staff—their group has rules. For the group to work well, everyone needs to keep the rules. Even though the students will have encountered these rules in their screening interview, take a moment to go through them now to check for understanding:

1. I will keep what we talk about private. We call this confidentiality.

2. I will stay in my seat.

3. I will keep my hands to myself.

4. I will wait for my turn to talk, and I will listen carefully when others talk.

5. I won't tease or put other people down.

6. I can pass during go-arounds.

7. I will come to every group session.

8. I will make up the class work I miss.

You can explain to the students that some of these rules may seem childish and that you really don't expect them to have trouble staying in their seats or keeping their hands to themselves.

Stress the importance of coming to every session and coming on time; also stress how important it is that they keep up their class work, since you will need the teachers' cooperation to allow you to have groups in the future.

Draw attention to the first rule regarding confidentiality. Remind the students that no one will know what they share in group, with some important exceptions. If they share in group information about suicide, homicide, child abuse, or sexual abuse, you are required by law to report that information to ensure safety. Once the students understand this and the other rules, have them sign and date their Group Rules Contracts. (see page 66).

Have the students place their contracts in their folders. Explain that new materials will be added to the folder each session, and that you will keep the folders until the end of the group sessions when the students can take them home. Tell the students that they can draw on their folders while waiting for the session to begin. (High school students often draw and color the names of their boyfriends and girlfriends!)

Keep the group rules poster and display it every time the group meets.

CENTERING EXERCISE

Since most of the students will be unfamiliar with a centering exercise, give them—and yourself—time to get into it. Explain that you will begin each group session with a centering exercise, a way to relax and let go of the stresses and frustrations encountered during the day. Point out that some of the centering exercises will reinforce what you teach about feelings and anger management. Also point out that the centering exercises are techniques the students can use on their own to manage stress and anxiety. Explain that some students create their own centering exercises, and that two students in Virginia developed the one called the "Rainbow".

Begin by inviting the students to relax and by telling them that the name of this exercise is "White-Water Rafting."

WHITE-WATER RAFTING

Okay, close your eyes. Imagine that you're floating down a river in a one-person boat, an inflatable kayak called a duck. You've been placed in the river by a guide, who has told you that this is a safe stretch of water. He's given you the equipment you need: a paddle, a helmet, and a life jacket, and shown you how to use them. He has told you that he will meet you a few miles down the river, and to enjoy yourself. When you first start paddling, you go around in circles, but soon you can make the kayak go in the right direction.

Right now, you're floating along in a long, calm pool of the river. No one else is around. The sky above is very clear and bright blue. The surrounding mountains are steep and green. It's a true beautiful wilderness area. You feel very safe in the calm pool, so safe

Exercise continued on next page.

Exercise continued from previous page.

that you take off your life jacket and helmet. You lie back in the kayak and put your feet up, soaking in the sunshine, and listening to the quietness. You feel very relaxed.

As you float along, you hear a noise. The sound is coming from around a bend in the river. You can't see what's around the bend. As you drift closer, the sound grows louder. It's the sound of rushing water. You begin to worry. You wonder if your guide placed you in the wrong part of the river. As the sound gets even louder, you worry more, wondering if it's a waterfall. You feel your heart beating faster and faster.

You sit up at attention. You fasten your life jacket and buckle your helmet. You grab your paddle and get yourself ready to go through whatever lies ahead. As the noise becomes even louder, you slip around the bend in the river. It's white water, all right!

You and the kayak leap into the white water. The kayak gives you a great ride around the rocks and through the rushing water. Waves break over the top of the kayak, but they don't stop you. You're feeling strong and excited. In a moment, you've passed through the rapids and you're floating gently in another of the river's calm pools.

You feel excited, and confident, and satisfied. You feel proud of yourself. You were able to get through something that was frightening because it was unknown. You got through very successfully, using the tools you'd been given and the skills you developed. You feel so good that you are sitting on top of the world! So, let that excitement, pride, confidence, and satisfaction wash all over you right now.

Point out that sometimes students who participate in group often feel scared at the beginning because they don't know what it will be like. Say that you expect them to have feelings of pride, confidence, and satisfaction by the time the group is over.

ICE-BREAKER

Involve the students in an ice-breaker. Have them get their index cards from their folders. Display the poster with the questions. Ask the group members to write their name (what they

want to be called), age, and grade in the center of the card. In the upper right-hand corner, have them write who lives with them in their house. In the lower right-hand corner, ask the students to write where they would be if they could be anywhere they wanted to be. In the lower left-hand corner, have them write what they would like to be or do when they finish school. In the upper left-hand corner, have them write three "-ing" words that describe themselves (for example, laughing, talking, playing the piano).

When the students finish writing, have them form pairs—if a student is left out, pair up with him or her yourself. Explain that they are to interview each other. Then they will go around and introduce their partner to the group, telling the group their partner's name and the other things they learned about him or her. To role-model for the students, begin by sharing the information about your partner.

This safe and nonthreatening activity helps the students feel comfortable about sharing information and introduces them to the go-around technique, which will be used throughout the program.

Exploring the Material

MINI-LECTURE AND DISCUSSION
Violence and Aggression

Present the following material, which appears on Handout 1A ("Violence and Aggression"), to the students. You might have the students read the handout to themselves quickly or read it together as a group. Or you may want to present the information in your own words. In that case, give the students the handout at the end of the session.

Violence and Aggression

What is violence?

Violence is a form of human aggression. It is behavior with the intent to harm someone or something. Aggression can be verbal; words can be vicious weapons.

Emotional Violence; Instrumental Violence

Aggression is categorized as emotional or as instrumental. *Emotional* or *expressive aggression* is reactive. People commit acts of emotional aggression in response to pain, a threat, or frustration. People use this kind of aggression or violence to express anger. In emotional anger, the stimulus to anger activates the fight-or-flight response: it causes the brain and hormones to order the heart to pump faster and to send more blood with food and oxygen to the muscles. The palms sweat, and the face flushes red with anger. A teenager who gets angry and hits his or her brother or sister is showing emotional aggression.

Instrumental aggression is used to attain a goal or an award. Instrumental aggression is proactive. People who commit acts of instrumental aggression may not be angry. A teenager who commits an act of violence to obtain membership in a gang is committing instrumental aggression. A hit man or an assassin who kills in cold blood is committing instrumental aggression. A soldier who is violent in order to defend his or her country is also committing instrumental aggression. There is low arousal by the central nervous system in instrumental aggression. It is a cold-blooded, reward-seeking form of aggression.

Range of Aggressive or Violent Behavior

Aggression or violence can range from verbal acts, like yelling and screaming, to slapping, to choking, to the use of weapons, to a fatal act.

Some acts of aggression are **crimes**. The FBI lists four kinds of violent crime: murder, forcible rape, robbery, and aggravated assault.

Murder is the willful killing of one human being by another.

Forcible rape is the carnal knowledge of a female forcibly and against her will.

Robbery is the taking of anything of value from a person by force or threat of violence or by putting the victim in fear.

Aggravated assault is an unlawful attack for the purpose of inflicting severe aggravated bodily injury. This type of assault usually is accompanied by the use of a weapon. In comparison, a simple assault is one where no weapon is used and which does not result in serious injury to the victim.

Where Violence Occurs

Surveys show that more violence occurs in cities than in rural areas; more violence occurs in crowded areas of the city than in less dense areas of the city. Violent crimes are also more frequent in areas where there are illegal markets, such as for prostitution and drugs. And, studies show that 70 percent of juvenile offenders, offenders between the ages of 10 and 17, come from single-parent families that lack a sense of closeness and togetherness.

When Violent Behavior Is Justified

The Semai tribe in Malaya is a society that does not condone violence. They may provide a model of when violence is appropriate. The Semai tribe is so nonviolent that not a single murder has ever been recorded among them; they have no need for a police force. However, when their country was threatened in World War II, they fought against the Communists, very violently, to protect their home. After the war, they went back to gentle, nonviolent ways.

Ask the students to take Handout 1B ("Scenarios") from their folders. Use Scenarios 1 and 2 to help the students understand the difference between emotional and instrumental aggression. Ask a student to read Scenario 1.

Scenario 1

One time Jeff, a freshman, was angry because the sophomores on the bus were making fun of him, calling him names and telling him he was stupid. Jeff started to get very angry. His heart started beating faster, he started breathing quickly, and his hands got sweaty. All he could think of was how angry he was and how embarrassing it was for the guys to call him names, especially in front of the other kids on the bus, including that cute girl in his English class. Jeff started to call the guys names. Finally, he punched the guy who was the ringleader.

To aid in the discussion, ask the students to consider the following questions.

1. **Is what Jeff did violent?** (Yes, he was trying to hurt the sophomores who were calling him names.)

Remind the students that aggression can be emotional, a way to react to anger or to express anger. Emotional aggression involves the central nervous system and prepares the body for the fight-or-flight response. Or aggression can be instrumental or proactive, designed to attain a goal. This kind of aggression is a cold-blooded, reward-seeking form of aggression.

2. **Is Jeff's act of aggression, punching the sophomore, an act of emotional or instrumental violence?** (It was emotional, done in response to the sophomores calling him names.)

3. **Did Jeff take time to cool down and think between the feeling of being angry and his behavior, or punching the sophomore?** (No, he just reacted quickly, without taking time to think.)

4. **What else could Jeff have done with his anger in this situation?** (If the students can't think of any alternatives, say that future

groups will teach them helpful, nonviolent ways to deal with anger.)

Now ask another student to read Scenario 2.

Scenario 2

Nick, a 16-year-old-boy, lives in the inner city of a large metropolitan area. He has never known his father. His mother works two jobs, as a cleaning woman in a large hospital, and at McDonald's, so he doesn't see her very much. Nick's family lives in a small apartment, and he has to share a bedroom with his three younger brothers. Nick doesn't get good grades, so he doesn't go to school very often. He has some buddies in a gang called ExMen, and they want him to join. Nick likes the idea of belonging to a gang. In order to join, Nick has to go through initiation. For the ExMen, initiation requires that Nick go to a shopping mall, find a woman, cut her Achilles tendon so she can't run away, and then rape her. Nick does this, so now he is a member of the ExMen. At last he feels like he has a family.

To aid in discussion, ask the following questions.

1. **Is Nick's act of cutting a woman's Achilles tendon and then raping her an act of violence?** (Yes, it was intended to do harm.)

2. **Was this act of violence emotional or instrumental?** (It was instrumental, since the purpose of the act was for initiation into the gang. Nick wasn't angry with the woman, whom he didn't even know.)

3. **How is Nick's cutting a woman's Achilles tendon and then raping her different from Jeff's punching a schoolmate on the school bus?** (Jeff was reacting out of anger; his act of aggression was emotional or expressive aggression. Nick's aggression was instrumental, or proactive, to achieve the goal of gang membership.)

4. **Is there a difference in the degree of violence shown in Jeff's and Nick's behavior? Would Nick's acts be considered violent crimes by the FBI; if so, what crimes?** (Expect the students to answer that Jeff's punching another guy was a minor incident

compared with Nick's act, which is probably an aggravated assault and forcible rape.)

5. **Is Nick's act of violence justifiable?** (Accept the group members' opinions as value judgments showing their current beliefs about violence.)

6. **What do you think are some causes of Nick's violent behavior?** (Living in a single-parent family and in a crowded city; also, living in a high crime area. Not having much time with his mother because she's always working; low income and crowded housing.)

Use Scenario 3 to point out that not all emotional aggression results in violence, but it can lead to other harmful behaviors. Ask a student to read Scenario 3.

Scenario 3

One time in class, Evie was quietly doing her work, but the girls next to her were goofing off like crazy. The teacher thought it was Evie and sent her to the office. Evie believes that the teacher has something against her and is always on her case. This time was especially unfair because for once Evie wasn't doing anything wrong. Evie was so angry that she did not work at all in the rest of her classes that day.

To start discussion, ask these questions.

1. **How did Evie feel when the teacher sent her to the office?** (Angry.)

2. **What did Evie do when she was angry?** (She didn't work at all in the rest of her classes that day.)

3. **Was Evie's not working all day emotional, to express her anger, or instrumental, to achieve a goal?** (It was emotional, since she was expressing her anger by not working.)

4. **Some behaviors can be harmful, even if they are not violent. Was Evie's not working in school all day a violent behavior?** (No, it was not violent because it did not do physical harm to anyone. However, it was a harmful behavior.)

5. **Whom did Evie's behavior harm the most?** (It harmed Evie because her grades suffered.)

Use Scenario 4 to point out that violent behavior is sometimes justified. Ask a student to read Scenario 4.

Scenario 4

Kenny, age 22, is a soldier in the U.S. Army. His job is to fire the guns on tanks. During the Desert Storm war, Kenny's tank saw a lot of action, and he fired on, and hit, several enemy tanks.

Ask the following questions to aid in discussion.

1. **Is Kenny's behavior, firing on enemy tanks, instrumental or emotional aggression?** (Instrumental, to achieve the purpose of winning the war.)

2. **Do you think Kenny's behavior is justified?** (Accept the students' value judgments.)

Factors in Development of Violent Behavior

On a chalkboard or newsprint, set up headings as in Handout 1C. (The following page is a duplicate of the students' Handout 1C on page 69.) Ask the group members to brainstorm factors that might influence an individual's decision to use violence, which are called risk factors, and factors that might influence an individual not to use violence, which are called protective factors. Ask them to think about factors on the personal level; on the family level; on the social level, which includes their extended family, their school, their peers, and their neighborhood; and on the societal level. As the students respond, help them to understand which level is appropriate for each factor, and whether it is a risk factor or a protective factor. After the students have finished, have them compare their ideas with the list of risk factors and protective factors on Handout 1C.

Risk Factors and Protective Factors for Aggressive Behavior

RISK FACTORS

PROTECTIVE FACTORS

Personal Level

pregnancy complications
low birthweight
fearless temperament
impulsive behavior
poor concentration
poor ability to delay gratification
low IQ
risk-taking behavior
low empathy
abnormally frequent watching of violence on television
bullying behavior in childhood

shy temperament
high IQ
being firstborn

Family Level

harsh, inconsistent discipline
lack of parental nurturance
physical abuse or neglect
poor supervision
early separation of children from parents
violent or criminal behavior by family members

small, stable family
lack of family conflict
high income
affectionate caregivers

Social Level

peer rejection
early school failure
poverty
poor housing
high crime neighborhood

good peer relationships
school success
living in low crime area
good housing

Societal Level

violence accepted in society
violence glorified in mass media
easy accessibility of firearms
economic inequalities

society does not accept violence
violence is not glorified on television
and in movies

(Chart derived from material in *Understanding and Preventing Violence*, 1993.)

To help the students further understand risk factors, ask them to look again at Scenario 2, and review what they know about Nick. **What risk factors might have influenced his decision to act violently?** (Living with a mother who works two jobs; not seeing his father; low income; crowded housing; high crime area.)

Tell the group members that various factors influence violent behavior. It is important to stress, however, that a single factor does not necessarily cause violent behavior. It may take several factors, on several levels, to interact in a way that leads a person to develop violent behavior. For instance, a child with low birthweight and birth-related central nervous system problems may develop violent behavior, but only if the child is also raised in an unstable, nonintact family. Describe how temperament can influence violent behavior. When toddlers encounter unfamiliar children and adults, some are shy and restrained ("inhibited"), while others are relatively fearless ("uninhibited"). Fearless behavior has been found to be a risk factor for children with low socioeconomic status, whereas fearfulness may act as a protective factor against aggression. Temperament may explain why only a proportion of children from high-risk homes and neighborhoods develops antisocial or violent behavior.

Point out that while a high proportion of delinquents, particularly violent delinquents, and of violent adult criminals, suffered extreme abuse in childhood, most physically abused children do not go on to become violent. And, only a third of people who were abused in childhood become abusers themselves. Researchers are identifying protective factors that help people choose not to be aggressive or violent, or to abuse their children as they were abused.

As an example, ask the group members to brainstorm protective factors that would help a person who had been abused as a child not to abuse his or her own children. Tell the group that these protective factors occur on four levels as well. Write the four headings on a chalkboard or newsprint: personal, family, social, societal. After

the students have given their ideas, complete the list from Handout 1D ("Protective Factors for Child Abuse").

Protective Factors for Child Abuse

Personal Level

high IQ
an awareness of early abusive experiences
a resolve not to repeat the abuse
a history of a positive relationship with one caregiver
special talents
physical attractiveness
good interpersonal skills

Family Level

healthy children
supportive spouse
economic security

Social Level

good social supports
few stressful events
strong, supportive religious affiliation
positive school experiences and peer relations as a child
therapeutic interventions

Societal Level

culture opposed to violence
economic prosperity
culture that helps parents

(Chart derived from Kaufman and Zigler, "The intergenerational transmission of child abuse" in Cicchetti and Carlson, eds. 1989. *Child Maltreatment: Theory and Research on the Causes and Consequences of Child Abuse and Neglect.*)

Stress that by examining these influences, group members can make sure they create protective influences for themselves—influences that lead them away from aggressive and violent behavior. Point out again that an awareness of childhood abuse (or being able to describe a family problem in words, such as a parent's chemical dependence or a parent's use of violent behavior) and a resolve not to repeat the abuse are significant and important protective factors. You hope that the students will resolve to learn behaviors besides aggression and violence.

ACTIVITY

Tell the students that they have a sheet in their folders to help them think about their own risk factors and protective factors regarding violence. Ask them to take out Handout 1E ("My Risk Factors and Protective Factors"). Give them a few minutes to complete this sheet. They can refer to Handouts 1C and 1D for ideas. When the students have completed the sheet, ask if anyone would like to share risk factors and protective factors.

Tell the students that this group will focus on the prevention of violence, especially on the personal level. You hope there will be improvement on the societal level, so that political and economic injustices that breed frustration will be eliminated. You hope that cultural values will shift, so that violence is not glorified on television and in movies, and parents will begin to teach their children to be nonviolent. You can also hope for improvement on the social or neighborhood level, for instance, an improvement in housing in the inner city, decreasing overcrowding.

But this group's attempt to change the system will start with them, a group of teenagers. In this group you will adopt the value that violence to express anger is not acceptable, and that violence is only acceptable if necessary for self-defense; you hope they will adopt that value as well. You will teach them effective ways to deal with emotional aggression: to take time to cool off, to look at what has angered them, to think about their choices for behavior, and to use alternative behaviors rather than hurting someone or something when they are angry. You will also look at ways to express anger that may not be violent, but are still harmful, so that they can learn more helpful ways to express anger.

BASIC FACTS

Ask the students to look at the List of Basic Facts. Tell the group members that each week they will learn new basic facts that carry the message of the session in easily remembered sentences. Explain that you will review the basic facts at the beginning of each session, and that you will ask them to explain what each means. Have students read the first three basic facts.

1. Violent behavior is intended to do harm. It can be emotional, to express anger, or instrumental, to attain a goal.

2. It is never acceptable to use violent or harmful behavior to express anger.

3. No matter what has influenced a person to be violent, it is his or her responsibility to choose to learn nonviolent and helpful ways to express anger.

Make sure the students understand the basic facts. If students disagree—and state that it is okay to use violence if they are angry—tell them that many people think this way and that is why violence is accepted in society. Point out that you hope the students will adopt the value that using violence or aggression to express anger is never justifiable.

ASSIGNMENT

Explain that the students will have a homework assignment each week. These assignments will help them practice what they learn in each session. They won't get graded for the homework, but they will get more out of the group if they do the assignments. The assignments should take only a minute or two each day. Tell the group members that each week you will ask them what they learned by doing the assignment.

Ask the students to pull out Assignment 1. Read the directions to the group: "There are two parts to this assignment. First, write a sentence about when you think it is okay to use violence. Second, each day, observe one time you get angry. Write down what you do. If it is an act of aggression or violence, write if it is expressive or instrumental. Next week, in group, be ready to discuss what you learned about how you handle anger."

Tell the students that Assignment 1 will help them learn to pay attention to what they do when they get angry. Tell them that observing themselves is the first step in changing the way they behave when angry. You don't want this to be a big chore, but you do expect them to write down a short sentence about how they act when angry each day. Next week, you will ask them to share what they learned about how they handle anger. Tell the group members to take the assignment sheet with them and to bring it to group next week.

Wrapping Up

CENTERING EXERCISE

Settle the students and introduce them to a new centering exercise, "Breathing Through Your Feet." Tell the students that they can use this centering exercise anywhere, and no one will know they are using it. It's an effective one to use if they're angry and want to calm down. It's also helpful to use if they feel nervous about giving a report in front of the class.

BREATHING THROUGH YOUR FEET

Imagine that you have tiny holes all over the bottom of your feet. Your shoes are dotted with tiny holes too. Now, breathe air up through those holes—all the way up to your ankles, through your knees, past your waist, right into your stomach. Hold that air in your stomach. Feel how refreshing it is. Now push the air all the way back down your body—down through your legs, past your knees and ankles, all the way down to and out through your feet.

Lead the students through this process five times, for a total of five deep breaths; give directions softly; make sure that the students inhale and exhale evenly and slowly. If students have been angry, you can have them breathe in calm, peaceful, relaxed air, and breathe out anger, or frustration, or worry, or anxiety, and again breathe in calm, peaceful, secure air. Finally,

conclude the exercise by saying:

You've learned the technique of breathing through your feet. This technique can give you power. Whenever you feel angry, or scared, or anxious, you can use breathing through your feet to help you calm down and relax.

(Adapted from *The Stress-Proof Child*, by Saunders and Remsberg, 1984.)

AFFIRMATION

Involve the group in an affirmation. Stand and join in a circle with the students, holding hands. Go around and have each student share something he or she liked about the group. Start the affirmation yourself: "One thing I liked about the group today was. . . ."

CLOSING

Remain standing in a circle with the students holding hands and lead the group in the closing activity. You'll use this same activity to end all group sessions.

Tell the students that you're going to make a silent wish for the student on your right. Then when you've made the wish, gently squeeze the student's hand. The student makes a silent wish for the person on his or her right, then gently squeezes the student's hand, and so on. Continue around the circle until a wish and squeeze come back to you. Usually, students follow the lead of group leaders who expect them to perform this activity. However, if the adolescents in your group do not want to hold hands, allow them to stand next to each other in a circle and to pass the wish by a pat on the shoulder, or elbow, or in any appropriate way they choose.

Collect the folders. Explain that you will keep the folders until the next group session.

Fill out a copy of the Process and Progress Form (see page 211) or the Progress Notes (see page 212), if you are an experienced leader, as soon as you can after leading the session.

Group Rules Contract

1. I will keep what we talk about private. We call this confidentiality.

2. I will stay in my seat.

3. I will keep my hands to myself.

4. I will wait for my turn to talk and listen carefully when other people talk.

5. I won't tease or put other people down.

6. I can pass during go-arounds if I want.

7. I will come to every session.

8. I will make up the class work I miss.

_____

Name

_____

Date

Violence and Aggression

What is violence?

Violence is a form of human aggression. It is behavior with the intent to harm someone or something. Aggression can be verbal; words can be vicious weapons.

Emotional Violence; Instrumental Violence

Aggression is categorized as *emotional* or as *instrumental*. *Emotional* or *expressive aggression* is reactive. People commit acts of emotional aggression in response to pain, a threat, or frustration. People use this kind of aggression or violence to express anger. In emotional anger, the stimulus to anger activates the fight-or-flight response: it causes the brain and hormones to order the heart to pump faster and to send more blood with food and oxygen to the muscles. The palms sweat, and the face flushes red with anger. A teenager who gets angry and hits his or her brother or sister is showing emotional aggression.

Instrumental aggression is used to attain a goal or an award. Instrumental aggression is proactive. People who commit acts of instrumental aggression may not be angry. A teenager who commits an act of violence to obtain membership in a gang is committing instrumental aggression. A hit man or an assassin who kills in cold blood is committing instrumental aggression. A soldier who is violent in order to defend his or her country is also committing instrumental aggression. There is low arousal by the central nervous system in instrumental aggression. It is a cold-blooded, reward-seeking form of aggression.

Range of Aggressive or Violent Behavior

Aggression or violence can range from verbal acts, like yelling and screaming, to slapping, to choking, to the use of weapons, to a fatal act.

Some acts of aggression are **crimes**. The FBI lists four kinds of violent crime: murder, forcible rape, robbery, and aggravated assault.

Murder is the willful killing of one human being by another.

Forcible rape is the carnal knowledge of a female forcibly and against her will.

Robbery is the taking of anything of value from a person by force or threat of violence or by putting the victim in fear.

Aggravated assault is an unlawful attack for the purpose of inflicting severe aggravated bodily injury. This type of assault usually is accompanied by the use of a weapon. In comparison, a simple assault is one where no weapon is used and which does not result in serious injury to the victim.

Where Violence Occurs

Surveys show that more violence occurs in cities than in rural areas; more violence occurs in crowded areas of the city than in less dense areas of the city. Violent crimes are also more frequent in areas where there are illegal markets, such as for prostitution and drugs. And, studies show that 70 percent of juvenile offenders, offenders between the ages of 10 and 17, come from single-parent families that lack a sense of closeness and togetherness.

When Violent Behavior Is Justified

The Semai tribe in Malaya is a society that does not condone violence. They may provide a model of when violence is appropriate. The Semai tribe is so nonviolent that not a single murder has ever been recorded among them; they have no need for a police force. However, when their country was threatened in World War II, they fought against the Communists, very violently, to protect their home. After the war, they went back to gentle, nonviolent ways.

Scenarios

Scenario 1

One time Jeff, a freshman, was angry because the sophomores on the bus were making fun of him, calling him names and telling him he was stupid. Jeff started to get very angry. His heart started beating faster, he started breathing quickly, and his hands got sweaty. All he could think of was how angry he was and how embarrassing it was for the guys to call him names, especially in front of the other kids on the bus, including that cute girl in his English class. Jeff started to call the guys names. Finally, he punched the guy who was the ringleader.

Scenario 2

Nick, a 16-year-old-boy, lives in the inner city of a large metropolitan area. He has never known his father. His mother works two jobs, as a cleaning woman in a large hospital, and at McDonald's, so he doesn't see her very much. Nick's family lives in a small apartment, and he has to share a bedroom with his three younger brothers. Nick doesn't get good grades, so he doesn't go to school very often. He has some buddies in a gang called ExMen, and they want him to join. Nick likes the idea of belonging to a gang. In order to join, Nick has to go through initiation. For the ExMen, initiation requires that Nick go to a shopping mall, find a woman, cut her Achilles tendon so she can't run away, and then rape her. Nick does this, so now he is a member of the ExMen. At last he feels like he has a family.

Scenario 3

One time in class, Evie was quietly doing her work, but the girls next to her were goofing off like crazy. The teacher thought it was Evie and sent her to the office. Evie believes that the teacher has something against her and is always on her case. This time was especially unfair because for once Evie wasn't doing anything wrong. Evie was so angry that she did not work at all in the rest of her classes that day.

Scenario 4

Kenny, age 22, is a soldier in the U.S. Army. His job is to fire the guns on tanks. During the Desert Storm war, Kenny's tank saw a lot of action, and he fired on, and hit, several enemy tanks.

Risk Factors and Protective Factors for Aggressive Behavior

RISK FACTORS	PROTECTIVE FACTORS

Personal Level

pregnancy complications	shy temperament
low birthweight	high IQ
fearless temperament	being firstborn
impulsive behavior	
poor concentration	
poor ability to delay gratification	
low IQ	
risk-taking behavior	
low empathy	
abnormally frequent watching of violence on television	
bullying behavior in childhood	

Family Level

harsh, inconsistent discipline	small, stable family
lack of parental nurturance	lack of family conflict
physical abuse or neglect	high income
poor supervision	affectionate caregivers
early separation of children from parents	
violent or criminal behavior by family members	

Social Level

peer rejection	good peer relationships
early school failure	school success
poverty	living in low crime area
poor housing	good housing
high crime neighborhood	

Societal Level

violence accepted in society	society does not accept violence
violence glorified in mass media	violence is not glorified on television
easy accessibility of firearms	and in movies
economic inequalities	

(Chart derived from material in *Understanding and Preventing Violence*, 1993.)

Protective Factors for Child Abuse

Personal Level

high IQ
an awareness of early abusive experiences
a resolve not to repeat the abuse
a history of a positive relationship with one caregiver
special talents
physical attractiveness
good interpersonal skills

Family Level

healthy children
supportive spouse
economic security

Social Level

good social supports
few stressful events
strong, supportive religious affiliation
positive school experiences and peer relations as a child
therapeutic interventions

Societal Level

culture opposed to violence
economic prosperity
culture that helps parents

(Chart derived from Kaufman and Zigler, "The intergenerational transmission of child abuse" in Cicchetti and Carlson, eds. 1989. *Child Maltreatment: Theory and Research on the Causes and Consequences of Child Abuse and Neglect.*)

My Risk Factors
and Protective Factors

RISK FACTORS   **PROTECTIVE FACTORS**

Personal Level

_____   _____
_____   _____
_____   _____
_____   _____
_____   _____
_____   _____
_____   _____

Family Level

_____   _____
_____   _____
_____   _____
_____   _____
_____   _____
_____   _____
_____   _____

Social Level

_____   _____
_____   _____
_____   _____
_____   _____
_____   _____
_____   _____

Societal Level

_____   _____
_____   _____
_____   _____
_____   _____
_____   _____

There are two parts to this assignment.

1. Write a sentence about when you think it is okay to use violence.

_____

_____

_____

_____

_____

2. Each day, observe one time you get angry. Write down what you do. If it is an act of aggression or violence, write if it is expressive or instrumental. Next week be ready to discuss what you learned about how you handle anger.

Day one

_____

_____

_____

_____

_____

Day two

_____

_____

_____

_____

_____

_____

Day three

_____

_____

_____

_____

_____

_____

Day four

_____

_____

_____

_____

Day five

_____

_____

_____

_____

_____

Day six

_____

_____

_____

_____

_____

_____

Day seven

_____

_____

_____

_____

_____

_____

Other feelings or comments

_____

_____

_____

_____

Feelings

Objectives

To help the students:

• identify a variety of feelings

• realize that anger is a normal feeling

• discover that feelings aren't good or bad, or right or wrong; they just are

• learn to put thinking between feeling and behavior

Session at a Glance

1. Group Rules: review if necessary—1 minute

2. Centering Exercise: "The Clouds"—
   2 minutes

3. Feelings Check-in: look at Feeling Wheel—
   4 minutes

4. Basic Facts Review—2 minutes

5. Assignment Review—4 minutes

6. Mini-lecture and Discussion—15 minutes

7. Activity: discuss examples of negative and positive thinking—8 minutes

8. Basic Facts: read Basic Facts 4 and 5; discuss—1 minute

9. Assignment—1 minute

10. Centering Exercise: repeat "The Clouds"—
    2 minutes

11. Affirmation: share a negative or incorrect self-talk, how you can change it to positive and correct, and how that will influence your feelings and your behavior—4 minutes

12. Closing: pass a silent wish—1 minute

Preparation

• Display the posterboard copy of the group rules.

• Have posters for Basic Facts 1-3 available. (Or the List of Basic Facts, already in the folders; or index cards with a basic fact on each one.)

• Have chalkboard and chalk or newsprint and a marker available.

- Include in each student's folder:

  —the Feeling Wheel

  —Handout 2A ("Feelings")

  —Handout 2B ("Scenarios")

  —Handout 2C ("Three Components of Emotion")

  —Handout 2D ("Your Examples")

  —Assignment 2.

- Staple the students' Group Rules Contract to the inside of the folder, on the right side.

- Have each student's folder, pencil and crayons or markers at his or her place.

- Read through the session plan before meeting.

Background and Guidelines

In the first session, the group members learned that some violence is expressive or emotional; it is a reaction to something that made the person angry. Many people who choose violent behavior have not learned to put thinking between their feelings and their behavior: they feel, and then react. This session teaches the students how to stop impulsive, aggressive, or violent behavior by putting positive thinking between feeling and behavior. This session also helps them learn what to do with feelings.

EMOTION REGULATION AND SWALLOWING FEELINGS

As discussed in the section on adolescent development, one of the tasks of childhood is emotion regulation. Putting emotions into words helps people to moderate feelings, both positive and negative. Many of the students in your group have not learned how to regulate their emotions; their parents may not have learned how to regulate their emotions

either. Many people minimize or deny their feelings or pretend they are without feelings. Many people fear feelings. They may fear that they will be overwhelmed by their feelings or that they may lose control of themselves. These people may try to swallow their feelings. However, no matter how hard people try to hold their feelings down, the feelings don't go away. Sometimes they show themselves in physical aches and pains (somatizing). Other times they get expressed through external acting out (fighting, disrespect, delinquent behavior). Or they may be expressed internally (depression, suicidal thoughts).

FEELINGS ARE TEMPORARY

Many people who try to avoid feelings do so thinking that feelings are permanent. They are not. Unfortunately, many people often behave or take action based on this misconception. For instance, very depressed people may attempt suicide because they believe their depression is a permanent condition. Very angry people may commit acts of violence, not realizing that their anger will eventually lessen. Feelings are not permanent; they are temporary. As part of mastering the task of emotion regulation, adolescents need to understand that they can learn to tolerate uncomfortable feelings until the feelings pass or until they can do something to make themselves feel better.

PEOPLE CAN DO THINGS TO FEEL BETTER

A brainstorming activity in this session emphasizes the point that students who are sad or angry can choose to do something to make themselves feel better. If you, the group leader, understand that you, too, are responsible for doing what you need to do in order to feel better, and if you have an extensive repertoire of behaviors to help you feel better (exercising, listening to music, talking with friends, playing sports, taking a bubble bath, and so on), you'll be more effective as a group leader. So be ready to share with the students the variety of behaviors and activities you use to feel better. Be sure to reinforce the concept that if you feel sad or angry, you can do something that will make you feel better. This is important to help teens gain a sense of control and mastery and to help them develop an internal locus of control.

ANGER IS NORMAL

In this session, the students learn that feelings are natural and normal, and that they shouldn't be judgmental about the way they feel. They also learn that anger is a normal feeling that most people experience 12 to 14 times a day. The group members learn that while they should not judge themselves as bad for being angry, they can make a judgment about their behavior, which might be considered to be good or bad. At the same time, the students also begin to understand that they can be responsible for the way they express their feelings. They can use some feelings to work for them; they can express other feelings so they can let them go.

FEELINGS CAN BE INTENSE AND DIFFICULT

As a group leader, you should be ready for some intense feelings from the students throughout the 11 sessions of the group. For example, it's not uncommon to hear a teen from a divorced family vehemently say, "I hate my mom. She won't let me see my dad. I wish she were dead." If you hear statements like this, don't succumb to the temptation to tell the student not to feel a certain way. Doing so discounts and invalidates his or her feelings. Never tell the students not to feel what they say they're feeling. Instead, help them see that they need to identify, validate, accept, tolerate, and express their anger in helpful ways.

For example, if a student is angry about parental violence, and speaks of this anger in group, *identify the feeling:* "I can tell you're feeling angry"; *validate it:* "Most kids feel angry like you do if they have seen their father beat up their mother"; *tolerate the anger:* "Tell me more about how angry you felt when your dad lost his temper"; and *encourage the teen to express his or her anger*

in a helpful way: "Some kids in your situation write in their journal or paint a picture of how angry they feel," or "Some kids go to the gym and work out when they're feeling angry," or "Some kids write their parents a letter, which they don't send, telling them exactly what they think." Leading the students through this process helps them let go of their anger.

This session simplifies the process (identification, validation, acceptance, toleration, and expression) for the students. They learn that instead of swallowing their feelings, it's better to recognize and accept them. They think about the best way to express their feelings—by sharing them with someone they trust, by writing or drawing, or by just sitting with the feelings until they pass. They also learn that they can use some feelings. For instance, adolescents who are feeling guilty about shoplifting can use their guilt dynamically to help them change their behavior so they will not shoplift again. With your help, the students can discover (1) words to recognize and identify (name) their feelings; (2) ways to accept their feelings (remember, feelings aren't right or wrong—they just are); and (3) appropriate ways to express their feelings.

THREE COMPONENTS OF EMOTION: FEELING, THINKING OR SELF-TALK, AND BEHAVIOR

As you lead the students through this session, keep in mind that a particular emotion possesses three components: feeling, thinking, and behavior. People can't control the feelings they get, but they are able to control their behavior. Sometimes, examining their thinking can help people control their behavior. For example, teens may feel sad because their parents are sad. Seeing the sadness of their parents, the teens think (or "self-talk"): "I can't be happy if my parents are sad." Their behavior might be crying or withdrawing into inactivity. But adolescents can examine their thinking and change their self-talk: "I can't be responsible for the way my parents feel. My parents feel sad, but I don't have to feel sad. I'm different from my parents. I'm responsible for my feelings. If I do feel sad, I can choose to do something to help me feel better (call a friend, read, listen to music, exercise)."

The mini-lecture in this session is relatively short to allow plenty of time for the activity. This session's activity focuses on the thinking, or self-talk, that accompanies feelings and that leads to behavior. The scenarios give examples of teenagers who have a feeling, their negative self-talk, and the behavior that follows; and their positive self-talk, and the behavior that follows. Becoming aware of positive and negative thinking, or self-talk, is an important cognitive-behavioral technique to help the students learn to choose their behavior. It will enhance their ability to control their behavior, and to feel they can control what they do; both are self-esteem boosters.

Although students generally struggle with understanding the concept of negative and positive self-talk, and the different behaviors that follow from each, it is well worth the time to help them make this connection so that they can do it on their own in the future. Encourage the students' participation and help them see how the three different components (feeling, thinking, and behaving) apply to each feeling. Help the teens to identify negative or incorrect thinking or self-talk, to see how it can be replaced by positive or correct thinking or self-talk, and to understand how both positive thinking and negative thinking affect feelings and behavior.

Beginning the Session

GROUP RULES

Welcome the students and begin with a quick review of the group rules. Draw attention to the poster listing the group rules. If you feel that it is necessary, call on different students to read them one at a time. Check for understanding before moving on.

CENTERING EXERCISE

Open the centering exercise by asking the group members if they used "Breathing Through Your Feet" in the past week. Then, lead the students in a new centering exercise, "The Clouds."

THE CLOUDS

Close your eyes and relax. This centering exercise can help you learn how to handle your feelings.

Imagine that it's a warm sunny day and that you are on the beach. You have been riding a dune buggy on the sand dunes and have had a great time. Now, you sit on a beach chair and let the waves come up to your feet. Just relax and imagine how warm and sunny it is.

Now, look up and see a blue sky dotted with clouds. You remember the game you used to play when you were a kid, when you would try to see objects in the clouds. Today, you decide to pretend that you're the sky and that those clouds are like the feelings you have. Watch the clouds move across the sky. See how they come and go. They are like your feelings. They come and go, too, like clouds in the sky.

Look what's coming now. It's a big storm cloud, filling the sky. It's filled with thunder and lightning. Your feeling of anger is like that cloud. It's a loud, crashing, shocking, frightening feeling! You wonder if you will be struck by lightning. The roar of the thunder makes you feel small and vulnerable. Eventually, though, the big storm cloud goes away. The sun begins to shine, and the sky is bright blue again.

Slowly, a rain cloud approaches. Soon it's raining—just a few drops; then a steady sheet of rain falls on the water. The sky looks gray and sad. Before you know it, a heavy, steady rain is falling. You remember how you felt when your best friend moved away, or when you broke up with a boyfriend or a girlfriend, or maybe even when a close friend was killed in a car accident. You felt sad, just like the clouds in a rainy sky, and you felt that you would be sad forever, just like sometimes it seems that it will rain forever. But the rain cloud doesn't last forever, just like sadness doesn't last forever. Eventually, the rain stops. The sky turns from gray to blue once again.

Now imagine that you're spending the night on the beach. It's the middle of the night. The wind is blowing. The moon is shining. You feel very unprotected out on the beach. Lots of clouds fill the sky. These are frightening clouds. They make strange, monsterlike shapes

Exercise continued on next page.

Exercise continued from previous page.

against the moonlight. These clouds are like your feelings of being scared or worried or afraid. You worry about how strong the wind is. Eventually, the wind dies down. The frightening clouds are going away. The moon is shining brightly, and you feel safe on the beach again. You fall back asleep.

Now it's daytime again, and you're sitting on your beach chair. The sky above is blue and beautiful. The clouds in the sky are white and fluffy, like big marshmallows. They go dancing across the sky. These clouds are like feelings of happiness, cheerfulness, or even love. They make you feel warm and happy inside. They put a smile on your face. But these clouds drift away too. Soon, the sky is blue and clear once more.

Your feelings are like clouds in the sky. They come, just like clouds do. Sooner or later, they go away, just like the clouds.

FEELINGS CHECK-IN

Do a feelings check-in with the students. Have them take out their Feeling Wheels. Tell the students that every week, they will look at the wheel and decide how they are feeling that day. Then everybody will give a brief description of how he or she is doing. Tell the students that if they want, they can color in the section on the Feeling Wheel that describes how they're feeling today. Remind the teens that they might have more than one feeling, since it's possible to have more than one feeling at a time. If they're having a feeling not named on the wheel, they can add a bubble to the outside of the wheel and name their feeling.

When the students finish, have a go-around. Begin by sharing your own feelings. Then, invite each student to share his or her feelings. Teenagers often list many feelings. For the interests of time, ask them to name the feelings they have, but then pick only two to discuss. Be sure to accept each student's feeling(s) and to affirm each student. Explain that they will use this same copy of the Feeling Wheel every time they meet. Ask the students to return the wheels to their folders.

BASIC FACTS REVIEW

To help the students review their last session and the basic facts learned so far, show them posters with Basic Facts 1, 2, and 3; or ask them to look at the List of Basic Facts and review the first three; or use index cards, on which you have written the basic facts, one to a card.

In a go-around, ask a student to read Basic Fact 1 aloud and to explain what it means. If the student has trouble explaining the fact, don't contradict or judge, simply clarify his or her explanation. Repeat the procedure for the next basic fact. This review ensures that the students understand and integrate the basic facts that have been taught. It is also easy preparation for the presentation and provides a lead-in for the session material.

ASSIGNMENT REVIEW

Ask the students if they brought their assignments from last week. Remind them that they were to (1) write their values about the use of violence, and (2) observe one time each day when they got angry and, if they were aggressive, whether their behavior was expressive or instrumental. In a go-around, ask the students to share their values about violence and what they learned about how they handle anger. If the students forgot to do the assignment, ask them to try to remember one time in the past week that they got angry and to describe what they did. Help them to decide if they were aggressive, and, if so, if the aggression was expressive or instrumental. If the students share harmful or violent ways of handling their anger, gently point that out. Remind them of Basic Fact 2, "It is never acceptable to use violent or harmful behavior to express anger." Tell them that the purpose of the group is to give them alternatives to violent behavior. Remind them that they will have a simple assignment each week that will help them choose better ways to handle anger.

Exploring the Material

MINI-LECTURE
Feelings

Recall that last week the students discussed violence. They learned that some violent behavior is emotional, or expressive; it is used to express anger; the violent behavior is a reaction to something that made the person angry. People who express anger through violence usually have not learned to put thinking between their feelings and their behavior; they feel, and then react. In this session the students will learn the three components of emotions: feelings, thinking or self-talk, and behavior. They will look at anger as a normal feeling, and they will look at how thinking, or self-talk, can be positive or negative. They will see how thinking influences feelings and behavior.

Present the following information, which appears on Handout 2A ("Feelings"), to the group. Call on the students to read the information orally or explain the information in your own words. If you choose to explain the material yourself, give the students the handout at the end of the session.

People have many kinds of feelings. Happiness, sadness, fear, anger, jealousy, relief, and disappointment are just a few of the feelings people have. All of these feelings are normal, including anger. In order to handle feelings well, people—including teens—have to be able to recognize their feelings and to put them into words.

Swallowing Feelings

Many people do not put their feelings into words; they may not even admit to themselves that they are having a feeling. These people swallow feelings down by minimizing, denying, or burying them. People who do this may get depressed, or they may get physically sick, or they may explode at something else.

Some people are afraid of feelings. They may fear the pain that accompanies feelings, especially feelings of sadness. Some people fear they will be overwhelmed by their feelings; or they may fear they will lose control: they may fear that if they let themselves feel anger, they will not be able to control their behavior. However, no matter how afraid people are of their feelings, the feelings don't go away. Sometimes they show themselves in physical aches and pains; or people may act out their feelings by fighting or by using alcohol or other drugs; or they may turn their feelings in and become depressed.

Feelings Are Temporary

Many people think that when they get a feeling, they will have it forever—many people make suicide attempts when they are very depressed and think the depression will last forever. Very angry people may commit acts of violence, not realizing that eventually their anger will die down.

Feelings are really temporary and fleeting; they don't last forever. Feelings come, but then they go. So, teenagers can just wait until a difficult feeling passes. Teens can also do something to make themselves feel better.

People Can Do Things to Feel Better

Most people do not understand they can do something about some feelings they might have. For instance, teenagers who have fights with their parents often feel better when they call their friends and complain about their parents. Some days, people wake up in an "up" mood, when they feel happy. But other days, people wake up in a "down" mood; they may feel angry or sad. It's important for teens to learn what they can do to help themselves feel better if they wake up in a sad or an angry mood. Teens might play sports, listen to music, dance, call their friends, or write a poem to help themselves feel better. It's important for adults to have fun things to do as well.

At this point, ask the students to brainstorm things they like to do to feel better if they wake up sad or blue. Start by sharing some things you do that help you feel better. One of the major benefits of group participation is learning from the ideas that the other group members have. Ask the students to pull out Assignment 2 and to fill in Number 1 as you do the brainstorming.

Continue the mini-lecture.

Anger Is a Normal Feeling

Adolescents may have intense feelings that can be very difficult to have. Some teens live in families where they feel intense anger, even hatred for their parents; they then often feel guilty and ashamed because they think they are bad to hate their parents. Anger is not a bad feeling; feelings are not good or bad; they just are. But, feelings like anger, hate, rage, and even sadness, panic, and grief can be very difficult to have. They are normal feelings that most people have at least some of the time.

People can't control what feelings they get, so they have to learn to accept them. But they are responsible for their behavior, which they can and should control. So it is okay for teens to feel anger, or even hate; but it is not okay for them to act in violent ways. It is okay for adolescents to feel angry at their parents; but it is not okay for them to hit their parents.

Three Components of Emotion

Feelings have three components: feeling, thinking, and behaving. Teenagers who act out a lot in school—talk back to teachers, break school rules, fight with peers, skip school, don't do schoolwork—are probably not putting thinking between their feeling of anger and their behavior. They may be feeling angry about something like their parents' divorce or a parent's alcoholism, but they may not be aware of the feeling. They may just be acting it out. Some teens may feel very sad, or even depressed. Their behavior might be to feel exhausted and lie around and do nothing.

Sometimes teens need to look at their thinking before they can handle their feelings. They may need to see if their thinking is straight or if it is incorrect. They may realize they have negative thinking, for instance, always expecting the worst or putting themselves down. They need to realize that their thinking is incorrect, or a false belief, or a misconception.

Ask the students to pull out Handout 2B ("Scenarios"). Ask a group member to read Scenario 1, Part 1.

Scenario 1, Part 1

Janice is a junior in high school. She has been going out with Frank, but she doesn't like him anymore. Janice finally gets the courage to tell Frank she doesn't want to go out with him. Frank still wants to be friends and talk to her on the phone. Now Janice is afraid she'll hurt his feelings if she doesn't talk to him. Every time he calls, he keeps asking her to go out with him again, and he keeps her on the phone for hours. Janice gets angrier and angrier, but she can't do anything about it. She feels rotten about herself because she is hurting Frank's feelings. She also feels powerless because she keeps on talking to him, even though she doesn't want to.

Ask the group members the following questions to help them understand the difference between negative and positive, or incorrect and correct, thinking.

1. **What is Janice feeling?** (Anger, low self-esteem, powerlessness.)

2. **What is Janice thinking?** (That she can't stop talking to Frank on the phone because it would hurt his feelings.)

3. **What is Janice's behavior?** (She continues to talk to Frank on the phone even though she doesn't want to.)

Now ask another group member to read Part 2.

Scenario 1, Part 2

Janice goes to a group and learns how to decide what she wants, how to communicate her feelings, and how to set limits, which means being able to say no. Here's what Janice thinks now: "I can't be responsible for Frank's feelings. I don't want to keep on dating him, even if he wants to. I can tell him nicely that I don't want to keep on seeing him."

When Frank calls again, Janice tells him: "Frank, I think you're a good person, but I don't have a special feeling for you. I'm too young to be attached to only one person, and I want to date other people. I'm sorry if your feelings get hurt, but I won't be able to date you, or to spend a lot of time on the phone with you. I hope you find someone else who does have a special feeling for you."

Ask the students the following discussion questions.

1. **What is Janice thinking now?** (That she can't be responsible for Frank's feelings; that she can decide what she wants; that she can tell Frank her feelings without blaming or accusing him; and that she can tell Frank nicely that she doesn't want to go out with him anymore.)

2. **What is Janice's behavior now?** (Janice shares her feelings and sets limits with Frank.)

3. **What do you imagine Janice's feelings are now?** (Janice probably feels a little sad and guilty for hurting Frank, but she also feels free of a burden she doesn't want. She feels proud that she could share her feelings and stand up for herself in a polite way.)

Explain to the group that in order to learn how to deal with their feelings, teens have to learn to put thinking between their feelings and their behavior. They have to learn what their negative thinking, or self-talk is, and what their positive self-talk is. They also have to learn techniques to handle their feelings. It helps to learn how to *recognize* (identify or put a name to feelings), *accept* (tell yourself it's okay to have feelings), *tolerate* (just sit with the feeling because it will pass), or *share* (express the feeling in a helpful way) all feelings, including anger. You may also need to look at your thinking. Sometimes you need to change your thinking in order to handle your feelings.

DISCUSSION

Lead a discussion to help the students better understand the facts—the key concepts—presented. As the group discusses, remember to go around, making sure that each student has an opportunity to add to the discussion. Encourage participation, but don't force it. Remember the group rule that allows a student to pass. Accept all ideas and answers, explaining or clarifying information where necessary to reinforce learning or to correct misconceptions. Questions like the following will aid the discussion.

- **What does it mean to swallow a feeling?** (To pretend that you don't have it; to bury it inside; to try to hide the feeling.)

- **What happens when you swallow feelings?** (You might feel physically sick; you might feel sad; you might explode in anger at others.)

- **What does it mean to recognize feelings?** (To know what you're feeling and to put a name to the feeling.)

- **What are some different feelings teens have?** (Accept all reasonable replies. If a student mentions "bad" or "good," however, point out that these are not feelings or feeling words—they're judgment words.)

- **What are the three components of an emotion?** (Feeling, thinking, and behaving.)

- **Give an example of how thinking, or self-talk, can change feelings and behavior.** (A teenage girl who thinks she has to keep going out with a boy just so she won't hurt his feelings has incorrect thinking. She can correct her thinking by realizing that she can decide whether she wants to date him; if she doesn't, she can tell him that politely.)

- **What does it mean to accept a feeling?** (To tell yourself that no matter what you're feeling, it's okay to have that feeling.)

- **What does it mean to tolerate a feeling?** (To sit with a feeling until it passes.)

- **What are some ways you can share feelings?** (Accept all reasonable replies, for example: talk to a friend; paint a picture; write a story; write a poem.)

- **Do feelings last forever?** (No, they're temporary. Sooner or later they pass. Or, if the feeling is uncomfortable, you can do something to feel better.)

- **Can you control the feelings you get?** (No, feelings just come to you. You can look at your thinking—or "self-talk"—and change it from negative to positive; you can control your behavior or actions, but not your feelings.)

- **What are some things you can do to help yourself feel better?** (Help the students recall the brainstorming—talk to friends, play games, read a good book, get some exercise.)

ACTIVITY

Ask the students to get out their copies of Handout 2C ("Three Components of Emotion"). Explain that the purpose of this activity is to help them become aware of positive thinking and negative thinking and their effect on both feelings and behavior.

The activity will also show how to change negative thinking to positive. Ask the group members to look at the examples given. Explain that in the first example the teen thinks negatively or incorrectly that she is responsible for her friends. She feels guilty and tries to take on her friends' problems. If she changes her thinking to positive and correct, she realizes that she can only control her own behavior and can only offer support to friends. Her behavior is to take care of herself and her feeling is relief. Ask group members to explain the second and third examples.

Example 1:

Marcy is a good friend of Paula and Joanna. Paula is having real problems. Her mother smokes marijuana all the time; her brother is on probation; and Paula is beginning to try marijuana herself. Joanna's boyfriend is pressuring her to have sex. Marcy is afraid Joanna is going to get pregnant.

NEGATIVE THINKING
Feeling: guilt
Negative thinking or self-talk: "The world is my fault."
Behavior: take on friends' problems

POSITIVE THINKING
Feeling: guilt
Positive thinking or self-talk: "I can only be responsible for myself. I can care for my friends, but I can't control them."
Changed behavior: talk to friends to help them, but don't take on their problems
Changed feeling: relief

Now ask the students to think of one or two situations of their own. Have them write their feel-

Example 2:

Bill usually looks sad when he's walking to his classes. Bill's father is in a work-release program, after getting his fourth DWI. Bill is afraid his father is going to divorce his mother when he gets out.

NEGATIVE THINKING
Feeling: sadness
Negative thinking or self-talk: "The sun will never shine."
Behavior: isolation

POSITIVE THINKING
Feeling: sadness
Positive thinking or self-talk: "I am sad, but I can do something about it."
Changed behavior: go shoot baskets with friends
Changed feeling: relaxed

ing, their negative thinking or self-talk, and their behavior, using Handout 2D. Ask them to change the negative or incorrect thinking to positive or correct. Have them write that down, as well as the corresponding changed feeling and behavior. Give the students three minutes to do this activity, and help them during this period. Then have a go-around, allowing each student to report what he or she wrote. Point out that they can't control the feelings they get, but they can learn to control what they do with them— how they think about them and how they behave or act on them.

Example 3:

Phil is a freshman on the soccer team. He was a good player in middle school, but now he spends a lot of time on the bench. The upperclassmen on the team are always putting the freshmen down. Phil is getting tired of their insults.

NEGATIVE THINKING
Feeling: anger
Negative thinking or self-talk: "How dare they!"
Behavior: cause pain/damage

POSITIVE THINKING
Feeling: anger
Positive thinking or self-talk: "I can tell them how I feel" or "I can use my anger to improve my skills in soccer."
Changed behavior: ask upperclassman for help in improving skills; work out every day
Changed feeling: empowered

Conclude the activity by asking the students to put their handouts in their folders.

BASIC FACTS

Tell the students to look at the List of Basic Facts. Ask a group member to read Basic Facts 4 and 5.

4. Feelings aren't good or bad, or right or wrong; they just are.

5. Putting thinking between your feeling and your behavior enables you to choose helpful ways to express feelings.

Briefly discuss each fact, checking for understanding.

ASSIGNMENT

Have the group members take Assignment 2 out of the folders. Read the directions: "1. Write things you can do to make yourself feel better if you wake up in a down mood. 2. Over the next week, once each day, observe your feelings, thinking or self-talk, and behavior. Decide if your thinking is positive or negative. Then fill in the chart." Explain again that you don't want the students to spend too much time on this, but you do want them to be observing their feelings, thinking, and behavior. You will ask what they observed next week, just as you did this week.

Wrapping Up

CENTERING EXERCISE

Settle the students and then repeat "The Clouds" (page 76).

AFFIRMATION

Involve the group in an affirmation. Stand and join in a circle with the students holding hands. Go around and have group members share a negative or incorrect belief or self-talk they have, how they can change it to positive and correct, and how that will influence their feelings or behavior. Start the affirmation yourself: "One negative or incorrect belief or self-talk that I have (or have had) is. . . . I can change it from negative to positive and correct by saying to myself. . . . This will influence my feelings or behavior by. . . . " You will need to role-model this complicated but effective affirmation. Group members will probably also need your help to get all three parts as they go through it themselves.

CLOSING

Remain standing in a circle with the students, holding hands, and lead the group in the closing activity. Tell the students that you're going to make a silent wish for the student on your right. Then, when you've made the wish, gently squeeze the student's hand. The student makes a silent wish for the person on his or her right, then gently squeezes that student's hand, and so on. Continue around the circle until a wish and squeeze come back to you. If necessary, the students can pass the wish in any appropriate way they choose.

Collect the folders. Fill out a copy of the Process and Progress Form (page 211) or the Progress Notes (page 212), if you are an experienced leader, as soon as you can after the session.

Feeling Wheel

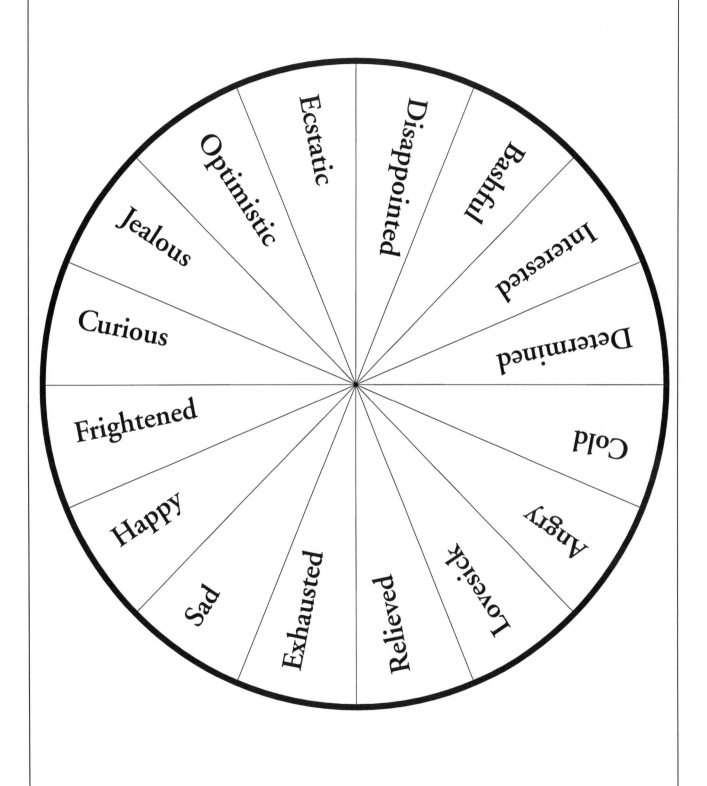

Feelings

People have many kinds of feelings. Happiness, sadness, fear, anger, jealousy, relief, and disappointment are just a few of the feelings people have. All these feelings are normal, including anger. In order to handle feelings well, people—including teens—have to be able to recognize their feelings and to put them into words.

Swallowing Feelings

Many people do not put their feelings into words; they may not even admit to themselves that they are having a feeling. These people swallow feelings down by minimizing, denying, or burying them. People who do this may get depressed, or they may get physically sick, or they may explode at something else.

Some people are afraid of feelings. They may fear the pain that accompanies feelings, especially feelings of sadness. Some people fear they will be overwhelmed by their feelings; or they may fear they will lose control: they may fear that if they let themselves feel anger, they will not be able to control their behavior. However, no matter how afraid people are of their feelings, the feelings don't go away. Sometimes they show themselves in physical aches and pains; or people may act out their feelings by fighting or by using alcohol or other drugs; or they may turn their feelings in and become depressed.

Feelings Are Temporary

Many people think that when they get a feeling, they will have it forever—many people make suicide attempts when they are very depressed and think the depression will last forever. Very angry people may commit acts of violence, not realizing that eventually their anger will die down.

Feelings are really temporary and fleeting; they don't last forever. Feelings come, but then they go. So, teenagers can just wait until a difficult feeling passes. Teens can also do something to make themselves feel better.

People Can Do Things to Feel Better

Most people do not understand they can do something about some feelings they might have. For instance, teenagers who have fights with their parents often feel better when they call their friends and complain about their parents. Some days, people wake up in an "up" mood, when they feel happy. But other days, people wake up in a "down" mood; they may feel angry or sad. It's important for teens to learn what they can do to help themselves feel better if they wake up in a sad or an angry mood. Teens might play sports, listen to music, dance, call their friends, or write a poem to help themselves feel better. It's important for adults to have fun things to do as well.

Anger Is a Normal Feeling

Adolescents may have intense feelings that can be very difficult to have. Some teens live in families where they feel intense anger, even hatred for their parents; they then often feel guilty and ashamed because they think they are bad to hate their parents. Anger is not a bad feeling; feelings are not good or bad; they just are. But, feelings like anger, hate, rage, and even sadness, panic, and grief can be very difficult to have. They are normal feelings that most people have at least some of the time.

People can't control what feelings they get, so they have to learn to accept them. But they are responsible for their behavior, which they can and should control. So it is okay for teens to feel anger, or even hate; but it is not okay for them to act in violent ways. It is okay for adolescents to feel very angry at their parents; but it is not okay for them to hit their parents.

Three Components of Emotion

Feelings have three components: feeling, thinking, and behaving. Teenagers who act out a lot in school—talk back to teachers, break school rules, fight with peers, skip school, don't do school work—are probably not putting thinking between their feeling of anger and their behavior. They may be feeling angry about something like their parents' divorce or a parent's alcoholism, but they may not be aware of the feeling. They may just be acting it out. Some teens may feel very sad, or even depressed. Their behavior might be to feel exhausted and lie around and do nothing.

Sometimes teens need to look at their thinking before they can handle their feelings. They may need to see if their thinking is straight or if it is incorrect. They may realize they have negative thinking, for instance, always expecting the worst or putting themselves down. They need to realize that their thinking is incorrect, or a false belief, or a misconception.

Scenarios

Part 1

Janice is a junior in high school. She has been going out with Frank, but she doesn't like him anymore. Janice finally gets the courage to tell Frank she doesn't want to go out with him. Frank still wants to be friends and talk to her on the phone. Now Janice is afraid she'll hurt his feelings if she doesn't talk to him. Every time he calls, he keeps asking her to go out with him again, and he keeps her on the phone for hours. Janice gets angrier and angrier, but she can't do anything about it. She feels rotten about herself because she is hurting Frank's feelings. She also feels powerless because she keeps on talking to him, even though she doesn't want to.

Part 2

Janice goes to a group and learns how to decide what she wants, how to communicate her feelings, and how to set limits, which means being able to say no. Here's what Janice thinks now: "I can't be responsible for Frank's feelings. I don't want to keep on dating him, even if he wants to. I can tell him nicely that I don't want to keep on seeing him."

When Frank calls again, Janice tells him: "Frank, I think you're a good person, but I don't have a special feeling for you. I'm too young to be attached to only one person, and I want to date other people. I'm sorry if your feelings get hurt, but I won't be able to date you, or to spend a lot of time on the phone with you. I hope you find someone else who does have a special feeling for you."

Three Components of Emotion

Every emotion has three components or parts: feeling, thinking, and behavior. Your thinking affects your feelings and behavior. Study these examples of how teens change negative thinking to positive thinking and how that affects their feelings and behavior.

EXAMPLE 1: Marcy is a good friend of Paula and Joanna. Paula is having real problems. Her mother smokes marijuana all the time; her brother is on probation; and Paula is beginning to try marijuana herself. Joanna's boyfriend is pressuring her to have sex. Marcy is afraid Joanna is going to get pregnant.

Negative Thinking	Positive Thinking
Feeling: guilt **Negative thinking or self-talk:** "The world is my fault." **Behavior:** take on friends' problems	**Feeling:** guilt **Positive thinking or self-talk:** "I can only be responsible for myself. I can care for my friends, but I can't control them." **Changed behavior:** talk to friends to help them, but don't take on their problems **Changed feeling:** relief

EXAMPLE 2: Bill usually looks sad when he's walking to his classes. Bill's father is in a work-release program, after getting his fourth DWI. Bill is afraid his father is going to divorce his mother when he gets out.

Negative Thinking	Positive Thinking
Feeling: sadness **Negative thinking or self-talk:** "The sun will never shine." **Behavior:** isolation	**Feeling:** sadness **Positive thinking or self-talk:** "I am sad, but I can do something about it." **Changed behavior:** go shoot baskets with friends **Changed feeling:** relaxed

EXAMPLE 3: Phil is a freshman on the soccer team. He was a good player in middle school, but now he spends a lot of time on the bench. The upperclassmen on the team are always putting the freshmen down. Phil is getting tired of their insults.

Negative Thinking	Positive Thinking
Feeling: anger **Negative thinking or self-talk:** "How dare they!" **Behavior:** cause pain/damage	**Feeling:** anger **Positive thinking or self-talk:** "I can tell them how I feel" or "I can use my anger to improve my skills in soccer." **Changed behavior:** ask upperclassmen for help in improving skills; work out every day **Changed feeling:** empowered

Your Examples

Think of one or two situations of your own or someone else's. Tell how you or another person could change negative thinking to positive thinking. Tell how that would affect feeling and behavior.

1. Situation:

Feeling:
Negative thinking or self-talk:
Behavior:
Feeling:
Positive thinking or self-talk:
Changed behavior:
Changed feeling:

2. Situation:

Feeling:
Negative thinking or self-talk:
Behavior:
Feeling:
Positive thinking or self-talk:
Changed behavior:
Changed feeling:

1. Write things you can do to make yourself feel better if you wake up in a down mood.

_____

_____

_____

_____

2. Over the next week, once each day, observe your feelings, thinking or self-talk, and behavior. Decide if your thinking is positive or negative. Then fill in the chart.

DAY ONE

Situation	
Feelings	
Thinking	
Behavior	

DAY TWO

Situation	
Feelings	
Thinking	
Behavior	

DAY THREE

Situation	
Feelings	
Thinking	
Behavior	

DAY FOUR

Situation	
Feelings	
Thinking	
Behavior	

DAY FIVE

Situation	
Feelings	
Thinking	
Behavior	

DAY SIX

Situation	
Feelings	
Thinking	
Behavior	

DAY SEVEN

Situation	
Feelings	
Thinking	
Behavior	

Six Different Styles of Expressing Anger

Objectives

To help the students:

• identify styles people use to express anger

• identify ways that the parents' style of expressing anger might influence their children's behavior

Session at a Glance

1. Group Rules: review if necessary—1 minute

2. Centering Exercise: "The Icicle"—2 minutes

3. Feelings Check-in: look at Feeling Wheel—4 minutes

4. Basic Facts Review—4 minutes

5. Assignment Review—4 minutes

6. Mini-lecture and Discussion—16 minutes

7. Activity: write about anger styles and discuss in a go-around—5 minutes

8. Basic Facts: read Basic Facts 6, 7, and 8; discuss—2 minutes

9. Assignment—1 minute

10. Centering Exercise: repeat "The Icicle"—2 minutes

11. Affirmation: share one style you have used to express anger—3 minutes

12. Closing: pass a silent wish—1 minute

Preparation

• Display the posterboard copy of the group rules.

• Have posters with Basic Facts 1-5 available. (Or the List of Basic Facts, already in the folders; or index cards with a basic fact on each one.)

• Have chalkboard and chalk or newsprint and a marker available.

• Add the following materials to each folder:

—Handout 3A ("Six Anger Styles")

—Handout 3B ("Anger Styles in My Life")

—Assignment 3.

- Have the folder, pencils, and crayons or markers at each student's place.

- Read through the session plan before meeting.

Background and Guidelines

This session begins the process of helping group members learn how to put positive thinking between their feelings of being angry and their behavior. It also introduces techniques to be problem solvers: to resolve conflicts in nonaggressive, proactive, constructive ways.

The underlying thesis is that anger is a normal feeling that everyone experiences around 12 to 14 times a day. People can express their anger in many different ways; aggression and violence are just one way. People can choose ways to express anger that may not be aggressive, but are just as damaging, or harmful, or nonconstructive. A teenage girl who burns herself with cigarettes or who cuts her arms with a knife may be expressing anger; just as a teenage boy who shuts down academically and allows his grades to fall may be expressing anger. The group members may have parents who are passive-aggressive; that is, they do not speak to anyone in the family for days if they are angry. Many of the group members, and their parents, may deal with their anger reactively and without thinking carefully about their options.

SIX ANGER STYLES

This session describes six styles of expressing anger. Teens are usually able to quickly identify family members and friends who use these styles; they are also able to identify the styles they use. The anger styles described here are the *stuffer*, who avoids conflict and may deny anger; the *withdrawer*, who is passive aggressive, who withdraws from interaction to express anger, or who doesn't do chores or schoolwork

to express anger; the *blamer*, who projects anger onto someone else by calling names, attacking, or using put downs; the *triangler*, who incites other people to be angry; the *exploder*, who uses violence or aggression; and the *problem solver*, who puts anger to a positive use, who thinks carefully before expressing anger, and who has good problem-solving skills.

In her book *The Dance of Anger*, Harriet Lerner (1985) discusses two common ways that women tend to deal with anger: (1) by denying, swallowing, or internalizing anger, and often becoming depressed; or (2) by nagging and complaining excessively, which often serve only to perpetuate the problem. Lerner points out that neither way of dealing with anger is very effective; she recommends that women "use their anger energy in the service of their own dignity and growth." In order to do this, she describes a four-step process:

1. Clarify the true sources of anger.

2. Learn communication skills.

3. Learn to observe and interrupt nonproductive patterns of interaction.

4. Anticipate countermoves or "Change back!" reactions from others.

This session focuses primarily on Step 3, helping group members to observe their patterns of expressing anger, a necessary first step before they can learn and put into practice more effective patterns of expressing anger.

Stuffers hold their anger in and deny that they are angry. Some people habitually do not allow themselves to experience anger, and instead allow themselves to feel sad, or hurt, or betrayed. These people may repress their anger, thereby becoming especially vulnerable to depression, somatic complaints, and other emotional problems. The teenager who denies feelings of sadness after the death of a grandparent or a parental divorce may be stuffing his or her feelings in.

Withdrawers deal with anxiety, or anger, by cutting themselves off emotionally and/or geographically. These people, whom Lerner describes as "Distancers," tend to intensify work-related projects when anxiety rises in personal relationships. They have difficulty showing their needy, vulnerable, and dependent sides, and they may cut off a relationship entirely when things get intense. Insisting that they work on a problem generally entrenches them more into their cut-off position. Teenagers who refuse to do their chores or their schoolwork may be shutting themselves off in a passive way.

When Lerner describes **Blamers**, she uses the phrase "de-self." De-selfed people don't have a sense of clarity about their own decisions and control over choices. They tend to hold other people responsible for their own feelings and actions and see others as the sole obstacle to making changes. They may expend high levels of energy trying to change someone who does not want to change; they may engage in cycles of fighting that relieve tension but perpetuate old patterns. Blamers give up a sense of an internal locus of control, projecting their power onto someone else. They avoid responsibility by doing so, but also give up any power to make things better. Teens may blame their poor grades on the teacher, saying the teacher loses homework or doesn't explain things clearly. They give the teacher the responsibility for the grades, but also give up their ability to improve their grades.

Trianglers reduce anxiety in a relationship by focusing on a third party. They pull another person or an unrelated issue into the situation, instead of dealing directly or appropriately with a relationship problem. Triangles can occur in families, in peer groups, and in workplaces. An angry wife who complains about her distant, uninvolved husband to the couple's teenage son may be triangling the child in. Or a mother who is having a relationship problem with her husband may focus on her teenage son's behavior or grades rather than on the real problem. An adolescent girl who has a fight with her best friend and cuts off from her and becomes friendly with another girl may be triangling.

Exploders express anger through aggression or violence. The exploder may have a short fuse. The exploder's repeated patterns of fighting tend to be ineffective in solving problems and instead may simply perpetuate the pattern.

Problem solvers have good problem-solving skills. They can state their feelings appropriately. They do not try to change other people, but have a clear sense of boundaries and can set clear and appropriate limits. The problem solver is also able to accept someone else's anger.

AMBIVALENCE

This session introduces the notion of ambivalence. Often, teenagers who live in violent homes—or in any home where parents use stuffing, withdrawing, blaming, triangling, or exploding—have mixed feelings toward their parents. Some teens have intense feelings of both love and hatred toward their parents, which, in turn, are often accompanied by feelings of guilt due to their hatred. Remember to accept both the positive and negative feelings the students may express about their parents. Help the students recognize that having such opposite feelings at the same time is confusing, but normal.

PROBLEM-SOLVING SKILLS

This session encourages the students to commit to becoming problem solvers in dealing with anger. Session 4 will describe five basic problem-solving skills the students can use. The session will also provide scenarios for the group members to practice these skills.

91

Beginning the Session

GROUP RULES

Welcome the students and begin with a quick review of the group rules. Draw attention to the poster listing the group rules. If you feel that it is necessary, call on different students to read them one at a time. Check for understanding before moving on.

CENTERING EXERCISE

Settle the students. Then lead them in the following centering exercise called "The Icicle." Tell them that this centering exercise will help them to calm down, relax, and be able to think if they get angry or upset. They can use this exercise without anyone else knowing.

THE ICICLE

Close your eyes. Tighten the muscles in your feet and legs really tight: make your feet and legs as stiff as an icicle. *(Pause.)* Now let that cold and stiff icicle melt. Let it melt, drip by drip, into a calm, peaceful puddle. Let your legs get loose and very relaxed, and imagine what they would feel like as part of a puddle. *(Pause.)* Now tighten your chest, stomach, and trunk area: make it as stiff as an icicle. *(Pause.)* Now let that icicle melt, slowly, drip by drip, into a puddle. *(Pause.)* Put your arms straight out in front of you, make fists, and pretend that your arms are icicles. *(Pause.)* Now let those icicles melt; let them drip into a puddle, and imagine what they feel like as they drip into a calm, peaceful puddle. *(Pause.)* Tighten the muscles in your shoulders, neck, and head; tighten them into a stiff, cold icicle. Make them very stiff and tight. *(Pause.)* Now let them relax and melt, slowly, very slowly into a puddle. *(Pause.)*

Now take every muscle in your whole body: make them just as stiff and tight as you can. Make your whole body into an icicle. *(Pause.)* Now let yourself melt, from the tip of your toes to the top of your head. Let all your muscles melt, drip by drip, into a puddle. Let yourself get very loose and relaxed, like smooth water in a puddle. Imagine that your whole body is a calm, quiet, peaceful puddle. *(Pause.)*

Remind the students that they can use this technique in class and at home to help them put thinking between their feelings and their behavior.

FEELINGS CHECK-IN

Do a feelings check-in with the students. Have them take out their Feeling Wheels. Ask the group members to decide how they are feeling today. Remind the students that if they want, they can color in the section on the Feeling Wheel that describes how they're feeling. Also remind the teens that they might have more than one feeling, since it's possible to have more than one feeling at a time. Tell the students that if they're having a feeling not named on the wheel, they can add a bubble to the outside of the wheel and name their feeling.

When the students finish, have a go-around. Begin by sharing your own feelings. Then, invite each student to share his or her feelings. Teenagers often list many feelings. For the interests of time, ask them to name the feelings they have, but then pick only two to discuss. Be sure to accept each student's feeling(s) and to affirm each student. Ask the students to return the wheels to their folders.

BASIC FACTS REVIEW

Review Basic Facts 1-5. Use the List of Basic Facts, or index cards.

In a go-around, ask a student to read Basic Fact 1 aloud and to explain what it means. If the student has trouble explaining the fact, don't contradict or judge, simply clarify his or her explanation. Repeat the procedure for the next basic fact. This review ensures that the students understand and integrate the basic facts that have been taught. It is also easy preparation for the presentation and provides a lead-in for the session material.

ASSIGNMENT REVIEW

Ask the students if they brought their assignments from last week. Remind them that they were to write down several things they can do to feel better if they wake up in a down mood. They were also supposed to observe their feelings, thinking, and behavior, and decide if their thinking was positive or negative. In a go-around, ask the students to share what they do to make themselves feel better, and what they learned about their feelings, thinking, and behavior. If the students forgot to do the assignment, ask them to try to remember one feeling they had in the past week, what their thinking was, whether it was positive or negative, and what their behavior was. Remind the group members that the purpose of the group is to give them alternatives to violent behavior, and putting positive thinking between feelings and behavior is a way to start developing alternatives. The students will have a simple assignment each week that will help them choose better ways to handle anger.

Exploring the Material

MINI-LECTURE AND DISCUSSION
Six Anger Styles

Recall that in Session 2 the students learned that anger is a normal feeling. Most people get angry 12 to 14 times a day. Teenagers, and adults, have different styles of handling anger. Some people express their anger through aggression and violence; they intend to harm someone else. Some people express anger in ways that are not violent, but may still be harmful. Everybody has the choice to express anger in helpful or harmful ways. Tell the students that in this session they will look at six different styles people use to express anger. Most are harmful. Some people use several different styles, at different times.

Ask the students to take out Handout 3A ("Six Anger Styles"). Ask a group member to start by reading the paragraph about stuffers. As you introduce the different styles of handling anger, write the name of each style on the chalkboard.

Stuffers

Stuffers are conflict avoiders, people who deny or bury their anger; their motto is "peace at any price." They often have lots of tension under the surface. The underlying problem is never addressed and therefore can't be solved. People who stuff their anger so much may become depressed, or they may become physically sick, with stomachaches, or headaches, or other physical complaints. Teens who have parents who stuff their anger don't have the opportunity to learn how to problem-solve.

Use these discussion questions to help the students understand the material.

1. **Do conflict avoiders get angry?** (Yes, but they stuff it and may try to deny it or bury it; sometimes they avoid conflict at great cost.)

2. **What problems go along with stuffing anger?** (Often there is great tension under the surface; stuffers may get depressed or develop physical symptoms; they never solve problems.)

3. **Can you give an example, without identifying the person, of someone you know who stuffs anger?** Describe a situation where the person stuffs anger and tell what happens.

Have another student read the material about withdrawers.

Withdrawers

Withdrawers use passive-aggressive means to express their anger. The term *passive-aggressive* means expressing anger in subtle, indirect ways. Some husbands are passive-aggressive: they don't talk to their wives for days when they are angry. Some teens who are angry about a divorce express their anger by letting their grades go down. Or some teens who are angry at their parents show their anger by not doing their chores or by not doing what they are told. These are subtle, not obvious, ways to show anger. Sometimes the withdrawers hurt themselves the most by their withdrawing—they suffer the consequences of not having a closer relationship when

Withdrawers continued on next page.

Withdrawers continued from previous page.

they don't communicate; they suffer the consequences of low grades. When parents are passive-aggressive, or withdraw, their children often feel guilty and responsible, and they are always wondering what they've done wrong. People who withdraw also miss out on the power of using their anger to work for them. They don't solve the underlying problem.

Use these discussion questions to help the students understand the material.

1. **How do passive-aggressive people express anger?** (By withdrawing and not talking at all; they say they'll do their chores, but they don't; they let their grades go down because they're angry at a teacher or at a parent, or at a situation like a divorce.)

2. **How might teens feel if their dad is a withdrawer?** (They might wonder what they've done wrong; they might feel guilty and responsible; they might be confused because they don't know what's going on.)

3. **Can you give an example, without identifying the person, of someone you know who withdraws when angry?** Describe a situation where the person withdraws and tell what happens.

Have another student read the paragraph about blamers.

Blamers

Blamers express their anger by blaming their problems on other people, by name calling, by attacking, or by putting other people down. Teens often blame their problems on their peers, their siblings, their parents, or their teachers. Parents often blame their problems on their children, their spouse, their own parents, or their work situation. Teenagers in families where one or both parents are blamers may have low self-esteem because they begin to believe what they are told. They may feel guilty and responsible for the family problems. Or they may become blamers, too, and never take responsibility for their own behavior.

Use these discussion questions to help the students process the material.

1. **How do blamers express their anger?** (They might yell at you, blame you, or put you down. They often blame their problems on other people.)

2. **How might children react if their parents are blamers?** (They might feel hurt and have low self-esteem; they may not learn to accept responsibility for their actions, but blame their problems on others. They may become blamers themselves.)

3. **Can you give an example, without identifying the person, of someone you know who blames when angry?** Describe a situation where the person blames and tell what happens.

Have another student read the paragraph about trianglers.

Trianglers

Trianglers express their anger in devious and manipulative ways. Instead of expressing their anger directly, they pull someone else in, or they try to get someone else to be angry. For instance, a mother who is angry at her husband may tell her son what the husband has done, so the son will be angry at the husband too.

Adolescents often use triangling. For example, Jenny might be angry because her best friend, Stephanie, said something to hurt her feelings. Rather than dealing with Stephanie directly, Jenny tells another friend, Maggie, something bad about Stephanie so that Maggie is mad at Stephanie too.

In families where there are trianglers, a lot of tension may be below the surface. Kids may have the feeling that they or someone else has done something wrong, but they don't know what.

Use these discussion questions to help the students process the material.

1. **How do trianglers express their anger?** (Indirectly. They tell a third party what they are angry about and try to get that person angry too.)

2. **How might teens react if their friends or parents are trianglers?** (They may end up in a lot of disagreements or sticky situations with their friends. If parents are trianglers, teens may experience a lot of underlying tension.)

3. **Can you give an example, without identifying the person, of someone you know who is a triangler?** Describe a situation where the person triangles and tell what happens.

Have another group member read the paragraph about exploders.

Exploders

Exploders use violence to express anger. This may range from pushing, shoving, kicking, and slapping to hitting, punching, choking, using a weapon, or even killing. These are all harmful behaviors. Teens who grow up in violent families are often scared that they or someone else is going to get hurt. They often intervene in order to rescue one parent, and sometimes the teens get hurt as well. Sometimes violent parents get angry at teens who try to rescue. If a teenage daughter is very close to a mother who is beaten by the father, the girl might believe that she should be beaten, too, and may not be able to set limits when she starts dating. Children in violent families worry about divorce; they also worry that someone will be hurt fatally and that the violent parent will go to jail.

Violent parents are often unpredictable in their violence. Their children never know what to expect. They are often hypervigilant, constantly scanning the mood of the violent parent, or of the family, to help them predict whether this is a safe time. Sometimes after violent fights with each other, the parents might get mad at the children, ignoring them, sending them to their room, or taking their anger out on them. Sometimes the parent directs the violence to the oldest son or daughter. The parent may beat the son or daughter, sometimes with the other parent watching. Teens in this position often wonder why their mother stands by and allows them to be beaten by their father. Teens in violent families often think their families are "different" and wish they could be like other families that they think are happy. Teens in these families also sometimes feel ashamed of their families, and ashamed of themselves, thinking something is the matter with them.

1. **How do exploders express their anger?** (They might become physically abusive and push, shove, kick, slap, hit, punch, choke, use a weapon, or even kill.)

2. **What are some issues for teens whose parents are exploders?** (They might become violent themselves or stay in relationships with someone who is violent. They might try to intervene and stop the fight—then they might get hurt themselves, or the parents might get angry with them. They often fear that their parents will divorce or that someone will get severely hurt or go to jail. Girls whose father batters their mother may not set limits with violent boyfriends. Teens in violent families often blame themselves for the family problems; they may think that their family is "different" or that something is the matter with them.)

3. **Can you give an example, without identifying the person, of someone you know who is an exploder?** Describe a situation where the person explodes and tell what happens.

Have another student read the paragraph about problem solvers.

Problem Solvers

Problem solvers admit that they are angry and then look at why they are angry. They put thinking between their feelings and their behavior. They see if they are angry about a problem they can solve; if so, they use their anger to give them power to change themselves. Problem solvers use their problem-solving skills in anger situations. If problem solvers have a problem they can't solve, they express their anger in helpful ways so they can let it go.

Teens who grow up in families where the parents are problem solvers will learn how to problem-solve when they are angry. They learn the consequences of their behavior; they don't feel put down; they feel safe; and they learn to use their anger to work for them.

Use these discussion questions to help the students process the material.

Use these discussion questions to help the students process the material.

1. **How do problem solvers handle anger?** (In a helpful way—they use their anger to change themselves. They use helpful ways to express anger and to solve problems.)

2. **Do problem solvers get angry?** (Of course. Everybody gets angry.)

3. **What's it like for teens to live in a family where the parents are problem solvers?** (They usually know what they've done wrong because their parents give them appropriate consequences. They learn how to solve problems.)

4. **Can you give an example, without identifying the person, of someone you know who is a problem solver?** Describe a situation where the person handles anger well and tell what happens.

Emphasize that one person may use these different styles at different times; or a person may tend to use one style all the time. In families, one person may tend to be an exploder while others may stuff their anger in order to avoid conflict. For example, the mother may be a blamer, putting down everyone else in the family, and the father may withdraw into his work and never say a word. Or the father may be violent and the mother may be a blamer.

Ambivalence

Write the term *ambivalence* on the chalkboard. Explain that people in families usually love the other people in the family, even if they are exploders, stuffers, withdrawers, trianglers, or blamers. They may love the person, but not like how the person expresses anger. This ability to have two opposite feelings at the same time is called ambivalence. It can sometimes be very confusing to teenagers, but it is very normal. Teens often get angry at how their parents express anger, especially if they blame or explode; these teens may love their parents, but dislike the behavior of blaming or violence. In the same way, parents can love their children, but dislike their behavior.

Point out that now that the group members are able to name the different anger styles, they can work on becoming aware of the different styles they use. The purpose of this group is to help them become problem solvers. In the next two sessions, they will learn problem-solving skills so that they can choose more helpful ways to deal with their anger.

ACTIVITY

Ask the students to take Handout 3B ("Anger Styles in My Life") out of their folders. Have a student read the directions aloud: "Think of someone you know who fits each category. On the lines provided, describe what that person would do if angry at a family member or friend. You don't have to identify the person, and you can use a different person for each style. Also, circle the names of the styles that describe how you express your anger." Give the students time to complete the activity independently, and, in a go-around, have them share examples of people who use the different styles, without necessarily identifying the person. Teenagers usually enjoy this activity and learn from the examples given by different group members.

Remember that the purpose of this activity is (1) to help the students understand that there are various styles of expressing anger; (2) to help them identify the different styles used by themselves, their parents and other family members, and their peers; and (3) to help them make a commitment to learn problem-solving techniques.

When the students have finished, have them return their handouts to their folders.

BASIC FACTS

Review the new basic facts for this session. Refer the students to the List of Basic Facts. Ask a group member to read the new basic facts.

6. Six ways to express anger are stuffing, withdrawing, blaming, triangling, exploding, and problem solving.

7. Parents usually love their children, even when the parents are choosing to use violent

or harmful ways to express their anger.

8. Children usually love their parents, although they may feel hate for the parents if the parents are using violent or harmful ways to express their anger.

Briefly discuss each fact, checking for understanding.

ASSIGNMENT

Have the group members take Assignment 3 out of their folders. Read the directions: "Over the next week, once each day, observe an anger style you use. Jot down if you were a stuffer, a withdrawer, a blamer, a triangler, an exploder, or a problem solver. This exercise will help you become aware of how you deal with anger. People need to be aware of their patterns before they can begin to change them."

Wrapping Up

CENTERING EXERCISE

Settle the students and repeat "The Icicle" (page 92).

AFFIRMATION

Involve the group in an affirmation. Stand and join in a circle with the students, holding hands. Go around and have the group members share an anger style they have used. Start the affirmation yourself: "One anger style I have used is. . . ."

CLOSING

Remain standing in a circle with the students holding hands and lead the group in the closing activity.

Tell the students that you're going to make a silent wish for the student on your right. Then when you've made the wish, gently squeeze the student's hand. The student makes a silent wish for the person on his or her right, then gently squeezes the student's hand, and so on. Continue around the circle until a wish and squeeze come back to you. If necessary, the students can pass the wish in any appropriate way they choose.

Collect the folders. Fill out a copy of the Process and Progress Form (page 211) or the Progress Notes (page 212), if you are an experienced leader, as soon as possible after leading the group.

Six Anger Styles

STUFFERS

Stuffers are conflict avoiders, people who deny or bury their anger; their motto is "peace at any price." They often have lots of tension under the surface. The underlying problem is never addressed and therefore can't be solved. People who stuff their anger so much may become depressed, or they may become physically sick, with stomachaches, or headaches, or other physical complaints. Teens who have parents who stuff their anger don't have the opportunity to learn how to problem-solve.

WITHDRAWERS

Withdrawers use passive-aggressive means to express their anger. The term passive-aggressive means expressing anger in subtle, indirect ways. Some husbands are passive-aggressive: they don't talk to their wives for days when they are angry. Some teens who are angry about a divorce express their anger by letting their grades go down. Or some teens who are angry at their parents show their anger by not doing their chores or by not doing what they are told. These are subtle, not obvious, ways to show anger.

Sometimes the withdrawers hurt themselves the most by their withdrawing—they suffer the consequences of not having a closer relationship when they don't communicate; they suffer the consequences of low grades. When parents are passive-aggressive, or withdraw, their children often feel guilty and responsible, and they are always wondering what they've done wrong. People who withdraw also miss out on the power of using their anger to work for them. They don't solve the underlying problem.

BLAMERS

Blamers express their anger by blaming their problems on other people, by name calling, by attacking, or by putting other people down. Teens often blame their problems on their peers, their siblings, their parents, or their teachers. Parents often blame their problems on their children, their spouse, their own parents, or their work situation. Teenagers in families where one or both parents are blamers may have low self-esteem because they begin to believe what they are told. They may feel guilty and responsible for the family problems. Or they may become blamers, too, and never take responsibility for their own behavior.

TRIANGLERS

Trianglers express their anger in devious and manipulative ways. Instead of expressing their anger directly, they pull someone else in, or they try to get someone else to be angry. For instance, a mother who is angry at her husband may tell her son what the husband has done, so the son will be angry at the husband too.

Adolescents often use triangling. For example, Jenny might be angry because her best friend, Stephanie, said something to hurt her feelings. Rather than dealing with Stephanie directly, Jenny tells another friend, Maggie, something bad about Stephanie so that Maggie is mad at Stephanie too.

In families where there are trianglers, a lot of tension may be below the surface. Kids may have the feeling that they or someone else has done something wrong, but they don't know what.

EXPLODERS

Exploders use violence to express anger. This may range from pushing, shoving, kicking, and slapping to hitting, punching, choking, using a weapon, or even killing. These are all harmful behaviors. Teens who grow up in violent families are often scared that they or someone else is going to get hurt. They often intervene in order to rescue one parent, and sometimes the teens get hurt as well. Sometimes violent parents get angry at teens who try to rescue. If a teenage daughter is very close to a mother who is beaten by the father, the girl might believe that she should be beaten, too, and may not be able to set limits when she starts dating. Children in violent families worry about divorce; they also worry that someone will be hurt fatally and that the violent parent will go to jail.

Violent parents are often unpredictable in their violence. Their children never know what to expect. They are often hypervigilant, constantly scanning the mood of the violent parent, or of the family, to help them predict whether this is a safe time. Sometimes after violent fights with each other, the parents might get mad at the children, ignoring them, sending them to their room, or taking their anger out on them. Sometimes the parent directs the violence to the oldest son or daughter. The parent may beat the son or daughter, sometimes with the other parent watching. Teens in this position often wonder why their mother stands by and allows them to be beaten by their father. Teens in violent families often think their families are "different" and wish they could be like other families that they think are happy. Teens in these families also sometimes feel ashamed of their families, and ashamed of themselves, thinking something is the matter with them.

PROBLEM SOLVERS

Problem solvers can admit that they are angry and then look at why they are angry. They put thinking between their feelings and their behavior. They see if they are angry about a problem they can solve; if so, they use their anger to give them power to change themselves. Problem solvers use their problem-solving skills in anger situations. If problem solvers have a problem they can't solve, they express their anger in helpful ways so they can let it go.

Teens who grow up in families where the parents are problem solvers will learn how to problem-solve when they are angry. They learn the consequences of their behavior; they don't feel put down; they feel safe; and they learn to use their anger to work for them.

Anger Styles in My Life

Think of someone you know who fits into each category. On the lines provided, describe what that person would do if angry at a family member or friend. You don't have to identify the person, and you can use a different person for each style. Also, circle the names of the styles that describe how you express your anger.

Stuffers
_____
_____
_____
_____
_____

Withdrawers
_____
_____
_____
_____
_____

Blamers
_____
_____
_____
_____
_____

Trianglers
_____
_____
_____
_____
_____

Exploders
_____
_____
_____
_____
_____

Problem Solvers
_____
_____
_____
_____
_____

Over the next week, once each day, observe an anger style you use. Jot down if you were a stuffer, a withdrawer, a blamer, a triangler, an exploder, or a problem solver. This exercise will help you become aware of how you deal with anger. People need to be aware of their patterns before they can begin to change them.

ANGER STYLE

Day one

Day two

Day three

Day four

Day five

Day six

Day seven

Other comments or observations

Skills to Problem-solve Anger Situations

Objectives

To help the students:

• realize the difference between problems they can change and problems they can't change

• learn three things they can do about problems they can't change

• learn the differences between passive, aggressive, and assertive behaviors

• learn five skills for problem solving

Session at a Glance

1. Group Rules: review if necessary—1 minute

2. Centering Exercise: "The Space Shuttle"—2 minutes

3. Feelings Check-in: look at Feeling Wheel—4 minutes

4. Basic Facts Review—3 minutes

5. Assignment Review—4 minutes

6. Mini-lecture, Role Plays, and Discussion—20 minutes

7. Basic Facts: read Basic Facts 9, 10, 11, and 12 aloud; discuss—2 minutes

8. Assignment—2 minutes

9. Centering Exercise: repeat "The Space Shuttle"—2 minutes

10. Affirmation: share one time you got angry and a problem-solving skill you could have used—3 minutes

11. Closing: pass a silent wish—1 minute

Preparation

• Display the posterboard copy of the group rules.

• Have posters with Basic Facts 1-8 available. (Or the List of Basic Facts or index cards with a basic fact on each one.)

• On a sheet of newsprint, list the steps in "chunking down" the problem-solving skills (page 111).

- Add the following materials to each folder:

  —Handout 4A ("Scenarios")

  —Handout 4B ("Five Problem-solving Skills")

  —Assignment 4

- Have the folder, pencil, and crayons or markers at each student's place.

- Read through the session plan before meeting.

Background and Guidelines

PROBLEMS THAT STUDENTS CAN'T CHANGE

In this session, the students learn to look at why they are angry and to decide if they are angry about something they can change or about something they can't change. They learn that they can't control some things that make them feel angry, such as parental divorce, chemical dependence, or violence; or the death of a close friend; or school regulations. In such cases, your task is to help the students realize they can learn to cope with the problem by accepting what they can't change, by learning to express their anger so they can let it go, and by doing something good for themselves.

For example, a teenager who is angry over his or her parents' divorce will be unable to do anything to change the divorce. To such a student you might say: "We teach students who are in a divorced situation the three Cs. Children can't cause, control, or change a parent's separation or divorce. Divorce is something children, even if they are teenagers, just have to accept. It's an adult decision that children can't change. But let's talk about some helpful ways to express your anger so you can let it go. Many teens in your situation write a letter to their parents—one they don't send—that tells them how angry they feel. Other teens whose parents are divorc-

ing use a pillow or a punching bag and punch it until they don't feel so angry. Now let's talk about how you can do something good for yourself. Remember what we talked about in Session 2? You could visit your best friend and listen to music, or you could play your favorite sport." The point here is to help the students see that they can use their anger to take care of themselves, rather than remaining in anger, powerlessness, and helplessness.

PROBLEMS THAT STUDENTS CAN CHANGE

In this session, the students also begin to see anger as an energy or power that they can use positively to work for them. They discover that they can use their anger to solve problems or to make powerful changes in themselves. They begin to see that they can change some problems by looking at their own behavior and by changing it. This session builds on Sessions 2 and 3. In Session 2, the students learned to look at their thinking and to see how that influenced their feelings and their behavior. In Session 3, the students learned to observe the styles they use to express anger. In this session, the students learn alternative behaviors they can use to deal with their anger. Their thinking between their feeling and behavior will help them to do this, as will their determination to avoid stuffing, withdrawing, blaming, triangling, or exploding.

PASSIVE, ASSERTIVE, AND AGGRESSIVE BEHAVIORS

The students learn the difference between passive, assertive, and aggressive behaviors. Much assertive behavior is mistakenly called aggressive. Persons who have *passive behavior* handle conflict by doing nothing. Persons who have *aggressive behavior* handle conflict by trying to harm the other person, either in words or action. Persons who have *assertive behavior* use problem-solving skills to stand up for themselves. A lot of your work with the students will help them develop assertive skills, especially as you teach them five problem-solving skills.

FIVE PROBLEM-SOLVING SKILLS

The session teaches five easy-to-remember skills that will help the students solve problems, especially in relationships. The five skills will allow them to be the problem solvers that were introduced last week and will improve their assertive skills.

I statements. These three-part statements describe how a person feels. The three parts are "I feel _____ when you _____ because _____."

Reflective listening. Reflective listening refers to the ability to listen to what someone else says. When teaching this, you help the students to realize that they can accept what others are feeling without reacting to them, or assuming responsibility for their feeling.

Kill-them-with-kindness sandwiches. This technique comes from Russell Barkley, author of a training program for parents of attention-deficit children. A kill-them-with-kindness sandwich is a three-part statement: (1) say something nice, (2) set the limit or boundary, or state your position, and (3) say something nice.

Apologizing. Research shows that acts of aggression are more likely to occur in situations where there are threats and counterthreats. A simple apology can prevent a situation from escalating into a violent one.

Negotiating a Compromise. Negotiating compromises is an important skill in a relationship. The process will be more successful if the two parties make a commitment to come to an agreement they can both live with. Each states his or her position, and they keep brainstorming ideas for solutions. Having time to think of different solutions often helps the negotiation process.

CHUNKING IT DOWN

It takes time to make changes in learning to deal with anger. People often want instant progress; school administrators often want instant improvement when students are in groups. Unfortunately, behavioral change takes time. The students won't be able to use these new skills immediately; it will take time for the students to develop the ability to use these skills. It helps to think of "chunking it down"—of looking at the process of behavioral change as requiring small steps that happen in stages (Gravitz and Bowden, 1985). Thus, group members will probably go through several steps before they develop the ability to use the problem-solving skills:

1. The teens observe their current behavior in anger situations.

2. The teens learn problem-solving skills to use in anger situations.

3. If the teens express anger aggressively, they process how they could have used the problem-solving skills in each particular situation. They may need the help of an adult to do this processing.

4. Then, the teens might begin to use some problem-solving skills in some anger situations; it may take two or three months for this to happen.

THE SCENARIOS

The scenarios in this session are common situations for teens. The first scenario demonstrates the difference between passive, aggressive, and assertive behavior. The subject is a teenage boy who begins to control and use violence against his girlfriend. This scenario will enable you to help girls learn how to set limits appropriately in their relationships. The next scenario demonstrates risk factors in anger situations and addresses the issue of using aggressive behavior to prove masculinity. The scenario plants the seed that it is manly to avoid a fight. The last scenario addresses a triangling situation.

In this session, you will ask the students to role-play the scenarios. Role playing will help make the session's concepts more real for the group members and will help them start to use problem-solving skills in their lives. If the students are reluctant to role-play, tell them that you will "coach" them on what to say.

The idea that anger can be used as a positive force will be a new one for most of the students. Expect some misunderstanding and resistance, especially as you introduce the problem-solving skills. If the group members make fun of the samples, ask them to help you make samples that use the language they would use. Be active and accepting during the session's role plays and discussion. Acknowledge the students' ideas about ways to express anger, but gently correct and redirect any harmful ideas. Help them tell the difference between problems they can't change (such as parental divorce) and problems they can change (such as having too much homework to do). Offer specific suggestions geared to the age and personalities of the students. For example: "Use your anger to give you power to control yourself when someone gets in your face," or "Use your anger to play football with more determination," or "Use your anger to get that social studies project started," or "Use your anger to think of a kill-them-with-kindness sandwich if you don't want to have sex with that boy."

Leaders who have mastered the ability to use anger to make positive changes for themselves will be better equipped to present the concepts in this session. For example, leaders who are angry about their professional standing might use that anger to take classes to improve advancement opportunities, and leaders who tend to be passive with their spouses might use their anger to acquire the power to speak clearly for themselves. Leaders who practice what they preach will find themselves very effective in helping the students understand this concept.

Remember, many of your group members are amply supplied with anger. Teaching them how to use their anger—and giving them alternative behaviors to aggression—is a great act of empowerment. This session begins the process of tapping into the power of anger. Session 5 goes further and gives the students a structured plan for choosing helpful ways to problem-solve or to express their anger so they can let it go.

Beginning the Session

GROUP RULES

Welcome the students and begin with a quick review of the group rules. Draw attention to the poster listing the group rules. If you feel that it is necessary, call on different students to read them one at a time. Check for understanding before moving on.

CENTERING EXERCISE

Lead the students in a new centering exercise, "The Space Shuttle."

This exercise will help you learn how to use your anger.

THE SPACE SHUTTLE

Close your eyes and relax. Imagine that you work for the people who send the space shuttle into outer space. You have an important job; your job is to put fuel into the space shuttle. The shuttle is parked on the launching pad and it's ready to go. It's going on a Star Trek mission, a mission to help people in the world live peacefully together. All it needs is fuel—plenty of fuel—to get going. But the fuel that this shuttle uses is your anger. The shuttle will only be successful if you get in touch with your anger and put it in the shuttle.

So, think of all the things that have happened to you today that might have made you angry. *(Give specific examples appropriate to the group.)* Feel how angry those things made you. Now, pump all that anger into the space shuttle tank.

Now think of all the things that you might have felt angry about over the past week. *(Give a few more examples.)* Imagine what that anger felt like, and pump it all into the shuttle.

Now think of all the things that you've felt angry about for the past year. Pump all that anger in.

Exercise continued on next page.

Exercise continued from previous page.

By now you've been able to feel a lot of the anger you've felt in the past, and you've pumped all of it into the shuttle. It's loaded with fuel. It's ready to blast off into outer space.

You go back to the control tower to watch the launch. The countdown is beginning: 5, 4, 3, 2, 1: blast-off! The shuttle takes off! The launch is successful. You feel great because you've used your anger in a very important way. You feel free because you've been able to let go of your anger. You feel peaceful. You feel calmer and more relaxed than you've felt in a long, long time. You also feel proud because you used your anger to work for you.

FEELINGS CHECK-IN

Do a feelings check-in with the students. Have them take out their Feeling Wheels. Ask the group members to decide how they are feeling today. Remind the students that if they want, they can color in the section on the Feeling Wheel that describes how they're feeling. Also remind the teens that they might have more than one feeling, since it's possible to have more than one feeling at a time. Tell the students that if they're having a feeling not named on the wheel, they can add a bubble to the outside of the wheel and name their feeling.

When the students finish, have a go-around. Begin by sharing your own feelings. Then, invite each student to share his or her feelings. Teenagers often list many feelings. For the interests of time, ask them to name the feelings they have, but then pick only two to discuss. Be sure to accept each student's feeling(s) and to affirm each student. Ask the students to return the wheels to their folders.

BASIC FACTS REVIEW

Review the basic facts learned so far. Use posters with Basic Facts 1-8, the List of Basic Facts, or the index cards.

In a go-around, ask a student to read Basic Fact 1 aloud and to explain what it means. If the stu-

dent has trouble explaining the fact, don't contradict or judge, simply clarify his or her explanation. Repeat the procedure for the next basic fact. This review ensures that the students understand and integrate the basic facts that have been taught. It is also easy preparation for the presentation and provides a lead-in for the session material.

ASSIGNMENT REVIEW

Ask the students to locate their assignment sheets from last week. Remind them that they were to observe the anger styles they used. They were to jot down once each day if they were a stuffer, a withdrawer, a blamer, a triangler, an exploder, or a problem solver. In a go-around, ask the students to share what they learned about how they deal with anger. If students forgot to do the assignment, ask them to try to remember one time they were angry and what style they used. Don't be judgmental if they used styles other than problem solving. Remind them that they need to be aware of their patterns of dealing with anger before they can change them.

Exploring the Material

MINI-LECTURE

Tell the group members that their goal today is to learn to be problem solvers who can deal with their anger in healthy, productive ways. Today they will look at two kinds of problems: problems they *can* change and problems they *can't* change. They will examine the differences between passive, assertive, and aggressive behavior. They will learn five easy-to-remember problem-solving skills they can use instead of aggressive behavior. They will look at how teens develop problem-solving skills slowly. Finally, they will also look at how they can use their anger as power to help them learn these skills.

Present the following information to the students in your own words.

Problems You Can't Change

When you're angry, the first thing to do is to see if it's a problem you can change or if it's a problem you can't change. If you're angry about a problem you can't change, you should:

1. **Accept what you can't change.**

2. **Express your anger (in a safe and helpful way) so you can let it go.**

3. **Do something good for yourself.**

For instance, if your parents have separated or divorced, or are violent, or are chemically dependent, you can't change these problems. You will have to accept what you can't change. You need to express your anger so you can let it go: punch a pillow, exercise, clean, prune hedges, draw a picture, or write a letter. Then do something good for yourself, like calling a friend, applying to college, getting your homework done, or playing Nintendo. If you're angry because your parents are nicer to a stepsister than to you, accept that you can't change their feelings. Then write a letter about how angry you are (but don't send it). Study to get good grades so you can make something of yourself.

Continue with the following information.

Problems You Can Change

If you're angry about a problem you can change, you can use your anger to work for you. Your anger can give you the power, or energy, to make changes in yourself and in your problem-solving skills.

For instance:

- You might be angry because you're caught in the middle between your divorced parents. They use you to send messages back and forth, like "Where's the child support?" You can use your anger to give yourself the power to set limits with them. Say: "Dad, I'm really glad you're my father, but I won't be able to pass messages between you and Mom because it makes me too uncomfortable. Maybe you need to talk to a counselor to figure out the best way to approach Mom. In the meantime, would you like to go to the movies with me?"

Problems You Can Change continued

- You might be angry about a big homework project. Use your anger to get started on a small piece of it.

- You might be angry when your friends get in your face because you've made a mistake. Use your anger to control yourself and give them an apology: "You know, I'm sorry. You're right; I messed up."

There is a lot of power and energy in anger. It can be used as a very positive force.

Write the words *passive*, *assertive*, and *aggressive* on the chalkboard. Then continue with the following information.

Passive, Assertive, and Aggressive Behaviors

It's important to learn the difference between behaviors that are passive, assertive, and aggressive. Imagine that you're about to leave your home to go to a concert by your favorite rock star. You get a phone call just as you're walking out the door. It's an old friend who lives out of state. The friend wants to discuss a big problem. If you really want to get to the concert but you stay on the phone and help the friend, you're being *passive*. If you start yelling at the friend, saying, "How dare you call me now. Don't you know I'm going to a really important concert? You are really rude to call me! Don't ever call me again!" you're being *aggressive*. If you say to the friend, "I'd really like to talk to you about your problem, but I have tickets for a great concert, and I need to leave now to be on time. I'm sorry I can't talk now, but how about if I call you tomorrow?" you're being *assertive*. To be able to manage your anger and solve problems, you need to be assertive—not passive or aggressive.

Have the students find Handout 4A ("Scenarios") in their folders. Ask a student to read Scenario 1.

Scenario 1

Crystal is a high school sophomore. Crystal's father is often jealous of her mother. He always wants to know where she's going and why she's late when she comes come from work. Sometimes Crystal's dad gets mad at her mother if she wears makeup or gets a new hairdo. Once, he even grabbed her and made her wash the makeup off. Sometimes Crystal's father is violent. He's pushed her mother against the wall. Sometimes her mother has bruises on her arms.

Crystal has been dating Steve, a senior, for about three months. Steve comes from a family where his father is boss. At first, Steve was nice to Crystal, but lately he's begun to be real bossy. He tells her to change her clothes if he doesn't like what she's wearing. A couple of weeks ago, he pushed her against the wall.

Have the students perform a role play to demonstrate the differences between passive, aggressive, and assertive behavior in this situation. Ask for two volunteers, one to play Crystal and one to play Steve. Draft two students if no one volunteers. Assure them that you will coach them about what to do.

Tell the students that Crystal will first act out a passive behavior. Have Steve tell Crystal he doesn't like her clothing, and have him push her against the wall. Ask Crystal and the group for ideas of how she should act if she is being passive. If they don't come up with any ideas, coach Crystal to say, "Steve, I'm sorry I'm wearing something you don't like. I'll go change right away, and I'll never wear it again. Please don't push me any more."

Ask these questions:

1. **What will Steve learn if Crystal is passive?** (He'll learn that he can boss her around and that it's okay if he pushes her.)

2. **How is Crystal likely to feel?** (Probably she'll feel bad about herself and very powerless.)

3. **What might happen to Crystal if she continues to act passive?** (She might end up in an abusive relationship like her mother.)

Now, ask Crystal to act out an aggressive behavior. Have Steve tell Crystal he doesn't like her clothing, and have him push her against the wall. Ask the group for ideas of what Crystal should do if she is being aggressive. Remind them that aggressive behavior is intended to do harm. If they don't come up with any ideas, coach Crystal to start yelling at Steve, "Don't tell me what to wear, you creep. How dare you tell me anything!" Have Crystal start pushing back at him and try to hit him. Coach Steve to push her back.

Ask the students these questions:

1. **What is likely to happen if Crystal is aggressive?** (It's likely that their disagreement will get worse and that they may become violent with each other; they'll stay angry.)

2. **How are Crystal and Steve likely to feel?** (Angry and resentful.)

Now, ask Crystal to act out an assertive behavior. Have Steve tell Crystal he doesn't like her clothing, and have him push her against the wall. Ask the group for ideas of what Crystal should do if she's being assertive. If they don't come up with any ideas, coach Steve to say, "Crystal, that blouse is really ugly. Go and change it right now." Have Crystal say, "Steve, I'm glad you're my boyfriend because I enjoy being with you, but I want to be in charge of what I wear, not you. It's important for me to feel independent. So, I'm going to wear what I want, and I hope you'll feel glad that I'm independent. I also need to let you know that I don't like it when you push me, and that is not something I'm going to allow anybody to do to me. I want you to remember that. I'm not going to let anybody push or shove me or hit me. I'm not going to let that be part of our relationship." Give Steve a chance to respond.

Ask the students these questions:

1. **What do you think will happen next between Steve and Crystal?** (There probably won't be an escalation of violence; Steve will probably decide whether he wants to keep on seeing Crystal.)

2. **How is Crystal feeling after being assertive?** (Probably a little afraid that Steve won't like her anymore. But she is probably glad that she stood up for herself about the blouse, and very glad that she set limits about violence in their relationship.)

Tell the students that they will learn about family violence in Session 6. Explain that violence in couples often starts out with minor episodes, such as Steve pushing Crystal. It then gets more serious and more frequent. Studies have shown that the best way to stop violence is for the victim to set strong, firm limits after the first, most minor incident. It's important for both males and females to set strong limits that they won't allow violence in their relationships.

Five Problem-solving Skills

Now introduce the five easy-to-remember skills that will help the students solve problems, especially in relationships. Have the students find Handout 4B ("Five Problem-solving Skills") in their folders. Read the summary statement at the beginning. Then call on volunteers to read the description and example of each skill. If you want, demonstrate these skills by having students role-play Trish and Tony as seen under "I statements" on Handout 4B and page 109. Assure them that you will coach them on what to say.

Now look at the next Scenario on Handout 4A. Tell the students that anger situations are likely to become violent if certain risk factors are present. These include the use of alcohol and other drugs, which impairs judgment and communication; the presence of firearms; the use of threats and counterthreats and insults; the exercise of coercive authority; and weapons displays. Point out that Scenario 2 is a common anger situation for teens. Many teenage boys consider

acting aggressively in a situation as proof of their manhood. The students will use Scenario 2 to imagine how the anger risk factors would influence the situation. Then they will have a chance to practice problem-solving skills. Ask a student to read Scenario 2, Part 1.

Scenario 2, Part 1

Carl and Michael are students in high school. They know each other from PE class. One day, they're playing basketball in a neighborhood park. As Michael is trying to take the ball away from Carl, he accidentally scratches Carl's eye. Carl is furious. He immediately punches Michael in the face, and calls him a stupid idiot.

Ask the students to imagine what this scenario would be like if the risk factors for violence were present. Ask two students to role-play the following situations:

• Carl and Michael are using alcohol or other drugs while playing.

• Carl threatens to hit Michael if he touches him again. Michael counterthreats by saying, "Oh yeah, wait til you see what I'll do to you."

• Carl tries to use coercive force. Coercive force is when one person uses physical power to control someone else.

• Carl and Michael display weapons. Carl pulls out a knife and holds it up in a threatening manner. Michael pulls out a metal chain and starts swinging it around.

• Both Carl and Michael have guns in their jackets.

Expect the role plays to include violence and an escalation of the violence. Ask Carl how he felt when he pulled out the knife and how he felt when he saw Michael pull out a metal chain. Ask Michael how he felt when he pulled out the metal chain and how he felt when he saw Carl pull out a knife.

Tell the students that the problem-solving skills give both Carl and Michael alternative behaviors to use that don't lead to aggression or violence.

FIVE PROBLEM-SOLVING SKILLS

Here are five easy-to-remember skills that will help you solve problems, especially in relationships. The five skills will allow you to be problem solvers and will improve your assertive skills.

1. **I statements:** describe how you feel.

2. **Reflective listening:** accept someone else's feelings, without reacting to them or feeling responsible for them.

3. **Kill-them-with-kindness sandwiches:** say something nice to the person; set the limit or say no politely; say something nice.

4. **Apologizing:** if you see that you have made a mistake, admit it and say you're sorry.

5. **Negotiating a compromise:** discuss the problem with the other person until you arrive at a decision you can both live with.

I Statements

I statements are three part statements that describe how a person feels. The three parts are: "I feel _____ when you _____because _____."

Example: Trish is angry with her boyfriend Tony because he's on the football team and she never gets to see him. If Trish uses an *I statement*, she might say: "Tony, I feel hurt when you're always with your football friends because I never get to see you any more." In comparison, if Trish uses a *you statement*, she might say something accusing: "Tony, you are a rude, mean jerk. You're selfish and insensitive. You don't spend as much time with me as you should." A person who hears a you statement is likely to feel attacked and may want to fight back. A person who hears an I statement is less likely to feel attacked.

Reflective Listening

Reflective listening refers to the ability to listen to what someone else says. Reflective listening enables you to realize that you can accept what other people are feeling without reacting to them or assuming responsibility for their feeling. Trish complains to her boyfriend, Tony, saying: "I'm really mad at you. Your sports are more important to you than I am. You're always at football practice, and you're always doing something with the other guys on the team. I want you to quit the team so you can spend more time with me." If Tony is using reflective listening, he will say something like: "It sounds like you're pretty angry with me. It must feel pretty bad. Tell me some more about what's going on, and what I've done to make you mad." But, if Tony is not using reflective listening, he might simply react to Trish's anger and get angry back. Then they will both be angry. Or if Tony feels responsible for fixing Trish's feelings, he might quit the team just to make her happy. Then he might lose out on something that's really important to him. Reflective listening allows him to accept her feeling, without taking the responsibility of making it better.

A Kill-Them-with-Kindness Sandwich

A kill-them-with-kindness sandwich is a three-part statement: (1) say something nice; (2) set the limit or boundary, or state your position; and (3) say something nice.

Example: Tony listens to Trish's complaints and then says: "Trish, I really like you a lot, and I'm glad you're my girlfriend. But I really like football, too, and I'm glad I'm on the team. I want to solve this problem so we can keep dating and I can keep playing. I think we're smart enough to come to a reasonable compromise." In this statement, Tony states his position clearly. He does not react to Trish's demands, but he doesn't give in to them either. He states what he wants and his wish for a reasonable compromise so they will both be happy.

Apologizing

Acts of aggression are more likely to occur in situations where there are threats and counterthreats. A simple **apology** can prevent a situation from escalating into a violent one.

Example: Tony says to Trish: "I'm sorry that I forgot about our date on Sunday afternoon. Some of the guys on the team wanted to play football, and I forgot all about taking you to the movies. I don't blame you for being angry. I really am sorry." If this is the first time Tony has stood Trish up, an apology might go a long way to helping the relationship. However, if forgetting dates is a pattern with Tony, Trish may need to set some limits in a kill-them-with-kindness sandwich herself.

Negotiating a Compromise

Negotiating compromises is an important skill in a relationship. The process will be more successful if the two parties make a commitment to come to an agreement they can both live with. Each states his or her position, and they keep brainstorming ideas for solutions. Having time to think of different solutions often helps the negotiation process.

Example: Tony and Trish keep talking about how they can solve the problem of seeing each other. Tony states that he wants to keep playing football. Trish states that she would like to have at least two dates with him a week, and to talk with him on the phone at least once a day. Tony looks at his calendar and says that he will probably only be able to go on one date a week during the football season, but that he would love to have two dates a week, or more, after the season is over. Tony responds to Trish's feelings, without reacting with anger, and without overreacting by giving up football, which is important to him.

Remind the students, however, that use of alcohol and other drugs impairs thinking, judgment, and decision making. If the angry person is under the influence, wait until the person is sober before using problem-solving skills.

Coach two students to show how the skills could work for both Carl and Michael. If the students complain that real teenagers would never say things like that, encourage them to use the skill in their own way and language.

1. *I statement.* Coach Carl to say to Michael: "It really hurt when you stuck your finger in my eye. It feels like my eye is bleeding."

2. *Reflective listening.* Coach Michael to say to Carl: "I can tell that your eye hurts and that you're pretty angry with me. I can see why you're angry. I hope your eye is okay."

3. *Kill-them-with-kindness sandwich.* Coach Carl to say to Michael: "Mike, I enjoy playing basketball with you; you're a good guard. But, I don't like it when your finger goes in my eye. I'd like to play with you again another time, but I'll need to ask you to be more careful."

4. *Apologizing.* Coach Michael to say to Carl: "I'm really sorry I stuck my finger in your eye. That happened to me once. It was called a corneal abrasion. I had to wear a patch over my eye for a day, but then it was okay. I'm sorry I scratched your eye." And coach Carl to say to Michael: "Michael, I'm sorry I called you a stupid idiot. I was angry, and I was scared about my eye, so I called you a name. I'm sorry."

5. *Negotiating a compromise.* Coach Carl to say to Michael: "I'd like to keep on playing basketball with you, after my eye gets better. But maybe we should set some guidelines for playing."

Ask the students which problem-solving skill seems to apply the best to this situation. Ask Carl and Michael how they felt when they were apologizing. Ask Carl how it felt when Michael was apologizing and ask Michael how it felt when Carl was apologizing.

Now have a student read Scenario 2, Part 2.

Scenario 2, Part 2

Michael is a boy who generally does not get into a lot of fights. He is taking karate, and he has been taught to use his karate skills only when absolutely necessary. He has been taught that it is more manly to walk away from a fight than to jump into a fight. When Carl punches Michael in the face, Michael decides not to punch Carl back because he is bigger than Carl and he knows he could hurt him.

Ask the students to discuss the issue of manhood in Scenario 2. Have them compare the actions of Carl in Part 1 with the actions of Michael in Part 2. Which boy shows more mature behavior? Michael chooses not to hit Carl back. What do the students think of Michael's masculinity?

Use Scenario 3 to provide the students with more practice in problem-solving skills. Ask a student to read Scenario 3.

Scenario 3

Susan and Kim are best friends. They spend a lot of time talking on the phone and doing things together. Then Susan meets Michelle, who just moved into town and is new in school. Susan seems to like Michelle and spends time with her instead of with Kim. Kim feels hurt and angry. She tells Michelle that Susan is not very nice.

Ask three girls to role-play Susan, Michelle, and Kim. Have Susan and Kim act out being best friends. Then have Michelle act out moving into town and being new in school. Finally, have Susan and Michelle act out spending time together and leaving Kim out.

1. *I statement.* Ask Kim to demonstrate an I statement that she could give Susan. Ask the group for an I statement if Kim doesn't come up with one. If they don't come up with any ideas, coach Kim to say: "Susan, I feel hurt when you spend more time with Michelle than with me. It makes me feel that you don't like me anymore."

2. *Reflective listening.* Ask Susan to demonstrate how she could use reflective listening in response to Kim's I statement. Ask the group for ideas if Susan doesn't come up with one. If they don't come up with any ideas, coach Susan to say, "Kim, it sounds like you're hurt. I can see how you would be upset that I have a new friend." Point out how Susan isn't taking responsibility for making Kim feel better, she's just naming and accepting Kim's feelings.

3. *Kill-them-with-kindness sandwich.* Ask Susan to demonstrate how she could use a kill-them-with-kindness sandwich with Kim. Ask the group for ideas if Susan doesn't come up with one. If they don't come up with any ideas, coach Susan to say, "Kim, we have been friends for a long time and I'm glad we're friends. But, I want to be friends with more than one person. I want to do things with a lot of friends. So, I want you to be my friend, but I also want to make new friends, like Michelle."

4. *Apologizing.* Ask Kim to demonstrate how she could apologize to Susan for saying bad things about her to Michelle. Ask the group for ideas if Kim doesn't come up with one. If they don't come up with any ideas, coach Kim to say, "Susan, I'm sorry I went behind your back and told Michelle bad things about you. I hope we can be friends again."

5. *Negotiating a compromise.* Ask Susan and Kim to demonstrate how to negotiate a compromise. Ask the group for ideas if Susan and Kim don't come up with any. If they don't come up with any ideas, coach Susan to say, "Kim, since I want to keep you

as my friend, but I want to make new friends, too, do you think we can solve this? Maybe you and I can still be good friends, but we could both make other friends too." Coach Kim to say, "That sounds like a good idea."

Chunking It Down

Tell the group members that it takes people a great deal of time to make changes in how they deal with anger. The students won't be able to use problem-solving skills immediately; it will take time for them to develop the ability to use these new skills. Introduce the concept of "chunking it down"—of looking at the process of behavioral change as requiring small steps that happen in stages.

Display the newsprint on which you've listed the steps in chunking down the problem-solving skills. Read through them with the group:

1. Observe your current behavior in anger situations.

2. Learn problem-solving skills to use in anger situations.

3. If you express anger aggressively, process how you could have used the problem-solving skills in each particular situation. You may need the help of an adult to do this processing.

4. Begin to use problem-solving skills in some anger situations. It may take two or three months for this to happen.

DISCUSSION

Lead a discussion to help the group members better understand the facts—the key concepts—presented. As the group discusses, remember to go around, making sure that each student has an opportunity to add to the discussion. Encourage participation, but don't force it. Remember the group rule that allows a student to pass. Accept all ideas and answers, explaining or clarifying information where necessary. To aid the discussion, you may wish to use questions like the following:

- **Is anger a normal feeling?** (Yes, people get angry as often as 12 to 14 times a day.)

- **What should you do when you feel angry?** (Look at why you're feeling angry and decide if it's a problem you can change or a problem you can't change.)

- **What should you do if you're feeling angry because of a problem you can't change?** (1. Accept what you can't change. 2. Express your anger so you can let it go. 3. Do something good for yourself.)

- **What should you do if it is a problem you can change?** (Use anger to work for you—to give you energy or power to make changes in yourself, to use problem-solving skills in the anger situation.)

- **What are the differences between passive, aggressive, and assertive behaviors?** (A person who has passive behavior handles conflict by doing nothing. A person who has aggressive behavior handles conflict by trying to harm the other person, either in words or action. A person who has assertive behavior uses problem-solving skills to stand up for himself or herself.)

- **What are five problem-solving skills?** (I statements, reflective listening, kill-them-with-kindness sandwiches, apologizing, and negotiating a compromise.)

- **What's an example of an I statement?** (Accept any appropriate response.)

- **What's an example of reflective listening?** (Accept any appropriate response.)

- **What's an example of a kill-them-with-kindness sandwich?** (Accept any appropriate response.)

- **What's an example of apologizing?** (Accept any appropriate response.)

- **What's an example of negotiating a compromise?** (Accept any appropriate response.)

- **What risk factors can make violence more likely in anger situations?** (The use of alcohol and other drugs; the presence of firearms; the use of threats, counterthreats, and insults; the use of coercive force; the display of weapons.)

- **What does "chunking it down" mean?** (Learning to use problem-solving skills in several small steps that happen in stages.)

Even if you choose not to use the above questions, make sure the discussion underscores these concepts.

BASIC FACTS

Review the new basic facts for this session. Refer the students to the List of Basic Facts. Ask four group members to read Basic Facts 9, 10, 11, and 12.

9. When teens are angry about a problem they can't change, they should:

   1. Accept what they can't change.

   2. Express their anger so they can let it go.

   3. Do something good for themselves.

10. When teens are angry about a problem they can change, they should use their anger to give them the power to make changes in themselves.

11. Five good problem-solving skills to use in anger situations are *I* statements, reflective listening, kill-them-with-kindness sandwiches, apologizing, and negotiating a compromise.

12. Chunking it down is a good way to start on a long-term goal.

Briefly discuss each fact, checking for understanding.

ASSIGNMENT

Have the group members take Assignment 4 out of their folders. Read the directions: "Over the next week, once each day, try to use assertive behavior in an anger situation. Try to use an *I* statement, reflective listening, a kill-them-with-kindness sandwich, apologizing, or negotiating a compromise. In the boxes below, tell about the problem-solving skill you used. If you don't remember to use one of these skills, jot down what you could have said." Remind the students that changing aggressive behavior takes chunking it down. This assignment will help them see how they can use the new skills they have learned.

Wrapping Up

CENTERING EXERCISE

Settle the students and then repeat "The Space Shuttle" (page 104).

AFFIRMATION

Involve the group in an affirmation. Stand and join in a circle with the students holding hands. Go around and have the students share a time they got angry and how they could have used a problem-solving skill. Begin the affirmation yourself: "One time that I got angry

was. . . . A problem-solving skill I could have used is. . . ." The students will need you to role model this effective affirmation. They will probably also need your help to see which skill they could have used.

CLOSING

Remain standing in a circle with the students holding hands and lead the group in the closing activity.

Tell the students that you're going to make a silent wish for the student on your right. Then, when you've made the wish, gently squeeze the student's hand. The student makes a silent wish for the person on his or her right, then gently squeezes that student's hand, and so on. Continue around the circle until a wish and squeeze come back to you. If necessary, the students can pass the wish in any appropriate way they choose.

Collect the folders. Fill out a copy of the Process and Progress Form (page 211) or the Progress Notes (page 212), if you are an experienced leader, as soon as possible after leading the group.

Scenarios

Scenario 1

Crystal is a high school sophomore. Crystal's father is often jealous of her mother. He always wants to know where she's going and why she's late when she comes home from work. Sometimes Crystal's dad gets mad at her mother if she wears makeup or gets a new hairdo. Once, he even grabbed her and made her wash the makeup off. Sometimes Crystal's father is violent. He's pushed her mother against the wall. Sometimes her mother has bruises on her arms.

Crystal has been dating Steve, a senior, for about three months. Steve comes from a family where his father is boss. At first, Steve was nice to Crystal, but lately he's begun to be real bossy. He tells her to change her clothes if he doesn't like what she's wearing. A couple of weeks ago, he pushed her against the wall.

Scenario 2, Part 1

Carl and Michael are students in high school. They know each other from PE class. One day, they're playing basketball in a neighborhood park. As Michael is trying to take the ball away from Carl, he accidentally scratches Carl's eye. Carl is furious. He immediately punches Michael in the face, and calls him a stupid idiot.

Scenario 2, Part 2

Michael is a boy who generally does not get into a lot of fights. He is taking karate, and he has been taught to use his karate skills only when absolutely necessary. He has been taught that it is more manly to walk away from a fight than to jump into a fight. When Carl punches Michael in the face, Michael decides not to punch Carl back because he is bigger than Carl and he knows he could hurt him.

Scenario 3

Susan and Kim are best friends. They spend a lot of time talking on the phone and doing things together. Then Susan meets Michelle, who just moved into town and is new in school. Susan seems to like Michelle and spends time with her instead of with Kim. Kim feels hurt and angry. She tells Michelle that Susan is not very nice.

FIVE PROBLEM-SOLVING SKILLS

Here are five easy-to-remember skills that will help you solve problems, especially in relationships. The five skills will allow you to be problem solvers and will improve your assertive skills.

1. **I statements:** describe how you feel.

2. **Reflective listening:** accept someone else's feelings, without reacting to them or feeling responsible for them.

3. **Kill-them-with-kindness sandwiches:** say something nice to the person; set the limit or say no politely; say something nice.

4. **Apologizing:** if you see that you have made a mistake, admit it and say you're sorry.

5. **Negotiating a compromise:** discuss the problem with the other person until you arrive at a decision you can both live with.

I Statements

I statements are three part statements that describe how a person feels. The three parts are: "I feel _____ when you _____ because _____."

Example: Trish is angry with her boyfriend Tony because he's on the football team and she never gets to see him. If Trish uses an *I statement*, she might say: "Tony, I feel hurt when you're always with your football friends because I never get to see you any

more." In comparison, if Trish uses a *you statement*, she might say something accusing: "Tony, you are a rude, mean jerk. You're selfish and insensitive. You don't spend as much time with me as you should." A person who hears a you statement is likely to feel attacked and may want to fight back. A person who hears an I statement is less likely to feel attacked.

Reflective Listening

Reflective listening refers to the ability to listen to what someone else says. Reflective listening enables you to realize that you can accept what other people are feeling without reacting to them or assuming responsibility for their feeling. Trish complains to her boyfriend, Tony, saying: "I'm really mad at you. Your sports are more important to you than I am. You're always at football prac- tice, and you're always doing something with the other guys on the team. I want you to quit the team so you can spend more time with me." If Tony is using reflective listening, he will say some-

thing like: "It sounds like you're pretty angry with me. It must feel pretty bad. Tell me some more about what's going on, and what I've done to make you mad." But, if Tony is not using reflective listening, he might simply react to Trish's anger and get angry back. Then they will both be angry. Or if Tony feels responsible for fixing Trish's feelings, he might quit the team just to make her happy. Then he might lose out on something that's really impor- tant to him. Reflective listening allows him to accept her feeling, without taking the responsibility of making it better.

A Kill-Them-with-Kindness Sandwich

A kill-them-with-kindness sandwich is a three-part statement: (1) say something nice; (2) set the limit or boundary, or state your position; and (3) say something nice.

Example: Tony listens to Trish's complaints and then says: "Trish, I really like you a lot, and I'm glad you're my girlfriend. But I really like football, too, and I'm glad I'm on the team. I want to

solve this problem so we can keep dating and I can keep play- ing. I think we're smart enough to come to a reasonable compro- mise." In this statement, Tony states his position clearly. He does not react to Trish's demands, but he doesn't give in to them either. He states what he wants and his wish for a reasonable compromise so they will both be happy.

Apologizing

Acts of aggression are more likely to occur in situations where there are threats and counterthreats. A simple **apology** can pre- vent a situation from escalating into a violent one.

Example: Tony says to Trish: "I'm sorry that I forgot about our date on Sunday afternoon. Some of the guys on the team wanted to play football, and I forgot all about taking you to the movies. I

don't blame you for being angry. I really am sorry." If this is the first time Tony has stood Trish up, an apology might go a long way to helping the relationship. However, if forgetting dates is a pattern with Tony, Trish may need to set some limits in a kill- them-with-kindness sandwich herself.

Negotiating a Compromise

Negotiating compromises is an important skill in a relationship. The process will be more successful if the two parties make a commitment to come to an agreement they can both live with. Each states his or her position, and they keep brainstorming ideas for solutions. Having time to think of different solutions often helps the negotiation process.

Example: Tony and Trish keep talking about how they can solve the problem of seeing each other. Tony states that he wants to

keep playing football. Trish states that she would like to have at least two dates with him a week, and to talk with him on the phone at least once a day. Tony looks at his calendar and says that he will probably only be able to go on one date a week dur- ing the football season, but that he would love to have two dates a week, or more, after the season is over. Tony responds to Trish's feelings, without reacting with anger, and without overre- acting by giving up football, which is important to him.

Over the next week, once each day, try to use assertive behavior in an anger situation. Try to use an *I* statement, reflective listening, kill-them-with-kindness sandwich, apologizing, or negotiating a compromise. In the boxes below, tell about the problem-solving skill you used. If you don't remember to use one of these skills, jot down what you could have said.

ASSERTIVE BEHAVIOR

Day one

Day two

Day three

Day four

Day five

Day six

Day seven

Other comments or observations

Anger Management Steps

Objectives

To help the students:

- learn an eight-step plan for managing anger

- understand that the anger management steps help teens put thinking between their feelings of anger and their behavior of anger

- practice ways to problem-solve anger situations

Session at a Glance

1. Group Rules: review if necessary—1 minute

2. Centering Exercise: "The Mountaintop"—2 minutes

3. Feelings Check-in: look at Feelings Wheel—4 minutes

4. Basic Facts Review—4 minutes

5. Assignment Review—4 minutes

6. Mini-lecture, Scenarios, and Discussion—18 minutes

7. Activity: make an index card with the anger management steps—3 minutes

8. Basic Facts: read Basic Facts 13 and 14; discuss—2 minutes

9. Assignment—1 minute

10. Centering Exercise: repeat "The Mountaintop"—2 minutes

11. Affirmation: share a time when you were angry and a helpful way you could have expressed that anger—3 minutes

12. Closing: pass a silent wish—1 minute

Preparation

- Display the posterboard copy of the group rules.

- Have posters with Basic Facts 1-12 available. (Or the List of Basic Facts, or index cards with a basic fact on each one.)

- Prior to the session make a poster. Title it "Anger Management Steps." List the anger management steps. (See Basic Fact 14.) Save this poster to use again should you decide to do Session 10.

- Add the following materials to each folder:
  —Handout 5A ("Anger Management Steps")
  —Handout 5B ("Scenarios")

—a 3" x 5" index card

—Assignment 5

- Have the folders, pencils, and crayons or markers at each student's place.

- Have chalkboard and chalk or newsprint and a marker available.

- Read through the session plan before meeting.

Background and Guidelines

Session 2 explored the cognitive-behavioral technique of putting thinking between feelings and behavior. Session 4 taught problem-solving skills. This session helps the students create a proactive plan to pull their learning together. It presents anger management steps so that the students can **think**, and then express their anger in helpful ways or problem-solve anger situations. The scenarios in this session allow them (1) to practice the steps of anger management, (2) to evaluate the consequences of anger styles such as stuffing, withdrawing, blaming, triangling, and exploding, and (3) to practice using the problem-solving skills. The plan shows the students how to put thinking between feeling angry and expressing anger.

As you lead the students through the session, help them become aware of the many different ways they can express their anger: in helpful ways, like problem solving or doing something good for themselves, or in harmful ways, like stuffing, withdrawing, blaming, triangling, or exploding. Specific examples will be of great help: "One student I knew was angry about his parents' divorce and the way they put each other down. He used a kill-them-with-kindness sandwich to say to each parent that he loved both of them and could not listen to either one say bad things about the other." Or "One time when I felt angry, I cleaned the bathroom, top to bottom; then I went out and jogged. While I was

jogging, I thought of different problem-solving skills to use, and I decided negotiating a compromise was the best solution." To help the group members evaluate the consequences of their expressions of anger, teach them to ask themselves: "Will this particular anger style or problem-solving skill be helpful or harmful?" During the session, you may notice that some students will describe harmful ways to express anger. Don't accept these harmful ways. Rather, gently encourage and redirect the students to find a helpful way to express their anger.

Emphasize that the anger management steps are something the students can use in real life: at home, on the game field, on the bus, and in the classroom. Let the students know that it's hard to change behavior right away. In fact, most people change their behavior quite slowly. The students can help themselves change their behavior by going through the anger management steps retroactively, even after they choose a harmful way to express anger. Doing so can help them figure out what would have been a more helpful choice to express their anger so they could let it go. It often takes people two to three months of processing the steps retroactively before they form the habit of using the plan at the time of anger.

Since students with behavioral problems may have difficulty in remembering the anger management steps and the problem-solving skills, and won't be able to change their behavior immediately, it's helpful to engage their teachers, principals, and student assistance teams in using the plan. Work with teachers and students to set up a plan so that the students will know exactly what choices they have with regard to expressing their anger. Explosive students may benefit from a plan that includes helpful choices such as journal writing, drawing a picture, or sitting in a time-out chair in the office or with a guidance counselor. Help teachers to choose behaviors that will work in a particular classroom and encourage them to help the students implement their plans when they feel angry. For instance, one teacher made files for all students, where they could keep letters they had written about their anger. It's also a good idea to teach the appropriate school personnel the six styles of expressing anger, the anger management steps, and the problem-solving skills, so they can help the student use them in each anger situation they encounter. As a matter of fact, an in-service on this information will prepare school personnel to help the students practice problem-solving skills on a daily basis.

Beginning the Session

GROUP RULES

Welcome the students and begin with a quick review of the group rules. Draw attention to the poster listing the group rules. If you feel that it is necessary, call on different students to read them one at a time. Check for understanding before moving on.

CENTERING EXERCISE

Lead the students in a new centering exercise, "The Mountaintop."

THE MOUNTAINTOP

Imagine that you're walking in the dark along a mountain trail. You feel very angry. Someone has told you that your best friend gave away a secret you had told him or her. You just can't believe that your friend would do that. You're just furious. You're breathing fast, and your heart is pumping loudly. As you walk up the trail, it's so dark you can barely see anything except the trail's outline. You feel like you could walk forever. You keep walking up the trail until you finally arrive at the top of the mountain. At least you think it's the top of the mountain because the trail seems to come to a level place.

Soon you can tell that you really are at the mountaintop, because it's beginning to get a little lighter. You're able to look out over the valleys and beyond to other mountaintops. Actually, it's quite pretty up there as dawn begins. You see more and more. You can see many mountaintops off in the distance. You sit down. Your

Exercise continued

heart is not pumping as loudly, and your breathing calms. You sit for a long time. You're beginning to see things from a new perspective in the light, and you begin to think about what it is you are feeling so angry about, also in a new light.

You think about whether it's true that your friend would give away such a secret. You think about how you can find out if it's true. You think about maybe asking your friend directly. You think if it is true, maybe you can't rely on that friend so much, and you won't tell that friend so much. You realize that nobody's perfect, not even your friends. Sometimes friends come through for you, but sometimes they don't. You make a plan for how you're going to deal with the possibility that your friend gave away an important secret.

Daylight finally breaks, and you watch as the sun rises. In the light, you see forests and rocks and mountains and valleys. You see things much more clearly than you could in the dark. You feel much calmer, now that you've made a plan for what to do with your anger at your friend. You head back down the mountain trail. Even though it's the same trail, it looks completely different to you. Now you can see the tall trees and the beautiful green bushes that surround it. You're feeling very calm and peaceful now.

Point out to the students that when people are really angry, often they can't see the situation clearly. If they wait a little while until the anger dies down, they can see different aspects of the situation more clearly.

FEELINGS CHECK-IN

Do a feelings check-in with the students. Have them take out their Feeling Wheels. Ask the group members to decide how they are feeling today. Remind the students that if they want, they can color in the section on the Feeling Wheel that describes how they're feeling today. Also remind the teens that they might have more than one feeling, since it's possible to have more than one feeling at a time. Tell the students that if they're having a feeling not named on the wheel, they can add a bubble to the outside of the wheel and name their feeling.

When the students finish, have a go-around. Begin by sharing your own feelings. Then, invite each student to share his or her feelings. Teenagers often list many feelings. In the interest of time, ask them to name the feelings they have, but then pick only two to discuss. Be sure to accept each student's feeling(s) and to affirm each student. Ask the students to return the wheels to their folders.

BASIC FACTS REVIEW

Review the basic facts learned so far. Use posters with Basic Facts 1-12, the List of Basic Facts, or index cards.

In a go-around, ask a student to read Basic Fact 1 aloud and to explain what it means. If the student has trouble explaining the fact, don't contradict or judge, simply clarify his or her explanation. Repeat the procedure for the next basic fact. This review ensures that the students understand and integrate the basic facts that have been taught. It is also easy preparation for the presentation and provides a lead-in for the session material.

ASSIGNMENT REVIEW

Ask the students to locate their assignment sheets from last week. Remind them that each day they were to try using assertive behavior in an anger situation. They were to try using an I statement, reflective listening, a kill-them-with-kindness sandwich, apologizing, or negotiating a compromise. In a go-around, ask the students to share the skills they used. If students forgot to do the assignment, ask them to remember one time they were angry and tell what problem-solving skill they could have used.

Exploring the Material

MINI-LECTURE

Remind the students that the goal of this group is to help them learn to deal with anger in ways that aren't aggressive. Recall that

some aggression is emotional or expressive and used to express anger. In this group, the students are learning how to handle anger in positive ways—in ways that aren't aggressive. They're also learning how to use problem-solving skills in anger situations. This session will focus on a specific plan to help them know what to do when they get angry.

Anger Management Plan

Present the following information, which appears on Handout 5A ("Anger Management Steps"), to the students. Have the students take turns reading the handout, or explain the material in your own words. If you choose to explain the material yourself, give the students Handout 5A at the end of the session.

Write *feeling, thinking,* and *behaving* on the chalkboard.

Anger Management Steps

Remember that anger is a normal feeling. It consists of feeling, thinking, and behaving. There is a difference between feeling angry, which is okay, and behavior—such as stuffing, withdrawing, blaming, triangling, or exploding—which may not be okay. These anger styles are usually not effective in helping you solve the problem that made you angry or in helping you get along with people and get what you want.

You can't control the feelings you get, but you can control your behavior. You may need to look at your thinking, or self-talk, and see if it is positive or negative. You may need to change your thinking to help you change behavior. You are responsible for your behavior when you are angry. No matter what might influence someone to use violent or aggressive behavior, it is still his or her responsibility to choose nonviolent and helpful ways to express anger. Each person is accountable for his or her behavior. You always have the choice to express your anger in a helpful or harmful way.

Some teens rush right from feeling to behaving. They get mad and hit someone, or put someone down, or yell. (Depending on the age and development of the group, you can call this minimal cognitive engagement.) So teenagers need to learn how to put thinking between their feelings of being angry and their behavior.

The **anger management steps** are a plan to help you put thinking between feeling angry and your behavior.

Continued on next page.

Display the poster you made, "Anger Management Steps." Refer to the poster as you introduce and explain the anger management steps.

Continued from previous page.

1. **Recognize that you're angry.**

2. **Accept your anger.**

3. **Practice relaxation.**

4. **Decide if it's a problem you can't change or a problem you can change.**

5. **Think about helpful and harmful ways to express the anger.**

6. **Evaluate the consequences.**

7. **Choose a best way.**

8. **Problem-solve or express your anger in a helpful way.**

Remember the principle of chunking it down. You will probably not be able to change your behavior right away. Behavioral change often comes slowly and inconsistently. Remember to set small, concrete goals if you want to change how you handle anger. For instance, a first goal can be to look at how you deal with anger. Do you stuff, withdraw, blame, triangle someone else in, explode, or problem-solve? Each time you notice how you deal with anger, think if you should have done it differently. If you didn't problem-solve, what could you have done to problem-solve? Could you have used your anger to give you the power to make changes in yourself? Or could you have accepted what you can't change, expressed your anger in a helpful way so you could let it go, and then done something good for yourself?

You can go through the steps of anger management even after you express anger in a harmful way. Sooner or later, you will begin to use your anger to work for you, or you will express it in a helpful way, or you will use problem-solving skills. Changing your behavior may take two or three months, so don't give up if you don't get the steps right away.

Practicing the Anger Management Steps

Have the students take out Handout 5B ("Scenarios"). Tell them that they will read and discuss some scenarios to see how to put the anger management steps into practice in an anger situation. Have a student read Scenario 1.

Scenario 1

Betsy, a junior at East High School, is on the softball team. Her boyfriend, Mark, goes to the same school. Betsy and Mark really like each other. They hold hands before and after Betsy's softball games. Sometimes they sneak a quick kiss before Betsy goes on the field. Betsy's softball coach, Mrs. Davis, doesn't like to see her players exhibiting behavior like holding hands and kissing. Mrs. Davis has told Betsy and Mark to stop such behavior. Betsy decides that she's going to do what she wants to do, and she and Mark continue to hold hands and kiss. Mrs. Davis puts Betsy on the bench for noncompliance to rules. Betsy is so angry that she can't see straight. She gets red and breathes fast. She plans to confront Mrs. Davis before practice and demand to be allowed to play, or else.

Use the following questions to process the anger management steps in this scenario.

1. **How can Betsy *recognize* that she's angry?** (She can look at the signals her body gives her. She can't see straight; she gets red; she breathes fast.)

2. **How can Betsy *accept* her anger?** (She can admit that she's angry; she can decide that her feeling of anger is normal.)

3. **What can Betsy do to *practice relaxation?*** (She can use a centering exercise, like "Breathing Through Your Feet," "The Icicle," or "The Clouds.")

4. **Is this a problem Betsy *can change?*** (Yes, Betsy can do something to be allowed to play again. She might try to change Mrs. Davis' mind, or Betsy and Mark can change their behavior.)

5. **If Betsy *thinks about ways to express her anger*, what might she think about?** (She might think about using problem-solving skills, such as an I statement, reflective listening, a kill-them-with-kindness sandwich, apologizing, or negotiating a compromise. She might see if any are appropriate for this situation. She might think of other ways she can express her anger, like stuffing, withdrawing, blaming, exploding, or triangling.

In this anger situation, Betsy could think of a lot of different things to do.)

a. She might do some *stuffing*—swallow her anger down and pretend she's not angry.

b. She might do some *withdrawing* and stop going to school until Mrs. Davis changes her mind.

c. She might do some *blaming* and yell at Mrs. Davis: "You're just a nosy old lady. You don't have the right to tell Mark and me what we can and can't do."

d. She might do some *triangling* and complain about Mrs. Davis to her friends, her parents, the guidance counselor, the other teachers, and the principal.

e. She might continue *exploding* and try to punch Mrs. Davis.

f. She might *express her anger by getting into fights* with other students all day.

g. She might *use a problem-solving skill*, like an I statement, reflective listening, a kill-them-with-kindness sandwich, apologizing, or negotiating a compromise. *(Have the students role-play each skill.)*

I statement: "Mrs. Davis, I feel angry when you won't let me play softball, just because Mark and I were holding hands."

Reflective listening: "Mrs. Davis, I can tell that you're disappointed that Mark and I were holding hands."

Kill-them-with-kindness sandwich: "Mrs. Davis, I think you're a good softball coach, and I'm glad I'm on your team, but I don't think you should keep me from playing just because we hold hands. So, I hope you'll start playing me again."

Apologizing: "Mrs. Davis, I'm sorry for holding hands with Mark and kissing him before I go on the field. I know that you have strict rules for your players when they're at ball games. Mark and I won't act like that at games or practice anymore."

Negotiating a compromise: "Mrs. Davis, I can understand that you don't like your players to be showing affection to their boyfriends before a game, but it's important to me. I feel I can play better if I know someone is supporting me. Do you think we could compromise on this?"

6. **How could Betsy *evaluate the consequences* of each of these actions?** (Betsy could take each action, think of what will happen if she does it, and decide if it would be *helpful or harmful*.)

a. If she *stuffs*, she might get depressed and feel helpless; she might explode with other students. That would be *harmful*.

b. If she *withdraws* and stops going to school, her grades will go down. Mrs. Davis won't care. It would be *harmful*.

c. If she *blames*, Mrs. Davis might get defensive and stronger in her position. That would be *harmful*.

d. If she does *triangling*, she can complain a lot, but it won't solve the problem. It won't be *helpful*.

e. If she *explodes* and punches Mrs. Davis, she'll probably get suspended. That would be *harmful*.

f. If she uses an *I statement,* she gets a chance to express how she feels. It might be *helpful*.

g. If she uses *reflective listening,* she lets Mrs. Davis know that she understands how her coach feels. It might be *helpful*.

h. It she uses a *kill-them-with-kindness sandwich,* Mrs. Davis will probably say, "Too bad, you don't make the rules. If you hold hands and kiss, you won't play." It would be *harmful*.

i. If she *apologizes,* Mrs. Davis might accept the apology and let Betsy play. It would be *helpful*.

j. If she tries to *negotiate a compromise,* it might work, but she doesn't have much leverage. It might be *helpful*.

7. **How could Betsy *choose a best way*?** (After she has a chance to calm down and think, and look at the consequences, she might decide the best thing to do is to apologize to Mrs. Davis for showing affection inappropriately in school.)

8. **How could Betsy *problem-solve or express her anger in a helpful way*?** (She might say, "Mrs. Davis, I'm sorry for holding hands with Mark and kissing him before I go on the field. I know that you have strict rules for your players when they're at ball games. Mark and I won't be acting like that at games anymore.")

Use Scenario 2 to process the anger management steps for a problem that can't be changed. Have a student read Scenario 2.

Scenario 2

Corey, a seventh grader, lives with his father and his stepmother. Corey's father spends a lot of time lying on the couch, watching TV, and drinking 40-ounce bottles of beer. Corey's father and stepmother fight a lot. His older sister, Tina, is always getting into trouble. Corey would like to play on the basketball team, but his father won't pick him up from practices and his stepmother doesn't drive. Corey spends a lot of his time being angry. He doesn't try very hard in school and he isn't very polite to the teachers.

Use the following questions to process the anger management steps for this scenario.

1. **How can Corey *recognize* that he's angry?** (He can think about why he's doing poorly in school and why he's rude to the teachers.)

2. **How can Corey *accept* his anger?** (He can admit that he's angry; he can decide that his feeling of anger is normal.)

3. **What can Corey do to *practice relaxation*?** (He can use a centering exercise.)

4. **Is this a problem Corey *can change*?** (No, he can't change his father's chemical dependence.)

5. **If Corey *thinks about ways to express his anger*, what might he think about?**

   a. He might do some *stuffing*—swallow his anger down and pretend he's not angry.

   b. He might continue *withdrawing* by skipping school.

   c. He might do some *blaming* and yell at his father: "You're nothing but a drunk. Why don't you ever get off of that couch!"

   d. He might do some *triangling* and complain about his father to his stepmother and sister.

   e. He might *explode* and try to punch his father.

   f. He might *express his anger by getting into fights* with his stepmother and sister.

   g. He might do the three things teens should do when they're angry about a problem they can't change.

   1. *Accept what he can't change.* Corey should realize that he didn't cause and can't control or change his dad's chemical dependence.

   2. *Express his anger* so he can let it go. Corey could write a letter about how angry he is, shoot baskets, or paint a picture of his anger.

   3. *Do something good for himself.* Corey could ask a friend's dad to pick him up after practice so he can be on the team; study so he can go to college; attend a group to learn how to cope with a parent's chemical dependence.

   h. Corey might *use a problem-solving skill.* For example, he might use an I statement to tell his dad how important being on the basketball team is to him.

6. **How could Corey *evaluate the consequences* of each of these actions?** (Corey could take each action, think of what will happen if he does it, and decide if it would be *helpful or harmful*.)

   a. If he *stuffs,* he might get depressed and feel helpless; he might explode in school or at home. That would be *harmful.*

   b. If he continues to *withdraw,* his grades will go down, and he won't pass his classes. His rude behavior might get him kicked out of class. That would be *harmful.*

   c. If he *blames,* his father might get angry with him. That would be *harmful.*

   d. If he does *triangling,* he will increase the tension in the family even more. That would be *harmful.*

   e. If he *explodes* and punches his father, his father will probably punch him back. The situation could become violent. That would be *harmful.*

   f. If he does the *three things teens should do when they're angry* about a problem they can't change, he will probably feel better and accomplish something positive. That would be *helpful.*

   g. If he tries a *problem-solving skill,* he might establish better communication with his father. That would be *helpful.* In general, however, the problem-solving skills wouldn't lend themselves to this situation.

7. **How could Corey *choose a best way?*** (Corey might decide to ask a friend's father to pick him up after basketball practice. That way he gets to do something he likes to do. Shooting baskets would be a good way to let off steam.)

8. **How could Corey *problem-solve or express his anger in a helpful way?*** (Corey should act on his decision to do something good for himself right away.)

If you have time, use Scenarios 3 and 4 to demonstrate further how to process the anger management steps. You might have the students role-play each step. In this case, give them plenty of coaching. Another possibility would be to ask the students for examples of anger situations common for students in their school. Have the group members apply the anger management steps to these situations.

Scenario 3

Jessa, a high school student, is dating Andy. Andy is putting a lot of pressure on her to be sexually active. Jessa really likes Andy and is flattered that he wants to go out with her, but she doesn't feel ready to be sexually active. It's also against her religious beliefs. She's angry that Andy is putting such pressure on her, but she doesn't want him to know how she feels. Jessa wants to keep things friendly and fun so that Andy will keep asking her out.

1. How can Jessa *recognize* that she's angry?

2. How can Jessa *accept* her anger?

3. How can Jessa *practice relaxation?*

4. Is this a problem Jessa *can change?* (Yes.)

5. How can Jessa *express her anger?*

She can use harmful ways, like stuffing, withdrawing, blaming, triangling, or exploding.

   a. What would Jessa do if she used *stuffing?*

   b. What would Jessa do if she used *withdrawing?*

   c. What would Jessa do if she used *blaming?*

   d. What would Jessa do if she used *triangling?*

   e. What would Jessa do if she used *exploding?*

Jessa can use problem-solving skills like an I statement, reflective listening, a kill-them-with-kindness sandwich, apologizing, or negotiating a compromise.

   a. How could Jessa use an *I statement?*

   b. How could Jessa use *reflective listening?*

   c. How could Jessa use a *kill-them-with-kindness sandwich?*

d. How could Jessa use an *apology?*

e. How could Jessa use *negotiating a compromise?*

6. **How could Jessa *evaluate the consequences of each method?***

   a. *Stuffing:* helpful or harmful?

   b. *Withdrawing:* helpful or harmful?

   c. *Blaming:* helpful or harmful?

   d. *Triangling:* helpful or harmful?

   e. *Exploding:* helpful or harmful?

   f. An *I statement:* helpful or harmful?

   g. *Reflective listening:* helpful or harmful?

   h. A *kill-them-with-kindness sandwich:* helpful or harmful?

   i. An *apology:* helpful or harmful?

   j. *Negotiating a compromise:* helpful or harmful?

7. **What might Jessa *choose as a best way?***

8. **Then, how could Jessa *problem-solve or express her anger?***

Scenario 4

Will's locker is next to Rick's. Rick is pretty obnoxious. He's always knocking things out of Will's hands, knocking books and papers out of his locker, and shutting the locker door on Will. Finally, Will is fed up. He yells for everyone in the hall to hear, "Rick! You stupid jerk! No wonder no one likes you!"

1. How can Will *recognize* that he's angry?

2. How can Will *accept* his anger?

3. How can Will *practice relaxation?*

4. Is this a problem Will *can change?* (Yes.)

5. How can Will *express his anger?*

He can use harmful ways, like stuffing, withdrawing, blaming, triangling, or exploding.

   a. What would Will do if he used *stuffing?*

   b. What would Will do if he used *withdrawing?*

   c. What would Will do if he used *blaming?*

d. What would Will do if he used *triangling?*

e. What would Will do if he used *exploding?*

Will can use problem-solving skills like an I statement, reflective listening, a kill-them-with-kindness sandwich, apologizing, or negotiating a compromise.

   a. How could Will use an *I statement?*

   b. How could Will use *reflective listening?*

   c. How could Will use a *kill-them-with-kindness sandwich?*

   d. How could Will use an *apology?*

   e. How could Will use *negotiating a compromise?*

6. **How could Will *evaluate the consequences of each method?***

   a. *Stuffing:* helpful or harmful?

   b. *Withdrawing:* helpful or harmful?

   c. *Blaming:* helpful or harmful?

   d. *Triangling:* helpful or harmful?

   e. *Exploding:* helpful or harmful?

   f. An *I statement:* helpful or harmful?

   g. *Reflective listening:* helpful or harmful?

   h. A *kill-them-with-kindness sandwich:* helpful or harmful?

   i. An *apology:* helpful or harmful?

   j. *Negotiating a compromise:* helpful or harmful?

7. **What might Will *choose as a best way?***

8. **Then, how could Will *problem-solve or express his anger?***

DISCUSSION

Lead a discussion to help the students better understand the facts—the key concepts—presented. As the group discusses, remember to go around, making sure that each student has an opportunity to add to the discussion. Encourage participation, but don't force it. Remember the group rule that allows a student to pass. Accept all ideas and answers, explaining or clarifying information where necessary. To aid the discussion, you may wish to use questions like the following:

- **What does it mean to manage your anger?** (It means having a plan to help you put thinking between feeling angry and doing angry things.)

- **What are the steps of managing anger or anger management?** (Note: Allow the students to use the poster you made as they respond: recognize that you're angry; accept your anger; practice relaxation; decide if it's a problem you can't change or a problem you can change; think about helpful and harmful ways to express the anger; evaluate the consequences; choose a best way; problem-solve or express your anger in a helpful way.)

- **What are some ways you might recognize that you're feeling angry?** (Accept all responsible replies; look for examples like the following: you might get hot, blush, sweat, feel tense, breathe hard, or feel your heart beating fast.)

- **How do you accept anger?** (Tell yourself it's okay to feel angry.)

- **What are some ways you can relax?** (Practice one of the centering exercises: "Breathing Through Your Feet," "The Icicle," "The Space Shuttle.")

- **What are some ways to express anger or to problem-solve?** Tell if they are helpful or harmful. (Accept all responsible replies.)

- **What does it mean to problem-solve or to choose a helpful way to express your anger?** (To use a problem-solving skill, like an I statement, reflective listening, a kill-them-with-kindness sandwich, apologizing, or negotiating a compromise. To choose a helpful way to express your anger means to pick a way that doesn't harm yourself or anyone or anything else.)

- **What does it mean to express your anger in a helpful way?** (To go ahead and act—to do your best choice.)

- **Why should you always try to problem-solve or to express your anger in a helpful way?** (So you can either solve the anger situation or let go of your anger without hurting yourself or anyone else.)

- **Do you think it will be easy to use these steps right away?** (Even if the students choose a harmful way to express anger, it will help them to think back over the steps. Doing so often enough will help them use the steps when they're actually angry. The steps will help them put thinking between feeling and their behavior. It may take the teens two or three months of practice to acquire this ability, so urge patience and perseverance.)

Even if you choose not to use the suggested questions, make sure the discussion underscores these concepts.

ACTIVITY

Have the students take the index cards out of their folders. Ask them to look at the List of Basic Facts. Then have them copy Basic Fact 14 (the eight anger-management steps) on one side of the card and Basic Fact 11 (the five problem-solving skills) on the other. Explain that the group members can fold their index cards and carry them in their pockets. Whenever they feel angry, they should look at the card to help them put thinking between feeling and action. Allow a few minutes for the students to complete their cards.

BASIC FACTS

Review the new basic facts for this session. Refer the students to the List of Basic Facts. Ask two group members to read Basic Facts 13 and 14.

13. The anger management steps help teens put thinking between the feeling of anger and the behavior of anger.

14. The anger management steps are:

1. Recognize that you're angry.

2. Accept your anger.

3. Practice relaxation.

4. Decide if it's a problem you can't change or a problem you can change.

5. Think about helpful and harmful ways to express the anger.

6. Evaluate the consequences.

7. Choose a best way.

8. Problem-solve or express your anger in a helpful way.

By this time, the students should be very familiar with these facts. Even so, spend some time going through them, briefly discussing each and checking for understanding.

ASSIGNMENT

H ave the group members take Assignment 5 out of their folders. Read the directions: "Over the next week, once each day, when you get angry, go through the anger management steps. Write down the best way for you to problem-solve or to express your anger." Remind the students that using the anger management steps even after they get angry will eventually help them to problem-solve or to express their anger in a helpful way when they are in an anger situation.

Wrapping Up

CENTERING EXERCISE

S ettle the students and then repeat "The Mountaintop" (page 119).

AFFIRMATION

I nvolve the group in an affirmation. Stand and join in a circle with the students holding hands. Go around and have the students share a time they felt angry and a helpful way they expressed—or could have expressed—their anger. Begin the affirmation yourself: "One time that I got angry was . . . A helpful way to express my anger would have been. . . ." The students will need you to role-model this affirmation. They will probably also need your help to see what would have been a helpful way to express anger.

CLOSING

R emain standing in a circle with the students, holding hands, and lead the group in the closing activity.

Tell the students that you're going to make a silent wish for the student on your right. Then, when you've made the wish, gently squeeze the student's hand. The student makes a silent wish for the person on his or her right, then gently squeezes that student's hand, and so on. Continue around the circle until a wish and squeeze come back to you. If necessary, the students can pass the wish in any appropriate way they choose.

Collect the folders. Fill out a copy of the Process and Progress Form (page 211) or the Progress Notes (page 212), if you are an experienced leader, as soon as possible after leading the group.

Anger Management Steps

Remember that anger is a normal feeling. It consists of feeling, thinking, and behaving. There is a difference between feeling angry, which is okay, and behavior—such as stuffing, withdrawing, blaming, triangling, or exploding—which may not be okay. These anger styles are usually not effective in helping you solve the problem that made you angry or in helping you get along with people and get what you want.

You can't control the feelings you get, but you can control your behavior. You may need to look at your thinking, or self-talk, and see if it is positive or negative. You may need to change your thinking to help you change behavior. You are responsible for your behavior when you are angry. No matter what might influence someone to use violent or aggressive behavior, it is still his or her responsibility to choose nonviolent and helpful ways to express anger. Each person is accountable for his or her behavior. You always have the choice to express your anger in a helpful or harmful way.

Some teens rush right from feeling to behaving. They get mad and hit someone, or put someone down, or yell. So teenagers need to learn how to put thinking between their feelings of being angry and their behavior.

The **anger management steps** are a plan to help you put thinking between feeling angry and your behavior.

1. Recognize that you're angry.
2. Accept your anger.
3. Practice relaxation.
4. Decide if it's a problem you can't change or a problem you can change.
5. Think about helpful and harmful ways to express the anger.
6. Evaluate the consequences.
7. Choose a best way.
8. Problem-solve or express your anger in a helpful way.

Remember the principle of chunking it down. You will probably not be able to change your behavior right away. Behavioral change often comes slowly and inconsistently. Remember to set small, concrete goals if you want to change how you handle anger. For instance, a first goal can be to look at how you deal with anger. Do you stuff, withdraw, blame, triangle someone else in, explode, or problem-solve? Each time you notice how you deal with anger, think if you should have done it differently. If you didn't problem-solve, what could you have done to problem-solve? Could you have used your anger to give you the power to make changes in yourself? Or could you have accepted what you can't change, expressed your anger in a helpful way so you could let it go, and then done something good for yourself?

You can go through the steps of anger management even after you express your anger in a harmful way. Sooner or later, you will begin to use your anger to work for you, or you will express it in a helpful way, or you will use problem-solving skills. Changing your behavior may take two or three months, so don't give up if you don't get the steps right away.

Scenarios

Scenario 1

Betsy, a junior at East High School, is on the softball team. Her boyfriend, Mark, goes to the same school. Betsy and Mark really like each other. They hold hands before and after Betsy's softball games. Sometimes they sneak a quick kiss before Betsy goes on the field. Betsy's softball coach, Mrs. Davis, doesn't like to see her players exhibiting behavior like holding hands and kissing. Mrs. Davis has told Betsy and Mark to stop such behavior. Betsy decides that she's going to do what she wants to do, and she and Mark continue to hold hands and kiss. Mrs. Davis puts Betsy on the bench for noncompliance to rules. Betsy is so angry that she can't see straight. She gets red and breathes fast. She plans to confront Mrs. Davis before practice and demand to be allowed to play, or else.

Scenario 2

Corey, a seventh grader, lives with his father and his stepmother. Corey's father spends a lot of time lying on the couch, watching TV, and drinking 40-ounce bottles of beer. Corey's father and stepmother fight a lot. His older sister, Tina, is always getting into trouble. Corey would like to play on the basketball team, but his father won't pick him up from practices and his stepmother doesn't drive. Corey spends a lot of his time being angry. He doesn't try very hard in school and he isn't very polite to the teachers.

Scenario 3

Jessa, a high school student, is dating Andy. Andy is putting a lot of pressure on her to be sexually active. Jessa really likes Andy and is flattered that he wants to go out with her, but she doesn't feel ready to be sexually active. It's also against her religious beliefs. She's angry that Andy is putting such pressure on her, but she doesn't want him to know how she feels. Jessa wants to keep things friendly and fun so that Andy will keep asking her out.

Scenario 4

Will's locker is next to Rick's. Rick is pretty obnoxious. He's always knocking things out of Will's hands, knocking books and papers out of his locker, and shutting the locker door on Will. Finally, Will is fed up. He yells for everyone in the hall to hear, "Rick! You stupid jerk! No wonder no one likes you!"

Over the next week, once each day, when you get angry, go through the anger management steps. Write down the best way for you to problem-solve or to express your anger.

The **anger management steps** are a plan to help you put thinking between feeling angry and your behavior.

1. Recognize that you're angry.
2. Accept your anger.
3. Practice relaxation.
4. Decide if it's a problem you can't change or a problem you can change.

5. Think about helpful and harmful ways to express the anger.
6. Evaluate the consequences.
7. Choose a best way.
8. Problem-solve or express your anger in a helpful way.

Five good problem-solving skills to use in anger situations are **I statements, reflective listening, kill-them-with-kindness sandwiches, apologizing,** and **negotiating a compromise.**

Day one

Day five

Day two

Day six

Day three

Day seven

Day four

Other comments or observations

SESSION • 6

Family Violence

Objectives

To help the students:

- recognize that family violence occurs in various forms

- understand that families have different values regarding family violence

- recognize possible causes of family violence

- make a commitment never to practice family violence in their own lives

Session at a Glance

1. Group Rules: review if necessary—1 minute

2. Centering Exercise: "The Pyramid"—2 minutes

3. Feelings Check-in: look at Feeling Wheel—4 minutes

4. Basic Facts Review—5 minutes

5. Assignment Review—5 minutes

6. Mini-lecture, Discussion, and Scenarios—19 minutes

7. Basic Facts: read Basic Facts 15 and 16; discuss—2 minutes

8. Assignment—1 minute

9. Centering Exercise: repeat "The Pyramid"—2 minutes

10. Affirmation: share something you learned in today's session—3 minutes

11. Closing: pass a silent wish—1 minute

Preparation

- Display the posterboard copy of the group rules.

- Have posters with Basic Facts 1-14 available. (Or the List of Basic Facts, or index cards with a basic fact on each one.)

- Add the following materials to each folder:

  —Handout 6A ("Family Violence")
  —Handout 6B ("Range of Family Violence")
  —Handout 6C ("Scenarios")
  —Assignment 6.

- Have the folders, pencil, and crayons or markers at each student's place.

- Read through the session plan before meeting.

Background and Guidelines

Sessions 1-5 focused on violence and the causes of violence. The sessions taught group members the value that violent or aggressive behavior is not an acceptable way to express anger. The sessions also gave the students proactive skills to deal with their anger in nonaggressive and helpful ways.

The next three sessions will focus on the violence and aggression that occur in families, the effects of this violence on family members, and how teens can develop coping strategies if they live in violent families.

This session presents an overview of family violence. It discusses the facts about domestic violence—its historical roots, its prevalence, and different types of domestic violence. The session provides scenarios that point out the range of domestic violence, from spanking to sexual abuse to battering. You will ask the students to look at their own values regarding family violence. You will again ask them to make a commitment to choose nonviolence in their own lives and to learn to use their anger to work for them.

FAMILY VIOLENCE DOES EXIST

Many people are very uncomfortable when talking about family violence, and they may deny or minimize the problem. Gelles and Straus (1988), two sociologists at the University of New Hampshire, conducted nationwide telephone surveys to study the incidence of family violence. They estimate that one woman in 22 (3.8 percent) is the victim of physically abusive violence each year. The average battered wife is attacked three times each year. Stacey and Shupe (1983) quote that "39,000 Americans died in the Vietnam conflict between 1967 and 1973; at the same time 17,570 Americans also died literally on the home front, from family violence. Most of these were women and children" (p. 3).

According to the FBI's *Crime in the United States,* 1991, almost half of the murder victims in 1991 were either related to (12 percent) or acquainted with (34 percent) their assailants.

EXPRESSIVE OR INSTRUMENTAL

Just as in aggression and violence, experts describe family violence as *expressive,* where family members become out of control in expressing their anger, or as *instrumental,* where family members use physical force or violence to control other family members.

MAJORITY OF FAMILY VIOLENCE IS MALE TO FEMALE

Although some women are physically violent to children and husbands, the majority of family violence is administered by men. Men also use the threat of violence to control their female partners. Stacey and Shupe quote Wolfgang's studies of homicides in Philadelphia in the 1950s. These studies showed that 65 percent of the homicides occurred among people who were intimate; 41 percent of the women were killed by their husbands, whereas only 10 percent of the men were killed by their wives. According to the FBI, among all female murder victims in 1991, 28 percent were slain by husbands or boyfriends. Four percent of the male victims were killed by wives or girlfriends.

INACTION BY POLICE AND COURTS

Studies have shown that the legal system has not taken the violence that occurs in families seriously. Police are more likely to make arrests for nonviolent acts outside the home than for violent offenses inside the home. This may have to do with the historical attitude that wives are the property of their husbands. It may also have to do with the ideals of the sanctity of the home and family privacy. In some instances, the courts have approved violence towards women. Until the 1950s, in Texas, Utah, and New Mexico, husbands were granted special immunity from prosecution if they murdered their wives after finding them in an adulterous situation. This same right was not granted to wives (Dobash and Dobash, 1979).

WHERE AND WHEN

Researchers have also looked at patterns of family violence in space and time. Gelles and Straus (1988) found:

- the typical location of marital violence is the kitchen

- the bedroom and living room are next

- the bedroom is the most likely place for a female to be killed

- the bathroom is the most frequently occupied room during domestic violence (it has a lock and provides a hiding place)

- physical conflict is most common between 8 p.m. and 11:30 p.m.

- dinnertime is a particularly dangerous time

- weekends and holidays, especially from Thanksgiving to New Year's Day, and Easter, are also "trouble times"

CONTINUUM FROM SPANKING TO DEATH

Some authors describe family violence as occurring on a continuum. On one continuum family violence ranges from parents spanking children with an open palm to parents administering severe physical discipline or deliberate and willful injury to children or sexually abusing them. On another continuum family violence ranges from husbands or wives emotionally abusing their spouses, to controlling behavior from husbands to wives, to physical harm in the form of slapping, punching, kicking, stabbing, or shooting.

WIFE BATTERING AND CHILD ABUSE: HISTORICAL PERSPECTIVE

Dobash and Dobash, two Scottish sociologists, looked at the history of wife beating in the Western world. In Roman society, a wife was the legal property of the husband, and he could require her to obey him. A Roman husband had the legal right to chastise, divorce, or kill his wife for engaging in behavior that he himself engaged in daily. She could be beaten for drunkenness, attending public games without his permission, or walking outdoors with her face uncovered.

While early Christianity did not endorse physical violence against women, it did promote the belief that women had an inferior voice and place to men. Paul wrote: "Let your women keep silence in the churches: for it is not permitted unto them to speak; but they are commanded to be under obedience, as also saith the law. And if they will learn anything, let them ask their husbands at home: for it is a shame for women to speak in the church." (1 Corinthians 14:34-35).

For many centuries, during the Dark and Middle Ages, as well as the Renaissance, "laws of chastisement" justified the physical punishment of women and reinforced their inferior status. Dobash and Dobash quote the marriage rules of Siena, Italy: "If your wife is of a servile disposition and has a crude shifty spirit, so that pleasant words have no effect, scold her sharply, bully and terrify her. And if this still doesn't work . . . take up a stick and beat her soundly, for it is better to punish the body and correct the soul than to damage the soul and spare the body" (p. 47).

The 16th-century Protestant Reformation perpetuated the physical discipline of women. Martin Luther said of his wife, "When Katie gets saucy, she gets nothing but a box on the ear" (p. 53).

English law also discriminated against women and allowed the use of physical coercion against married women. In the early years of the United States, state governments borrowed much of English law. The supreme court of Mississippi, for example, formalized a husband's right to batter his wife in 1824. Public debate over similar legal decisions in other states eventually led to a movement to reject a husband's legal right to chastise his wife. By the 1870s, courts were rejecting the legal justification of wife beating.

Child abuse has a similar historical pattern. As Stacey and Shupe point out, the Bible is filled with gory stories of infanticide and violence toward children: Abraham and Isaac, the pharaoh's child slaughter at Moses' birth, and Herod's slaughter of the innocents at Jesus' birth. In Roman society, the father's legal rights included maiming or killing his children as well as selling them as slaves or sacrificing them to the gods.

Children were seen as having rights only very recently. Just after the Civil War, a child, Mary Ellen, was found beaten, neglected, and malnourished in New York City. There was no agency devoted to the rights of children, so her case was argued in court by the Society for the Prevention of Cruelty to Animals. This led to the formation of the Society for the Prevention of Cruelty to Children in 1871. In 1960, Dr. Henry Kempe described the battered child syndrome and raised national awareness of the effects of child abuse.

The move to obtain voting rights for women as well as equal civil rights began in the early 1900s. By the 1970s, women began to be vocal about family violence and child abuse and, along with the Vietnam War and the environment, these became topics for national attention. In 1974 Congress passed the Child Abuse Prevention and Treatment Act. The first White House Conference on Domestic Violence was held in 1976. The attention to sexual harassment in the 1990s is the next step in developing a regard for women (and children) as persons, and not as property or objects.

In spite of the growing awareness of the last 20 years of family violence, both child abuse and wife beating continue.

STUDY OF BATTERED WOMEN IN A SHELTER, DALLAS

Stacey and Shupe (1983) studied women in a shelter for battered women in Dallas, Texas.

Progression of Family Violence

In the families studied, the battering situations usually began with the husband verbally abusing the wife. The situations progressed to the husband punching the wife and then to the husband using weapons, such as knives or guns. The violence began to occur more frequently: progressing from the woman being beaten several times a month to being beaten daily. Alcohol and drug use by the batterer was frequent during the violent episodes. Sexual domination was frequent, with 66 percent of the batterers demonstrating jealousy and possessiveness over their wives' clothing, appearance, and time; they generally suspected affairs. Job and financial pressures were also frequent.

Alcohol and Other Drug Use Present, But Not a Cause

Although alcohol and drug use by the batterer was frequent during the violent episodes, Stacey and Shupe agree with other researchers who do not attribute such violence to substance abuse. Using alcohol and other drugs can increase irritability and lower internal controls, but it does not cause violence. Gelles and Straus found that when alcohol is present in domestic violence the abuser most often has been drinking moderately; those who don't drink or who get drunk often are the least abusive partners and parents. Being intoxicated is often used as an excuse by violent men for their behavior.

Three Stages of Battering

The Dallas study verified that violence in families usually comes in three stages: a stage of building tension, the violent episode, and the honeymoon phase. The honeymoon stage refers to the period following the violent episode, when the batterer is filled with remorse and intimacy.

Battering Men

The battering men in Stacey and Shupe's study had difficulty arguing with women over even trivial issues without violence. Ninety percent were violent toward children, animals, and physical objects. They destroyed property, not just in emotional rages but also with a cold disregard for the rights and feelings of others. As children, 60 percent had witnessed physical violence between their parents. These were the men most likely to abuse their own children. Fifty percent of the men did not have the honeymoon stage; these men felt the beatings were justified. The most severe violence occurred among this group.

Battered Women

Some researchers describe learned helplessness as a condition of battered wives that makes them unable to leave abusive husbands. However, Stacey and Shupe found women who were active in seeking relief from the abuse. Some of these women stayed in the relationship out of affection for the man, and some because of the hope for improvement. However, the majority stayed because of "economic dependency, children . . . , direct coercion, and . . . indirect coercion, such as threats related to leaving, threats to children, or the man threatening to commit suicide" (pps. 55-56).

Researchers, including Gelles and Straus, have found that "the key to preventing severe violence is taking action against the first and more minor acts of physical aggression" (p. 155). Women who have conviction and determination that the violence must stop now seem to be able to find strategies or help sources that are effective in getting their spouses to stop the violence.

CHILDREN IN VIOLENT FAMILIES

Session 7 looks more specifically at the effects of family violence on children. Stated briefly, these children may have attachment problems, may be unable to regulate their emotions, may not have a realistic sense of themselves as independent and competent, may have aggression or withdrawal in peer relationships, and may have problems adapting to school, either socially or academically.

Adolescent girls may start to accept threats and violence from boyfriends who control them through this behavior. Other teens run away to avoid family violence; some act out in delinquent behavior. Some adolescent boys imitate behavior that has been modeled for them by assaulting their mother or siblings. Still other teens adopt parenting roles in the family, trying to protect their siblings from the violence (Jaffe et al., 1990).

CAUSES OF FAMILY VIOLENCE

Researchers have looked at the causes of family violence.

On the Personal Level

One theory is that aggression is a *normal instinct* in men and that violence is a necessary part of life in Western society; men are socialized to be aggressive; it is normal for men to use physical force to dominate women. *Psychological* explanations of family violence point to childhood experiences or marital relationships, often blaming women (mothers and wives) for male violence.

On the Family Level

Other researchers attribute family violence to the *generational transfer hypothesis,* or *learning theory:* children repeat the behavior of their parents. The *interpersonal theory* assumes that the two people in a relationship contribute to the violence by their behavior. Other theorists point out that this is blaming the victim (the woman) for the beating her husband gives her.

On the Social Level

Some researchers note the *subculture of violence,* where groups of people, such as gangs, believe that violence is normal and justified.

On the Societal Level

Some attribute family violence to the legacy of a *patriarchy*, the historical custom which regarded women and children as property and legalized wife beating and child abuse. Another theory looks at the *family as an institution* that uses force to achieve control; fathers and husbands usually perform this coercion because of their physical dominance.

Anger Management and Violence Prevention sees family violence, especially severe family violence, as a condition that must end. The students will be encouraged to make the value judgment that it is not acceptable for people to physically harm other people. Just as for violence in general, factors on the personal, family, social, and societal level contribute to family violence. Men and women who batter and abuse their spouse and children may have problems in regulating their emotions, in communicating their feelings, and in problem solving. But people can break the pattern of using physical force in relationships, whether it's used to express anger or to control others. Battered children have the responsibility to get help so that they can break the cycle of abuse. Teenagers who see parents expressing their anger violently have the responsibility to learn different ways to express their own anger so that they can break the cycle of violence. Teens can learn how to regulate their emotions and how to communicate their feelings and their anger in helpful ways, and they can learn to use problem-solving skills in anger situations.

This material was drawn from the following sources:

Crime in the United States, 1991: Uniform Crime Reports. Federal Bureau of Investigation, U.S. Department of Justice, Washington, D.C. 20535.

Dobash, R. E., and R. Dobash. 1979. *Violence Against Wives.* New York: Free Press.

Gelles, R. J., and M. A. Straus. 1988. *Intimate Violence.* New York: Simon & Schuster.

Jaffe, P. G., D. A. Wolfe, and S. K. Wilson. 1990. *Children of Battered Women.* Newbury Park, CA: Sage Publications.

Stacey, W. A., and A. Shupe. 1983. *The Family Secret.* Boston: Beacon Press.

Beginning the Session

GROUP RULES

Welcome the students and begin with a quick review of the group rules. Draw attention to the poster listing the group rules. If you feel that it is necessary, call on different students to read them one at a time. Check for understanding before moving on.

CENTERING EXERCISE

Lead the students in a new centering exercise, "The Pyramid."

THE PYRAMID

Today's centering exercise will help you get through periods of very intense feelings, such as panic. Imagine that you are in Mexico and that you are exploring some ancient Mayan ruins. It is amazing to see what these primitive people could build in the jungle in the 700s. One of the massive structures they built was a pyramid, about 500 feet tall, with a steep stone staircase on each of the four sides, and a temple on its flat top. You decide to climb the pyramid so you can get a better view of the other ruins and of the surrounding jungle. You start climbing up, and you move up the stairs very quickly. But, about halfway up, you are suddenly struck with a sense of panic, or terror. It's as if you're suddenly overcome with a fear of heights. You are sure that if you try to go down, you will fall off the pyramid and die. If you move up, you will fall off and die. You are paralyzed. The only thing worse than moving is staying where you are. There is nothing to hold onto except the steep stone staircase, so you bend down and slowly move up the stairs one at a time, holding on to higher stairs with your hands.

You finally make it to the top of the pyramid. You remain bent down, and touching the floor with your hand, you make it over to the temple, which you hold onto. You go around to the third side of the pyramid, where there is a thick wire cable that begins at the temple and goes down the surface of the stairs. You realize that if you don't go down, you will have to stay on top of the pyramid forever. You sit down on your behind, and you hold onto the cable and slowly inch out to the staircase. You go down

Exercise continued on next page.

Exercise continued from previous page.

the stairs one at a time, holding on desperately to the cable. Other people are coming up the pyramid, and some of them have stopped as if they are paralyzed. Others are coming up holding onto the cable. As you go down the pyramid, you breathe easier and easier. You know that you are safe as long as you can hold onto the cable.

Finally, you get to about 12 steps up from the bottom. You feel safe at this point, and you can let go of the cable. You stand up and walk erect down the rest of the steps. The feeling you have is of relief, because you didn't fall off and die. But you also feel proud, because you got through a period of panic by grounding yourself, by finding something to hold onto. You feel safe and secure now. You decide that if you are ever somewhere where you feel panic, you will just imagine that you are holding onto the cable of the pyramid's staircase. You will remember the sense of being grounded, which helped you feel safe and secure even during the period of panic.

FEELINGS CHECK-IN

Do a feelings check-in with the students. Have them take out their Feeling Wheels. Ask the group members to decide how they are feeling today. Remind the students that if they want, they can color in the section on the Feeling Wheel that describes how they're feeling today. Also remind the teens that they might have more than one feeling, since it's possible to have more than one feeling at a time. Tell the students that if they're having a feeling not named on the wheel, they can add a bubble to the outside of the wheel and name their feeling.

When the students finish, have a go-around. Begin by sharing your own feelings. Then, invite each student to share his or her feelings. Teenagers often list many feelings. For the interests of time, ask them to name the feelings they have, but then to pick only two to discuss. Be sure to accept each student's feeling(s) and to affirm each student. Ask the students to return the wheels to their folders.

BASIC FACTS REVIEW

Review Basic Facts 1-14. Use posters, the List of Basic Facts, or index cards.

In a go-around, ask a student to read Basic Fact 1 aloud and to explain what it means. If the student has trouble explaining the fact, don't contradict or judge, simply clarify his or her explanation. Repeat the procedure for the next basic fact. This review ensures that the students understand and integrate the basic facts that have been taught. It is also easy preparation for the presentation and provides a lead-in for the session material.

ASSIGNMENT REVIEW

Ask the students if they brought their assignments from last week. Remind them that they were to go through the steps of anger management when they got angry, and to write down the best way for them to problem-solve or to express their anger. In a go-around, ask each student to describe one incident from the past week. If students forgot to do the assignment, ask them to think of one time they were angry and a problem-solving skill they could have used, or a helpful way they could have expressed their anger. Remind the students that they can learn from each other, by seeing how other group members use the problem-solving skills. Also remind them of the principle of chunking it down—just going over the steps of anger management after an anger situation happens will help them to choose a helpful way to express anger in the future.

Exploring the Material

MINI-LECTURE

Tell the students that so far in this group they have focused on violence and the causes of violence. They have learned the value that

137

violent or aggressive behavior is not an acceptable way to express anger. They have also practiced proactive skills to deal with their anger in nonaggressive and helpful ways.

Explain that the next three sessions will focus on the violence and aggression that occur in families, the effects of this violence on family members, and how teens can develop coping strategies if they live in violent families. This session will present an overview of family violence. The students will discuss the facts about domestic violence—its historical roots, its prevalence, and different types of domestic violence. They will look at scenarios that point out the range of

domestic violence, from spanking to sexual abuse to battering. The group members will look at their own values regarding family violence. You will again ask them to make a commitment to choose nonviolence in their own lives and to learn to use their anger to work for them.

Facts About Family Violence

Present the following information to the students. Gear your presentation to the age and level of understanding of the group members. At the conclusion of the mini-lecture, show students Handout 6A ("Family Violence"), which summarizes facts about family violence.

Family Violence Does Exist

Many people are very uncomfortable when talking about family violence, and they may deny or minimize the problem. Family violence does exist, however. One study estimates that one woman in 22 (3.8 percent) is the victim of physically abusive violence each year. The average battered wife is attacked three times each year. Between 1967 and 1973, 39,000 Americans died in the Vietnam conflict. During the same time, another 17,570 Americans died from family violence. Most of these were women and children. According to the FBI's *Crime in the United States, 1991*, almost half of the murder victims in 1991 were either related to (12 percent) or acquainted with (34 percent) their assailants.

Expressive or Instrumental

Just as in aggression and violence, experts describe family violence as *expressive*, where family members become out of control in expressing their anger, or as *instrumental*, where family members use physical force or violence to control other family members.

Majority of Family Violence Is Male to Female

Although some women are physically violent to children and husbands, the majority of family violence is administered by men. Men also use the threat of violence to control their female partners. A study of homicides in Philadelphia in the 1950s showed that 65 percent occurred among people who were intimate; 41 percent of the women were killed by their husbands, whereas only 10 percent of the men were killed by their wives. According to the FBI, among all female murder victims in 1991, 28 percent were slain by husbands or boyfriends. Four percent of the male victims were killed by wives or girlfriends.

Inaction by Police and Courts

Studies have shown that the legal system has not taken the violence that occurs in families seriously. Police are more likely to make arrests for nonviolent acts outside the home than for violent offenses inside the home. This may have to do with the fact that throughout history wives have been seen as the property of their husbands. It may also have to do with the ideals of the sanctity of the home and family privacy. In some instances, the courts have approved violence towards women. Until the 1950s, in Texas, Utah, and New Mexico, husbands were granted special immunity from prosecution if they murdered their wives after finding them in an adulterous situation. This same right was not granted to wives.

Where and When

Researchers have also looked at patterns of family violence in space and time. They have found that

- the typical location of marital violence is the kitchen
- the bedroom and living room are next
- the bedroom is the most likely place for a female to be killed
- the bathroom is the most frequently occupied room during domestic violence (it has a lock and provides a hiding place)
- physical conflict is most common between 8 p.m. and 11:30 p.m.
- dinnertime is a particularly dangerous time
- weekends and holidays, especially from Thanksgiving to New Year's Day, and Easter, are also "trouble times"

Range of Family Violence

Ask the group members to find Handout 6B ("Range of Family Violence") in their folders. Use this handout to acquaint the students with the various forms of family violence and to help them examine their own values regarding family violence. In a go-around, have each student read one of the forms of violence. Ask the students if they can think of different examples of family violence to add to this list. They can write their examples in the space provided on the handout.

Have the students note the way in which the various forms of violence have been arranged. This order suggests that some forms of violence are worse than others and that violent behavior progresses through stages. Tell the students that they can reorder the forms of violence if they want. For instance, they might believe that spanking is more violent than yelling and screaming or that name calling and put downs are less violent than spanking. They can use the space on the handout to reorder the list. Ask the students to share their ideas. Remind them of the value judgment that no form of violence to express anger is acceptable.

RANGE OF FAMILY VIOLENCE

0 Not violent at all, talking the problem over calmly

1 Disciplining child by spanking with an open palm

2 Yelling and screaming

3 Name calling and put downs

4 Slapping with an open palm

5 Throwing things; destruction of furniture; injuring pets

6 Discipline of child by beating with a belt, extension cord, or switch; punching spouse and leaving bruises

7 Sexual abuse of children

8 Repeated acts of slapping, kicking, punching, or choking, and leaving broken arms, black eyes, etc.

9 Use of a weapon, such as a knife or gun

10 Extreme violence, resulting in death

Take a few minutes to get the students' opinions on spanking as a form of violence. Note that most people think that spanking children is an acceptable form of discipline. Some researchers, however, see spanking as a mild form of force that leads to other, more serious forms of violence.

Ask the students to take Handout 6C ("Scenarios") out of their folders. Have a student read Scenario 1.

Scenario 1

Dennis, age 8, is generally well behaved, but sometimes he gets into trouble. One day, he starts hammering a table at home. He hammers so hard that he makes big dents in it. Dennis' mother finds out that he has ruined the table, and she spanks him.

Ask the students if they think this spanking is justified.

Have another student read Scenario 2.

Scenario 2

One day Dennis is walking down the street. He accidentally bumps into a woman who is passing by him. She stops him and starts to spank him.

Ask the students if they think this spanking is all right.

Ask the students to be thinking of how much use of physical control or coercion (force) should be allowed between parents and children, between husbands and wives, and between peers or strangers.

Battering

Tell the students that they will look at an extreme form of violence—wife battering. Explain that wife battering is when men do severe physical injury to their wives or girlfriends. Continue with the mini-lecture.

Wife Battering and Child Abuse: Historical Perspective

Wife battering has had a long history in the Western world. In Roman society, a wife was the legal property of the husband, and he could require her to obey him. A Roman husband had the legal right to chastise, divorce, or kill his wife for engaging in behavior that he himself engaged in daily. She could be beaten for drunkenness, attending public games without his permission, or walking outdoors with her face uncovered.

The belief that wife battering was justifiable continued through the Dark Ages, the Middle Ages, and the Renaissance. The 16th-century Protestant Reformation also perpetuated the physical discipline of women. Martin Luther said of his wife, "When Katie gets saucy, she gets nothing but a box on the ear."

English law also discriminated against women and allowed the use of physical coercion against married women. In the early years of the United States, state governments borrowed much of English law. The supreme court of Mississippi, for example, formalized a husband's right to batter his wife in 1824. Public debate over similar legal decisions in other states eventually led to a movement to reject a husband's legal right to chastise his wife. By the 1870s, courts were rejecting the legal justification of wife beating.

Child abuse has a similar historical pattern. The Bible is filled with gory stories of infanticide and violence toward children: Abraham and Isaac, the pharaoh's child slaughter at Moses' birth, and Herod's slaughter of the innocents at Jesus' birth. In Roman society, the father's legal rights included maiming or killing his children as well as selling them as slaves or sacrificing them to the gods.

Children were seen as having rights only very recently. Just after the Civil War, a child, Mary Ellen, was found beaten, neglected, and malnourished in New York City. There was no agency devoted to the rights of children, so her case was argued in court by the Society for the Prevention of Cruelty to Animals. This led to the formation of the Society for the Prevention of Cruelty to Children in 1871.

The move to obtain voting rights for women as well as equal civil rights began in the early 1900s. By the 1970s, women began to be vocal about family violence and child abuse, and along with the Vietnam War and the environment, these became topics for national attention. In 1974 Congress passed the Child Abuse Prevention and Treatment Act. The first White House Conference on Domestic Violence was held in 1976. The attention to sexual harassment in the 1990s is the next step in developing a regard for women (and children) as persons, and not as property or objects.

In spite of the growing awareness of the last 20 years of family violence, both child abuse and wife beating continue.

Study of Battered Women in a Shelter, Dallas

Two sociologists studied women in a shelter for battered women in Dallas, Texas.

PROGRESSION OF FAMILY VIOLENCE

The researchers found that in the families studied, the battering situations usually began with the husband verbally abusing the wife. The violence progressed to the husband punching the wife and then to the husband using weapons, such as knives or guns. The violence began to occur more frequently: progressing from the woman being beaten several times a month to being beaten daily. Alcohol and drug use by the batterer was frequent during the violent episodes. Sexual domination was frequent, with 66 percent of the batterers demonstrating jealousy and possessiveness over their wives' clothing, appearance, and time; they generally suspected affairs. Job and financial pressures were also frequent.

ALCOHOL AND OTHER DRUG USE PRESENT, BUT NOT A CAUSE

Although alcohol and drug use by the batterer was frequent during the violent episodes, the researchers do not believe that the substance use caused the violence. Using alcohol and other drugs can increase irritability and lower internal controls, but it does not cause violence. Other researchers find that when alcohol is present in domestic violence the abuser most often has been drinking moderately; those who don't drink or who get drunk often are the least abusive partners and parents. Being intoxicated is often used as an excuse by violent men for their behavior.

THREE STAGES OF BATTERING

The Dallas study verified that violence in families usually comes in three stages: a stage of building tension, the violent episode, and the honeymoon phase. The honeymoon stage refers to the period following the violent episode, when the batterer is filled with remorse and wants to make up.

BATTERING MEN

The battering men in the study had difficulty arguing with women over even trivial issues without violence. Ninety percent were violent toward children, animals, and physical objects. They destroyed property, not just in emotional rages but also with a cold disregard for the rights and feelings of others. As children, 60 percent had witnessed physical violence between their parents. These were the men most likely to abuse their own children. Fifty percent of the men did not have the honeymoon stage; these men felt the beatings were justified. The most severe violence occurred among this group.

BATTERED WOMEN

Some researchers describe learned helplessness as a condition of battered wives that makes them unable to leave abusive husbands. However, the researchers in the Dallas study found women who were active in seeking relief from the abuse. Some of these women stayed in the relationship out of affection for the man, and some because of the hope for improvement. However, the majority stayed because of economic dependency, children, direct coercion, and indirect coercion, such as threats related to leaving, threats to children, or the man threatening to commit suicide.

Other researchers have found that the key to preventing severe violence is taking action against the first and more minor acts of physical aggression. Women who have conviction and determination that the violence must stop now seem to be able to find strategies or help sources that are effective in getting their spouses to stop the violence.

Children in Violent Families

In Session 7, we'll look more specifically at the effects of family violence on children. Stated briefly, children may have attachment problems, may be unable to regulate their emotions, may not have a realistic sense of themselves as independent and competent, may have aggression or withdrawal in peer relationships, and may have problems adapting to school, either socially or academically.

Adolescent girls may start to accept threats and violence from boyfriends who control them through this behavior. Other teens run away to avoid family violence; some act out in delinquent behavior. Some adolescent boys imitate behavior that has been modeled for them by assaulting their mother or siblings. Still other teens adopt parenting roles in the family, trying to protect their siblings from the violence.

THEORIES ABOUT THE CAUSES OF FAMILY VIOLENCE

Ask the students what they think causes family members to be violent. Write their responses on the chalkboard. Then continue with the mini-lecture.

Causes of Family Violence

Researchers have looked at the causes of family violence.

ON THE PERSONAL LEVEL

One theory is that aggression is a *normal instinct* in men, and violence is a necessary part of life in Western society; men are socialized to be aggressive; it is normal for men to use physical force to dominate women. *Psychological* explanations of family violence point to childhood experiences or marital relationships, often blaming women (mothers and wives) for male violence.

ON THE FAMILY LEVEL

Other researchers attribute family violence to the *generational transfer hypothesis*, or *learning theory*: children repeat the behavior of their parents. The *interpersonal theory* assumes that the two people in a relationship contribute to the violence by their behavior. Other theorists point out that this is blaming the victim (the woman) for the beating her husband gives her.

ON THE SOCIAL LEVEL

Some researchers note the *subculture of violence*, where groups of people, such as gangs, believe that violence is normal and justified.

ON THE SOCIETAL LEVEL

Some attribute family violence to the legacy of a *patriarchy*, the historical custom where women and children were seen as property, and wife beating and child abuse were legal. Another theory looks at the *family as an institution* that uses force to achieve control; fathers and husbands usually perform this coercion because of their physical dominance.

In this group, we will see family violence as a condition that must end. We will make the value judgment that it is not acceptable for people to physically harm other people. Just as for violence in general, factors on the personal, family, social, and societal level contribute to family violence. Men and women who batter and abuse their spouse and children may have problems in regulating their emotions, in communicating their feelings, and in problem solving. But, people can break the pattern of using physical force in relationships, whether it's used to express anger or to control others. Battered children have the responsibility to get help so that they can break the cycle of abuse. Teenagers who see parents expressing their anger violently have the responsibility to learn different ways to express their own anger so that they can break the cycle of violence. Teens can learn how to regulate their emotions and how to communicate their feelings and their anger in helpful ways, and they can learn to use problem-solving skills in anger situations. This group will urge each member to make a commitment to end the use of physical force in his or her life.

DISCUSSION

Ask the students to look at some scenarios of family violence. Use the questions following each scenario to generate discussion. Tell the students that there are no right or wrong answers to the discussion questions. They are designed to help them examine their own values about the degree of control and physical force family members should use on each other.

Ask a student to read Scenario 3.

Scenario 3

Larry, age 35, works in a factory. He is married to Karen, a 30-year-old woman who manages the deli at the local grocery store. Larry is very jealous of Karen. He is always telling her what clothing to wear. He gets angry with her when she puts on makeup. He always wants to know what she does on her time off from work and gets angry when she talks on the phone with her friends. Last week, he hit her in the face and gave her a black eye. He was angry because he didn't like her new sweater. He thought it was too tight.

1. Where do you think this incident stands in the range of family violence?

2. Do you think Larry hit Karen to express his anger or to try to control her?

3. Do you think it was okay for Larry to hit Karen in the face and give her a black eye?

4. Why do you think Karen stays with Larry?

5. What do you think Karen should do?

6. Can you think of some problem-solving skills that Karen could use? (If you want, have the students role-play the problem-solving skills.)

Ask another student to read Scenario 4.

Scenario 4

Charlene's parents lose their tempers a lot. Her father is always cursing and yelling at everybody. Her mother lets her little brother get away with everything. Charlene gets really upset when her mother buys things for her little brother and doesn't even take Charlene to the mall to look around. She yells at her mother a lot. When Charlene gets really angry, she goes to her room, slams her door, and starts throwing things. Last week, when she was having a fight with her mother, her mother came into the bathroom and hit Charlene on her back three times. Charlene was holding onto her hairbrush so hard that she broke it, and then her mother got mad about that. Charlene had to control herself so she wouldn't hit her mother with the hairbrush.

1. Where does this incident stand in the range of family violence?

2. How does this family express anger?

3. How do you think Charlene gets along with her friends?

4. What kind of a mother do you think Charlene will be?

5. What are some problem-solving skills Charlene could use?

Ask a student to read Scenario 5.

Scenario 5

Tom is a high school student who has a chip on his shoulder. He's always getting into somebody's face and is constantly in the principal's office for fighting. Tom's mother was severely battered by her boyfriend, and he saw her getting beaten up many times when he was a child. Later, when he was a teenager, his stepfather shot her to death. When Tom gets angry, he likes to hurt other people. He's planning to beat up one of his teachers. The teacher gave Tom an F on a test because he thought Tom was cheating, when Tom wasn't.

1. On the range of family violence, what kind of violence did Tom's mother experience?

2. What effect did this have on Tom?

3. Do you think Tom will grow up to be a man who batters his wife and abuses his children?

4. Can you think of a problem-solving skill that Tom could use with the teacher who gave him an F?

BASIC FACTS

Review the new basic facts for this session. Refer the students to the List of Basic Facts. Ask two group members to read Basic Facts 15 and 16.

15. No matter what you believe about the causes, family violence will end only if each person decides never to use violence in his or her own life.

16. To set limits against the use of force in a relationship, speak in a calm, rational way, firmly, and with conviction and determination.

Briefly discuss each fact, checking for understanding.

ASSIGNMENT

Have the group members take Assignment 6 out of their folders. Read the directions: "There are two parts to this assignment. In the first part, write down your values regarding the use of force in families.

• Do you think spanking is okay?

• Do you think it's okay for parents to use force to get children to do things?

• Do you think it's okay for husbands and wives to use force with each other?

• Do you think it's okay for teenage boys to push their girlfriends around?

In the second part, observe yourself and your peers, friends, and family. See if anyone you know uses force to get what they want. See if you can figure out what they, or you, could have done instead. Write it down." Remind the students that the group's purpose is to help them learn how to problem-solve anger situations, and how to come to agreements calmly and rationally. This assignment will give them the chance to apply what they have learned.

Wrapping Up

CENTERING EXERCISE

Settle the students and then repeat "The Pyramid" (page 136).

AFFIRMATION

Involve the group in an affirmation. Stand and join in a circle with the students, holding hands. Go around and have the students share something they learned in today's session. Begin the affirmation yourself: "One thing I learned in today's session is. . . ."

CLOSING

Remain standing in a circle with the students holding hands and lead the group in the closing activity.

Tell the students that you're going to make a silent wish for the student on your right. Then when you've made the wish, gently squeeze the student's hand. The student makes a silent wish for the person on his or her right, then gently squeezes the student's hand, and so on. Continue around the circle until a wish and squeeze come back to you. If necessary, the students can pass the wish in any appropriate way they choose.

Collect the folders. Fill out a copy of the Process and Progress Form (see page 211) or the Progress Notes (see page 213), if you are an experienced leader, as soon as possible after leading the group.

Family Violence

1. Family violence does exist. One study estimates that one in 22 women is physically abused by a husband or boyfriend each year. The average battered wife is attacked three times each year. According to the FBI, in 1991 almost half of the murder victims were either related to or acquainted with their assailants.

2. Family violence may be expressive or instrumental.

3. Men administer the majority of family violence. According to the FBI, among all female murder victims in 1991, 28 percent were killed by husbands or boyfriends, while only 4 percent of the male victims were killed by wives or girlfriends.

4. Studies have shown that the police and courts have generally not treated violent acts that occur in homes as serious crimes.

5. Researchers have found that family violence is more likely to occur at certain times of the day and year and in certain locations in the home.

6. Family violence takes many forms, including spanking; yelling and screaming; slapping, kicking, punching, and choking; and using weapons. Some researchers believe that family violence progresses through stages. Acts of violence become increasingly harmful and more frequent. Families differ on their attitudes toward violence.

7. In the history of the Western world, wife battering and child abuse have generally been culturally accepted. In many instances, battering has even been legally approved. Only in the past 100 years have society's attitudes begun to change. In the United States, a husband no longer has the legal right to batter his wife. Although wife battering and child abuse now receive much attention, the problem continues.

8. Some male batterers tend to become violent not only with women but also with children, animals, and physical objects. One study found that the most severe violence is administered by men who feel their actions are justified and who feel no remorse for their actions.

9. Battered women stay in the violent relationship not because they like to be hurt but because they are financially dependent or their male partners have used force or the threat of force to make them stay.

10. Children and adolescents who grow up in violent families are likely to experience severe personal and social problems. Learning coping strategies can help these young people survive emotionally and grow up to be healthy.

11. Several theories attempt to explain the causes of family violence. These theories include the idea that aggression is a normal instinct for men, that violence is a learned behavior, that certain groups condone and encourage violence, and that violence or the threat of violence is necessary to maintain order in families and society.

Range of Family Violence

Study the range of family violence. If you can think of other examples of family violence, write them in the space below. If you think the acts of violence should be in a different order, rewrite them in the space below.

0 Not violent at all, talking the problem over calmly

1 Disciplining child by spanking with an open palm

2 Yelling and screaming

3 Name calling and put downs

4 Slapping with an open palm

5 Throwing things; destruction of furniture; injuring pets

6 Discipline of child by beating with a belt, extension cord, or switch; punching spouse and leaving bruises

7 Sexual abuse of children

8 Repeated acts of slapping, kicking, punching, or choking and leaving broken arms, black eyes, etc.

9 Use of a weapon, such as a knife or gun

10 Extreme violence, resulting in death

_____

_____

_____

_____

_____

_____

_____

_____

_____

_____

_____

_____

_____

_____

_____

_____

_____

_____

Scenarios

Scenario 1

Dennis, age 8, is generally well behaved, but sometimes he gets into trouble. One day, he starts hammering a table at home. He hammers so hard that he makes big dents in it. Dennis' mother finds out that he has ruined the table, and she spanks him.

Scenario 2

One day Dennis is walking down the street. He accidentally bumps into a woman who is passing by him. She stops him and starts to spank him.

Scenario 3

Larry, age 35, works in a factory. He is married to Karen, a 30-year-old woman who manages the deli at the local grocery store. Larry is very jealous of Karen. He is always telling her what clothing to wear. He gets angry with her when she puts on makeup. He always wants to know what she does on her time off from work and gets angry when she talks on the phone with her friends. Last week, he hit her in the face and gave her a black eye. He was angry because he didn't like her new sweater. He thought it was too tight.

Scenario 4

Charlene's parents lose their tempers a lot. Her father is always cursing and yelling at everybody. Her mother lets her little brother get away with everything. Charlene gets really upset when her mother buys things for her little brother and doesn't even take Charlene to the mall to look around. She yells at her mother a lot. When Charlene gets really angry, she goes to her room, slams her door, and starts throwing things. Last week, when she was having a fight with her mother, her mother came into the bathroom and hit Charlene on her back three times. Charlene was holding onto her hairbrush so hard that she broke it, and then her mother got mad about that. Charlene had to control herself so she wouldn't hit her mother with the hairbrush.

Scenario 5

Tom is a high school student who has a chip on his shoulder. He's always getting into somebody's face and is constantly in the principal's office for fighting. Tom's mother was severely battered by her boyfriend, and he saw her getting beaten up many times when he was a child. Later, when he was a teenager, his stepfather shot her to death. When Tom gets angry, he likes to hurt other people. He's planning to beat up one of his teachers. The teacher gave Tom an F on a test because he thought Tom was cheating, when Tom wasn't.

There are two parts to this assignment. In the first part, write down your values regarding the use of force in families.

• Do you think spanking is okay?
• Do you think it's okay for parents to use force to get children to do things?
• Do you think it's okay for husbands and wives to use force with each other?
• Do you think it's okay for teenage boys to push their girlfriends around?

_____

_____

_____

_____

In the second part, observe yourself and your peers, friends, and family. See if anyone you know uses force to get what they want. See if you can figure out what they, or you, could have done instead. Write it down.

Day one

Day two

Day three

Day four

Day five

Day six

Day seven

Other comments and observations

The Effects of Violence on Families: Family Sculptures

Objectives

To help the students:

- learn that teens can't cause, change, or control their parents' use of violence to express anger

- discover four things teens in violent families can do to take care of themselves

- become aware of survival roles, intermittent reinforcement, enmeshment, boundaries, closed family systems, and enabling

Session at a Glance

1. Group Rules: review—1 minute

2. Centering Exercise: "The Meadow"— 3 minutes

3. Feelings Check-in: look at Feeling Wheel— 4 minutes

4. Basic Facts Review—4 minutes

5. Assignment Review—4 minutes

6. Mini-lecture, Family Sculptures, and Discussion—18 minutes

7. Activity: identify key terms from the family sculptures—2 minutes

8. Basic Facts: read Basic Facts 17 and 18; discuss—2 minutes

9. Assignment—1 minute

10. Centering Exercise: "The Meadow"— 3 minutes

11. Affirmation: share one thing you will remember from today's session—2 minutes

12. Closing: pass a silent wish—1 minute

Preparation

- Display the posterboard copy of the group rules.

- Have posters with Basic Facts 1-16 available. (Or the List of Basic Facts or the index cards.)

- Add the following materials to each folder:

    —Handout 7A ("Survival Roles")

    —Handout 7B ("Sculptures of Violent Families")

    —Assignment 7

- Have pencils, crayons or markers, and the folder ready at each student's place.

- Copy the three Cs (Basic Fact 17) and the four steps (Basic Fact 18) onto posterboard or newsprint to display during the session. Save these posters to use again should you decide to do Session 10.

- Have chalkboard and chalk or newsprint and a marker available.

- Have a hat for the family sculptures.

- Read through the session plan before meeting.

Background and Guidelines

THE THREE Cs AND THE FOUR STEPS

Because children don't possess the knowledge and perspective necessary to correctly identify the stresses in their family, they often try to create order out of the chaos that they do see. However, given their developmental levels, they generally do so in "childish," egocentric, and incorrect ways. Although adolescents are sometimes able to correctly identify the family's problems, and are becoming less egocentric, they still hold onto the misconceptions typical of younger children.

For example, adolescents often believe that their families' problems are their fault, that they've *caused* a parent's violence: " My mom and dad fight because I'm always getting into trouble." Or some adolescents try to *control* parental violence. They may attempt to intervene and stop the parents from fighting, risking injury to themselves as well as becoming the target of parental violence. Adolescents may also try to control the parents by trying to be their therapist, telling them to stop fighting or to seek professional help. Unfortunately, although adolescents may believe that they have the power nec-

essary to insist that a parent get help, they can't have such power. Thus, when teens are unsuccessful in their controlling efforts, they feel like failures and suffer low self-esteem.

When adolescents believe that they've caused a parent's violence, they often think that they can *change* it as well. Adolescents may try to create change through a variety of means: by getting good grades in school, by doing all the chores around the home, or by finding another way to bring honor to the family such as by performing well in sports, dance, or art. Again, these efforts won't be effective, and again the teens will feel like failures.

Students who begin to trust and talk about family violence are beginning to get better. Group members often feel uncomfortable talking about parental violence, but as they talk and the group leader normalizes their feelings, they begin the process of accepting their situations and learning to cope with their feelings.

You can correct the teens' misconceptions by teaching them the three Cs: children (1) *don't cause,* (2) *can't control,* and (3) *can't change a parent's use of violence.* Since this will be new information for many of the students, they may resist it. While respecting the students' feelings and opinions, you should be ready to help them understand that they don't have the power to cause, control, or change parental behavior. Acknowledge to the students that it would be wonderful if children could control or change another person's behavior. Unfortunately, children don't have that kind of power. Point out that not even the spouse of a violent person has such power. Help the students see that no one can control anyone else's behavior. People who use violence to express anger will change their behavior only when they realize the severe consequences of such behavior and decide they want to change.

By teaching the students the three Cs, you will also help them deal with *codependence, detachment,* and *empowerment.* It's important that you understand how each affects the teens.

Codependence

Although the term *codependence* is not introduced to the students, the material is designed to help them learn alternatives to codependent behavior. A person's behavior may be described as *codependent* when (1) the person feels responsible for another's feelings, problems, or behavior; or (2) the person doesn't take action on his or her own behalf, but simply reacts to the behaviors or feelings of another. Codependent people may be very controlling of another, or they may worry so much about another that they don't pay attention to themselves, thus never fulfilling their own potential.

In Session 2, the students discovered that they can do things to take care of themselves, and that they are responsible for handling their own feelings. Knowing this is the first step to learning alternatives to codependent behavior. By now, the students should realize that they don't have to depend on someone else for their feelings, but that they can be responsible for themselves, can learn how to deal effectively with feelings, especially anger, and can choose to do things that they enjoy.

Detachment

Learning the three Cs also helps the students begin the *detachment* process. This doesn't mean that children cut themselves off from their parents. Rather, they give up believing that they are responsible for a parent's problem. The students discover that they can love and care for a parent and can express that love and concern without having to control a parent or fix a parent's problem.

Empowerment

Finally, the three Cs *empower* the students. They help the teens begin to turn their focus away from the family's problems and to train it on themselves in positive and healthy ways. The session introduces four steps the students can take to empower themselves.

The four steps teens can take if they live in a violent family are:

1. Find a safe place for themselves.

2. Ask an adult for help if the parents are out of control with their violence.

3. Learn to put thinking between their feeling and their behavior.

4. Choose to learn nonviolent ways to express their own feelings, and learn to use problem-solving skills in anger situations.

Since many students think that such empowerment is a form of selfishness, be ready to help them see the difference between selfishness and self-preservation. For example, you might ask a student to imagine that he or she is one of three people on an island, with only one piece of cake to eat. Eating the whole piece is selfishness; giving it to the other two people and having none yourself is being a martyr; dividing the cake into three pieces and claiming your share is self-preservation.

The students need to realize that self-preservation is a positive activity and means taking care of themselves in age-appropriate ways. The students can't do this if they're engaged in the futile and overwhelming task of trying to fix their parents' problems.

Finally, make sure the students clearly get the message that they should not try to protect a parent from the violence of another parent. Realize, however, that most of the students will not like this message. They will want to intervene: "Do you think I'm just going to sit there and watch him beat on Mom?" Gently acknowledge that many teens feel this way, but universalize that children, even teenagers, can't protect parents. Strongly encourage the students to keep themselves safe and to ask an adult for help. It may be only after the students hear the facts in this session that they will begin to recognize the futility of trying to control parental violence.

FAMILY SCULPTURES

The heart of this session is five "family sculptures." The sculptures are a special type of role play. The students take the roles of family members: Dad, Mom, Sons, and Daughters. Another character, Violence, personifies the stress ever-present in the homes of at-risk families. You, as sculptor, position the students to illustrate patterns of behavior that families adopt to cope with stress. Your only prop—a hat—will indicate when the violent family member is calm and when the member is "exploding."

The family sculptures allow you to teach the students concepts such as survival roles and intermittent reinforcement, enmeshment, boundaries, closed family systems, and enabling in a vivid way. The sculptures, which were adapted from Rokelle Lerner, a therapist who has worked with children from alcoholic families, also apply to families affected by stresses arising from chemical dependence, divorce, and severe physical illness and to families that use other anger styles like stuffing, withdrawing, blaming, and triangling. Understanding more about each sculpture will help you explain the role playing to the students.

Violence

The first sculpture, *Violence*, shows how violent families tend to revolve around the person who has the violent behavior. The students recognize that one person—the violent family member—is controlling the behavior of other family members. When the behavior of the violent person changes, the behavior of the other family members changes as well. Children in such families often are not in control of their own behavior. Although the students can't control other family members—especially the violent member—they can learn skills to control themselves. They can learn to take action for themselves, rather than allowing themselves to be controlled (in feelings or behavior) by the family's violence.

SURVIVAL ROLES AND INTERMITTENT REINFORCEMENT

The *Violence* sculpture is used to introduce the behaviors adopted by children living in traumatic stress and first described in the chemical dependence literature. Children from families that use violence to express anger may experience traumatic shock as well as fear, anger, sadness, anxiety, loneliness, and hopelessness. They may take on "survival roles" in order to make life less painful. The roles typically described for children in a dysfunctional family are superhero, scapegoat, lost child, and clown.

Superheroes (or "overachievers" or "too-good-to-be-true" children) generally—and mistakenly—believe that if they are only good enough, or perfect enough, their families' problems will be solved. These children help out at home, get good grades, and try to be therapists to their parents. They do anything and everything they can to help parents solve their problems. These children live in the misconception that their behavior (if it's good enough) can control or cure parental behavior (get a parent to stop using violence). Superhero children generally end up feeling like failures because, no matter how good they are, their "perfect" behavior can never be good enough to make their parents stop fighting, using violence, or hurting as a result of violence.

Superheroes are outwardly successful. The family can point to them, feel proud, and say, "We're okay." Superheroes pay a price, however. Generally, they experience feelings of hurt, inadequacy, confusion, guilt, fear, and low self-esteem. Superheroes may become rigid and perfectionistic. They may overreact and become unduly upset over the slightest criticism from an authority figure (teacher, coach, clergy person). Superheroes seem able to do anything, except what they want to do most—make their family well.

Scapegoats tend to be the "lightning rods" for anger in a family. These children may act out their own anger by fighting or yelling at home or at school. They tend to get themselves in trouble and, in this way, draw the anger of the violent parent away from the spouse to themselves in a self-sacrificing rescue attempt. Scapegoats feel hurt and abandoned, angry and rejected, and totally inadequate; they possess little or no self-esteem.

Lost children may feel personally responsible for the parental chaos in a violent home. Rather than trying to control that chaos, however, lost children try becoming invisible. Invisible, they won't be held accountable for parental stress. These children might spend a lot of time by themselves, away from other family members, "lost" in their own worlds. They may become overeaters or underachievers in school, or they may become isolated and withdrawn, seeing themselves as alone, helpless, vulnerable, and powerless. Lost children give a family with violence some relief. Pointing to the quiet, lost child, a family can think that everything's all right in the family. On the inside, lost children feel unimportant, lonely, hurt, abandoned, fearful, and defeated.

Clowns provide comic relief for the family members by making them laugh. They focus attention away from the problem of the violent parent or deflect that violence through humor. These children generally see themselves as "jokes." Thus, they have low self-esteem and feel frightened, lonely, anxious, inadequate, and unimportant. Clowns may be diagnosed as having attention-deficit hyperactivity disorder, or they may have learning disabilities in school.

These survival roles aren't meant to be labels or rigid categories. In fact, children in violent families may exhibit characteristics of several different roles at the same time; or, over time, they may adopt different roles. For instance, a younger child who acts as a scapegoat may become a superhero after an older sibling (who has played the role) leaves home. Likewise, children from violent families may exhibit other traits that don't necessarily lend themselves to the roles identified here. These roles are stressed to alert you to behaviors typically found in children from troubled families, behaviors you might find in the members of your group.

In the sculpture, you coach the students to play a superhero, a scapegoat, a lost child, and a clown. Each role will be played twice. First, the violent father rewards the teen's behavior by staying calm. Then, the father responds to the teen's behavior by exploding. This is *intermittent reinforcement:* a pattern of rewarding behavior in sporadic, rather than consistent, ways. The teens are likely to continue their behavior in the hope that the dad will reward it by staying calm at least some of the time. Intermittent reinforcement explains why some teens, and adults, keep behaving in ways that appear self-defeating.

Enmeshment

The second sculpture, *Enmeshment,* shows extremely codependent behavior, where the family members assume responsibility for the feelings of the violent person or for other people in the family. The children are unable to set boundaries between themselves and their parents. For example, enmeshed children might assume parental feelings ("If Mom is sad, I must be sad too"). They might feel responsible for fixing parental problems ("I must try to do things to solve the problem or make my parents feel better"), or they might feel they have to conduct themselves in ways that will not disturb the violent person ("I can't ask for the car tonight or dad will explode").

Boundaries

Boundaries shows that when teens are enmeshed with one or both parents, they often fail to develop a separate identity, a sense of personal integrity, and the internal resources necessary to form relationships and to deal with life's stresses. To be healthy, teens must develop a sense of separateness and individuality that allows for closeness when needed. It is also healthy for teens to develop a sense of personal space and integrity that allows them to set limits in a relationship when they don't desire closeness. The kill-them-with-kindness sandwich, along with the three Cs and the four steps presented in this session, will help the students escape enmeshment, set appropriate boundaries, and learn to take care of themselves.

Scenarios accompany this sculpture that will help the students to set boundaries in situations they may face. Girls are coached to set limits in situations where their boyfriends are beginning to use violent behavior or want sexual activity. Boys are coached to set limits in situations where their friends are prodding them to engage in delinquent behavior.

Closed Family System

Closed Family System demonstrates a family trying to hide the violent behavior of the mother. To keep their dark secrets from being revealed, family members live by the rules "Don't talk; don't trust; don't feel." Students learn about these unwritten, unspoken rules in this sculpture. They also see the daughter in the family begin to break the rules: she talks about her family's problems. As teens open up about family problems, they feel embarrassment, guilt, shame, anger, rage, hurt, and fear. Remind the group members that although breaking the rules of the closed family system is uncomfortable, it's also the beginning of getting better. Teens who open up the closed family system by seeking help eventually will feel better because they're beginning to recognize, accept, and share their feelings.

Enabling

The final sculpture is *Enabling*. As you help the students present this sculpture, make the point that people who enable have positive motives—they want to keep the violent person calm, they want to protect the person, they want to preserve the family name. However, their rescuing behavior actually prevents the violent person from getting the help he or she needs. When family members stop enabling, the violent member will have to face the consequences of his or her behavior. This, in turn, increases the chances that the violent person will admit that he or she has a problem and will decide to get better.

The first time you conduct the family sculptures, follow the directions given. After you have led this session a few times, and are comfortable with the material, you can use your knowledge of the group members and the anger styles in their families to personalize these sculptures in an anonymous way. If the students want to, and if you feel comfortable, let them demonstrate what their own families would look like in a sculpture.

You may find that the students become quite involved in the family sculptures and that the sculptures take longer to perform than anticipated. In this case, you may split the session into two meeting times. Present the three Cs, the four steps, and the first sculpture (including the survival roles and intermittent reinforcement) in the first session. In the second week of the session, present the final four sculptures, the discussion questions, Handout 7B, and the basic facts. Use the same activities for beginning and wrapping up each session.

Beginning the Session

GROUP RULES

Welcome the students and begin with a quick review of the group rules. Draw attention to the poster listing the group rules. If you feel that it is necessary, call on different students to read them one at a time. Check for understanding before moving on.

CENTERING EXERCISE

Lead the students in a new centering exercise, "The Meadow."

THE MEADOW

Imagine that it's the month of April. You're in a meadow of soft green grass. The meadow is surrounded by beautiful dogwood trees—so full that the blossoms look like a snowfall. You can smell the fresh scent of spring in the air, and the smell of new spring

Exercise continued on next page.

Exercise continued from previous page.

grass. The sky above is bright blue and dotted with white fluffy clouds. You are there with a very good friend—somebody you really trust, like a mom or dad, a best friend, or maybe someone you were once close to who has died, like a grandparent or an aunt or uncle. You feel very safe and secure with this friend.

You begin to experience a difficult feeling—anger or sadness or even fear. Imagine that you are experiencing anger right now. Think of something that has happened that has made you very angry. Maybe you even feel rage. Your body feels angry: maybe your muscles are tight, or maybe you feel very hot. You tell your friend how angry you are. Your friend is so understanding that it's okay for you to be very angry, and you know that you will be safe. You feel so safe that you beat the ground with your fists. Eventually, you don't feel so angry.

Now, imagine that you are feeling sad. Imagine some losses that you have had. Maybe someone close to you has died; maybe your parents split up; maybe your best friend has moved away. Maybe you feel so sad that it feels like grief. You trust your friend so much that you feel safe to talk about your loss. Your friend doesn't tell you to get over it—doesn't tell you not to feel that way. Instead, your friend listens and understands how hard it is for you. You feel so safe that you can cry, maybe even sob, with your friend. After you have cried for a while, you don't feel quite so sad.

Now, imagine that you are feeling some fear. Maybe your parents are getting a separation. Maybe you're afraid there will be severe violence in your family. Maybe someone close to you has a serious illness. Maybe you're worried about the future for yourself. You tell your friend how scared you are, and even that you feel some panic. You may even begin to shake you're so scared. Your friend helps you stay grounded during this period of panic, and helps you remember that it's okay to feel this panic, but that it will pass. In a little while, the intense panic does pass.

After you've finished telling your friend about the feeling, experienced it in your body, and maybe even pounded, cried, or shook, you begin to feel better. You experience a sense of release, a calmness and peacefulness you haven't felt for a long time. You begin to be aware of the meadow again. It's as if you're seeing the dogwoods, the sky, and the clouds for the first time. You feel a sense of thanks and appreciation for the beauty of the surroundings, and for your friend. You again feel in control, calm and peaceful.

FEELINGS CHECK-IN

Do a feelings check-in with the students. Have them take out their Feeling Wheels. Ask the group members to decide how they are feeling today. Remind the students that if they want, they can color in the section on the Feeling Wheel that describes how they're feeling today. Also remind the teens that they might have more than one feeling, since it's possible to have more than one feeling at a time. Tell the students that if they're having a feeling not named on the wheel, they can add a bubble to the outside of the wheel and name their feeling.

When the students finish, have a go-around. Begin by sharing your own feelings. Then, invite each student to share his or her feelings. Teenagers often list many feelings. For the interests of time, ask them to name the feelings they have, but then pick only two to discuss. Be sure to accept each student's feeling(s) and to affirm each student. Ask the students to return the wheels to their folders.

BASIC FACTS REVIEW

Review the basic facts learned so far. Use posters with Basic Facts 1-16, the List of Basic Facts, or index cards.

In a go-around, ask a student to read Basic Fact 1 aloud and to explain what it means. If the student has trouble explaining the fact, don't contradict or judge, simply clarify his or her explanation. Repeat the procedure for the next basic fact. This review ensures that the students understand and integrate the basic facts that have been taught. It is also easy preparation for the presentation and provides a lead-in for the session material.

ASSIGNMENT REVIEW

Ask the students if they brought their assignments from last week. Remind them that they were to write down their values about family violence, by answering the following questions:

- Do you think spanking is okay?

- Do you think it's okay for parents to use force to get children to do things?

- Do you think it's okay for husbands and wives to use force with each other?

- Do you think it's okay for teenage boys to push their girlfriends around?

Have a go-around so the students can share their values.

In the second part of the assignment, the students observed themselves and their peers, friends, and families to see if anyone uses force to get what they want, and to figure out what else they could have done. In another go-around, ask the students what they observed. If the students forgot to do the assignment, ask if they can think of someone who uses force and what problem-solving skills that person could use instead.

Exploring the Material

MINI-LECTURE
The Three Cs and the Four Steps

To begin, point out that children who live in violent families may have special problems. They may have difficulty being close to others or being able to regulate their emotions. They may not have a realistic sense of themselves as independent and competent. They may be aggressive or withdraw in peer relationships, and they may have problems adapting in school, either socially or academically.

Explain that some adolescents assume parenting roles in the family, especially if the mother is the victim of violence and unable to fulfill her responsibilities. These teens may take over household chores and may try to intervene to protect the victim and other siblings. They risk

injury themselves and are rarely effective, often feeling like failures when the violence continues. Some teens run away to avoid family violence; others act out in delinquent behavior. Some adolescent boys imitate their father's behavior by assaulting their mother or siblings. Some adolescent girls may start to accept threats and violence from their boyfriends, who may be trying to control them.

Point out that even children living in a family where the parents use anger styles like stuffing, withdrawing, blaming, or triangling may feel guilty and responsible. They may feel like failures, may feel hurt, and may experience great anger. They often think the family's tension, anger, and discord are their fault.

Tell the students that teens living in such families need to learn the three Cs. The three Cs are written about parents who use violence, but they apply equally to any style of anger that the parent chooses.

Display the poster with the three Cs. Read through the steps and explain each one.

The Three Cs

1. Teens don't **cause** their parents to use violence to express anger. Teens can do things that make parents angry, but it's the parent's choice to stuff, withdraw, blame, triangle, explode, or problem-solve.

2. Teens can't **control** how their parents express anger. Parents who choose violence will be violent even if the teens try to calm them down or intervene in the fight. The teens may get hurt, and they often feel like failures because they can't succeed in the control efforts. Only the parent can control the parent's behavior.

3. Teens can't **change** their parent's use of violence to express anger. Teens can give consequences in the form of I statements, such as "I get scared when you fight. I'm afraid you're going to get a divorce. I'm angry that you can't solve your problems." But only parents can change their behavior.

Tell the students that since teens can't change their parents' choice to use violence to express anger, they can take some steps for themselves. Display the poster with the four steps and read each one.

The Four Steps

The four steps teens can take if they live in a violent family are:

1. Find a safe place for themselves.

2. Ask an adult for help if the parents are out of control with their violence.

3. Learn to put thinking between their feeling and their behavior.

4. Choose to learn nonviolent ways to express their own feelings, and learn to use problem-solving skills in anger situations.

Family Sculptures

Note that living in a family where the parents use anger styles like stuffing, withdrawing, blaming, triangling, or exploding can present some special challenges. Families sometimes develop patterns of behavior to cope with the stresses or challenges. Tell the students that you will help them form five family sculptures to demonstrate these patterns. Ask all the group members to take one of the following roles: Mom, Dad, Daughter, Son, and Violence; add as many Daughters and Sons as necessary. Point out that Violence represents the stress caused by the aggressive family member, but it could also represent the stress caused by chemical dependence, physical or mental illness, or divorce. As the students role-play the sculptures detailed below, write the titles on the chalkboard or newsprint.

SCULPTURE 1: VIOLENCE

Have Dad and Violence stand close, facing each other. Have Mom, the Daughters, and the Sons form a circle around Dad and Violence. Then ask them to revolve around Dad and Violence. Coach Dad and Violence to move across the room, back and forth, and have the family

members, still in a circle, allow themselves to be dragged along. Ask the students if they think this is a child-centered family. (It is not.) Point out that Dad is focused on Violence and his family is focused on them both. Explain that this is a sculpture of violence. Place a hat on Dad. Say, "Sometimes everything seems okay, and Dad acts normal. He helps the kids with their school projects and drives them to football and softball practice." Go on to say, "But sometimes when the kids come home from a game, if the parents are fighting, it's as if a volcano is exploding." (Take the hat off dramatically.)

SURVIVAL ROLES AND INTERMITTENT REINFORCEMENT

Point out that the people in the family are probably afraid of Dad and try to keep him calm so he won't explode. Ask the group members playing the children how they might try to keep Dad from exploding. Accept all replies. Point out that in many troubled families, the children adopt ways of behaving that have been called survival roles.

Four roles have been identified: Superheroes, Scapegoats, Lost Children, and Clowns. Have the students find Handout 7A ("Survival Roles") in their folders and quickly read the descriptions.

Superheroes. Tell the students that one of the teenagers may get good grades and do chores around the house, like mowing the lawn. Teens who try to be perfect are sometimes called Superheroes. Ask which group member wants to be the Superhero, and then have him or her stand next to Dad. Ask the Superhero what he or she will do to please Dad and to keep him calm. After the Superhero acts out a solution, put the hat on Dad, and say, "Sometimes Dad will be pleased and compliment the Superhero and even spend time with him or her." Ask the student what else the Superhero would do, and have the student act it out. This time, coach the Dad to explode. Take the hat off. Say, "But sometimes Dad might be in a bad mood and explode about the chores not being done well enough or the grades not being all A pluses."

Scapegoats. Tell the students that another role is that of the Scapegoat. Teens might get themselves in a lot of trouble so that their parents will forget about being angry with each other and be angry at their son or daughter instead. The Scapegoat takes the blame for the family's anger. Ask who would like to play the Scapegoat and what kind of trouble the student would like to get into. Coach Mom and Dad to respond appropriately when the teen gets into trouble by coming to school and by stopping their fighting with each other. (Put the hat on Dad.) Ask the student what else the Scapegoat might do. This time, have Mom and Dad ignore the Scapegoat and continue to fight with each other (explode the hat off) and maybe even fight with the teenager.

Lost children. Say that other teens in violent families might isolate themselves, spending most of their time in their bedroom by themselves, sometimes overeating. They may be trying to avoid causing any trouble, as well as trying to avoid the fighting. A teen who isolates himself or herself is called the Lost Child. Ask for a Lost Child, and have the student "hide" in his or her room. Coach Mom and Dad to be quietly doing what they usually do; Dad will have his hat on. Then have the Lost Child come home from school and go to his or her room. This time, coach Mom and Dad to start a fight, and explode the hat off Dad.

Clowns. Tell the students that other teens might try to keep everybody in the family happy by telling jokes or acting crazy. These teens are called the family Clown. Ask for a volunteer to play the Clown, and have the student act out what he or she would like to do. Coach the parents to respond appropriately and to laugh. Ask the Clown to do something else, and this time coach Dad to explode.

Point out that the efforts of the Superhero, Scapegoat, Lost Child, or Clown to get the Dad to stop the violent behavior sometimes seem to work. But other times they don't work at all. Sometimes Dad will react by being pleasant, or nonviolent, and sometimes he won't. This is called intermittent reinforcement. When behavior is rewarded by intermittent reinforcement, it is usually hard to extinguish. For instance, the Superhero will continue to struggle to be perfect, even if it doesn't work every time, because the next time might be the time it will work. Children of troubled parents often act in a self-defeating way, as long as it sometimes get their Dad to calm down or their Mom to smile. For the Scapegoat, the attention might be negative, but for some teens negative attention is better than none.

Emphasize that these roles are not necessarily rigid. Say that sometimes teens show behavior common to all of these roles. Also point out that some of these behaviors may not be completely harmful. It's okay to try to get good grades, if you're doing it for yourself. But if you get A's to try to get a parent to stop violent behavior, you'll never succeed, and you'll always feel like a failure. Humor is an important skill to develop; but you have to be serious some of the time.

SCULPTURE 2: ENMESHMENT

Ask everyone to form a line in this order: Dad, Violence, Mom, Daughters, Sons. Have everyone link arms closely. Take Dad's arm, and move him, and everyone else, in one direction. Say, "This violent family is so tightly connected to Dad and his violent behavior, that when Dad feels happy, the whole family feels happy." Move the line in the other direction. Say, "When Dad feels angry, the whole family feels angry." Move the line back again. "When Dad has a headache, the whole family takes aspirin." Tell the group that what's happening here is called enmeshment, when all the people in the violent family take on Dad's moods.

SCULPTURE 3: BOUNDARIES

Tell the students that in this family Dad is violent. One of the daughters feels very close to Mom and very protective of her. Have Mom and Daughter stand next to one another and lock arms tightly. Point out how close the two are. Say, "Can you tell where Mom ends and Daughter begins? No, you can't tell, and sometimes neither can they." Help the group see that a teenager who has no boundaries has little sense of who he or she is, that is, as a separate person from Mom. When Dad puts down and hits Mom, Daughter feels like it's happening to her. She believes that what Dad says about Mom is true for her too. Thus, Daughter will not have much self-worth and might get into trouble because she can't say no to others. So she could easily allow herself to be abused or to be talked into cheating at school, or shoplifting, or using alcohol or other drugs.

Explain to the group that one of their tasks as adolescents is to develop a sense of identity, of knowing who they are, what their values are, and how they want to live. Another way to think of boundaries is to think of a sense of personal space. Most people like to have their own space and to know that other people won't come into their space if we don't want them to. This is a boundary. Now have two students stand at opposite sides of the room. Tell them that you will walk toward each, one at a time. Explain that they may call out "Stop!" when you get too close. Walk toward one and stop when told. Ask the student how he or she knew to say stop. Accept the student's reply. Repeat for the other student. Point out that people have their own sense of territory and personal space, their boundaries.

Then tell the students that sometimes boundaries can change, depending on the emotion of the approaching person. Tell the students that you're going to approach them, and they can say stop whenever they want. Put an angry look on your face and walk toward the student saying how angry you feel. Stop when told. Ask the student how they knew when to say stop. Repeat with the other student. Then announce that you'll try it again. This time, put a sad look on your face, and turn and walk toward the other student while describing how sad you feel. Stop when told. Ask the student how he or she knew when to say stop. Point out that boundaries are something that are very individual and can depend on a person's emotions. Usually people want more space if someone approaching

them seems angry, but often they're willing to let a sad person come a little closer. Some people are willing to let the angry person get right in their face, but they want the sad person to stay far away.

Point out that some teenagers who live in violent families don't have a clear sense of their own boundaries. They don't realize that they can set limits. Tell the students that they will act out three different situations in which teens can set boundaries. The concept of boundaries can help teenage girls realize that they have the right not to allow even minor incidents of violence in their relationships. They also have the right to set limits regarding sexual activity so they don't go further than they want to or are ready to. Teenage boys need to understand the concept of boundaries so they can say no to friends who might be prodding them to do something they really don't want to do, whether it is vandalism or using alcohol or other drugs. Point out that kill-them-with-kindness sandwiches are effective ways to set boundaries.

Minor Violence. Ask a boy and a girl to act out a scene between a teenage girl and her boyfriend. Have the boy push the girl against the wall. Coach the girl to say to him: "I really like you, and I'm glad we're dating. But I need to let you know that it's not okay for you to push me against the wall when you get angry. I'm not going to allow violence, no matter how small, in any relationship that I'm in. We're going to have to find some other way to solve our problems besides you pushing me. I hope we can because I really enjoy spending time with you."

Remind the students that they learned last week that domestic violence often starts with very minor incidents, sometimes with the man being controlling, jealous, and possessive. The violence becomes more severe and more frequent. Also remind them that one major way of stopping the man's violence is for the woman to set calm, rational, but very firm, limits with conviction and determination that violence will not be part of their relationship.

Sexual Limits. Ask another boy and girl to role-play this scenario. Set up a situation where the boy is saying, "Come on, let's do it. You would if you really loved me." Coach the girl to say to him: "I really care about you, but I don't want to make love to you right now. I'm just not ready for that. But I would like to keep going out with you."

Turning Friends Down. Ask several boys to role-play this scenario. Set up a situation where a boy's friends are encouraging him to join them in delinquent behavior. Have the boy say to his friends: "I really like having you guys for friends, and I like hanging around together. But, I just can't go around breaking windows with you. With my luck we'd be caught, and then I'd have to spend the rest of my life mowing lawns to pay it off. Why don't we shoot baskets instead?"

SCULPTURE 4: CLOSED FAMILY SYSTEM

Say that in this sculpture Mom is violent with one Daughter. Have Dad, Sons, and the other Daughters link arms to form a tight circle around Mom, Violence, and Daughter. Then ask them to move slowly around in a circle. Have Mom pretend to slap Daughter. Explain that this family has many secrets. The family members must stay very close together so the secrets don't get out.

Ask the group:

• **Is this family going to let any outsiders in?** (No.)

• **Will Daughter be able to go to school and tell what her mother does?** (No.)

• **Suppose the parents are fighting so much that they break promises they make to the children. Are these children going to trust what their parents say?** (No.)

• **Suppose the children in this family tell the parents that they're scared that there's going to be a divorce, or that they're angry because the parents are always fighting. Do you think these parents are going to be able to accept their feelings?** (No.)

Point out that the children learn "don't talk, don't trust, and don't feel." These are unwritten rules in some violent families.

Now pull the Daughter out of the circle and say, "Daughter begins to talk to the people at school about what's going on at home. She feels conflicted, uncomfortable, and guilty because she is breaking the family rules. But breaking the family rules of don't talk, don't trust, don't feel is the only way she can take care of herself and start to get better."

SCULPTURE 5: ENABLING

Have Mom and the Sons and Daughters form a tight V, with Mom at the center or point of the V and the children on either side. Say, "This family loves Dad and tries to help him. When Dad is violent (explode the hat off Dad), the family members rescue him. Here's an example: Dad gives Mom a black eye. Mom doesn't tell anybody and stays in the house for a few days, until the swelling goes down." Ask Dad to stand with his back to the opening of the tight V. (Caution Mom and the children to be ready to catch Dad.) Then have Violence gently push Dad so that he falls back into the V, where the family will catch him. Say, "Mom rescues Dad by letting him get away with hitting. She doesn't call the police; she doesn't tell her family or his family; she gives no consequences, and she puts up with his inappropriate behavior. She may put up with his hitting her not because she likes it, but because she has no money, no job, and nowhere to go. She feels powerless."

Explain to the group that every time Dad is violent and the family members don't tell anyone, they are catching or rescuing him. Ask the students, "Is Dad ever going to change his violent behavior if the family keeps on catching him?" (No.) Tell the students that rescuing behavior like this is called enabling. Enabling means protecting someone from the consequences of his or her actions. Dad won't change his violent behavior until his family stops catching him, and he "falls" and hits the ground and experiences some pain. We call this consequences. People who protect their friends from the consequences of their behavior, like drinking or vandalism, are enabling.

When all the sculptures have been formed thank the students for their role-playing work.

DISCUSSION

Use questions such as these to check the students' understanding.

- **What are the survival roles?** (Four survival roles have been described: superhero, scapegoat, lost child, and clown. Children sometimes adopt these behaviors in order to survive in a troubled family; sometimes they adopt these behaviors to help the family get better.)

- **What is intermittent reinforcement?** (Sporadic, inconsistent rewarding of behavior. Sometimes parents will respond calmly and rationally to their child's behavior; other times they will respond violently and explosively to the same behavior. Children will keep on acting in a way that may not really help them, as long as it will sometimes get their violent parent to stop being violent.)

- **What is enmeshment?** (Feeling so close to someone else that you don't know where the other person ends and you begin. Children enmeshed with parents might assume parental feelings and try to solve parents' problems.)

- **What are boundaries?** (Having an identity of your own and being able to keep people away or to let them in.)

- **Do children who are enmeshed or overly close to parents have a good sense of boundaries?** (No, they usually don't see themselves as separate or complete, and they often have a hard time saying no.)

- **Is it good to have boundaries?** (Yes, teens need to be able to decide if they want people to come in close or stay away. Teens also need to respect other people's boundaries.)

- **What is a kill-them-with-kindness sandwich?** (A good, polite way to set limits or boundaries. You say something nice, set the boundary or limit, and say something nice again. For example: "I really care for you, but I don't want to make love to anybody right now. But I do want to keep on dating you.")

- **What is a closed family system?** (A closed family system enforces the rules "Don't talk; don't trust; don't feel.")

- **How do children feel when they begin to break these rules?** (They often feel uncomfortable, anxious, or guilty. But breaking these rules helps children get better. Eventually, the children will feel better as they begin to talk about their problems, trust a little at a time, and learn to recognize, accept, and share their feelings.)

- **What is enabling?** (Rescuing people from the consequences of their behavior.)

- **Will violent people change their behavior if they are rescued all the time?** (Probably not. They need to experience the consequences of what they're doing before they can admit they have a problem and decide they want to get better.)

Even if you decide not to use the suggested questions, make sure that you highlight these concepts and that the students are comfortable with them.

ACTIVITY

Have the students take Handout 7B ("Sculptures of Violent Families") from their folders. Explain that the purpose of this handout is to review terms introduced in the family sculptures. Have the students read each description and write in the correct term. You may have the students complete the handout individually, or you may complete it as a group. (Answers: 1. closed family system, 2. enmeshment, 3. survival roles, 4. enabling, 5. consequences, 6. violence, 7. lack of boundaries, 8. intermittent reinforcement.)

BASIC FACTS

Review the new basic facts for this session. Refer the students to the List of Basic Facts. Ask two group members to read Basic Facts 17 and 18.

17. The three Cs are:

    1. Teens don't **cause** their parents to use violence to express anger.

    2. Teens can't **control** how their parents express anger.

    3. Teens can't **change** their parents' use of violence to express anger.

18. The four steps teens can take if they live in a violent family are:

    1. Find a safe place for themselves.

    2. Ask an adult for help if the parents are out of control with their violence.

    3. Learn to put thinking between their feeling and their behavior.

    4. Choose to learn nonviolent ways to express their own feelings, and learn to use problem-solving skills in anger situations.

Briefly discuss each fact, checking for understanding.

ASSIGNMENT

Have the group members take Assignment 7 out of their folders. Read the directions: "Each day this week observe yourself, your family members, and your friends. Each day look for an example of one of the family patterns described today: violence; the survival roles of superhero, scapegoat, lost child, or clown; intermittent reinforcement; enmeshment; boundaries; a closed family system; or enabling. Write down what you observe." Tell the students that this assignment will help them become aware of patterns many families have.

Wrapping Up

CENTERING EXERCISE

Settle the students and then repeat "The Meadow" (page 154).

AFFIRMATION

Involve the group in an affirmation. Stand and join in a circle with the students, holding hands. Go around and have each student share something that he or she will remember from today's session. Start the affirmation yourself: "One fact or idea that I'll remember from today is. . . ."

CLOSING

Remain standing in a circle with the students, holding hands, and lead the group in the closing activity. Tell the students that you're going to make a silent wish for the student on your right. Then, when you've made the wish, gently squeeze the student's hand. The student makes a silent wish for the person on his or her right, then gently squeezes that student's hand, and so on. Continue around the circle until a wish and squeeze come back to you. If necessary, the students can pass the wish in any appropriate way they choose.

Collect the folders. Fill out a copy of the Process and Progress Form (page 211) or the Progress Notes (page 213), if you are an experienced leader, as soon as possible after leading the group.

Survival Roles

Children from families that use violence to express anger may experience traumatic shock as well as fear, anger, sadness, anxiety, loneliness, and hopelessness. They may take on "survival roles" to make life less painful. These survival roles are superhero, scapegoat, lost child, and clown.

Superheroes

Superheroes are sometimes called "overachievers" or "too-good-to-be-true children." They believe that if they are only good enough, or perfect enough, their families' problems will be solved. These children help out at home, get good grades, and try to be therapists to their parents. Superheroes are outwardly successful. The family can point to them, feel proud, and say, "We're okay." Superhero children, however, generally end up feeling like failures because, no matter how good they are, their "perfect" behavior can never be good enough to make their parents stop fighting, using violence, or hurting as a result of violence. Superheroes may become rigid and perfectionistic and overreact to the slightest criticism from an authority figure.

Scapegoats

Scapegoats try to take the blame for the family's anger. These children may act out their own anger by fighting or yelling at home or at school. They tend to get themselves in trouble, and, in this way, draw the anger of the violent parent away from the spouse to themselves. They sacrifice themselves in an attempt to save the abused parent. Scapegoats feel hurt and abandoned, angry and rejected, and totally inadequate; they possess little or no self-esteem.

Lost Children

Lost children may feel personally responsible for the parental chaos in a violent home. Rather than trying to control that chaos, however, lost children try becoming invisible. Invisible, they won't be held accountable for parental stress. These children might spend a lot of time by themselves, away from other family members, "lost" in their own worlds. They may become overeaters or underachievers in school. Lost children give a family with violence some relief. Pointing to the quiet, lost child, a family can think that everything's all right. On the inside, lost children feel unimportant, lonely, hurt, abandoned, fearful, and defeated.

Clowns

Clowns provide comic relief for the family. They try to make the family forget about the violence by making jokes and doing funny things. They might even make fun of themselves. Clowns focus attention away from the problem of the violent parent, or deflect that violence, through humor. These children generally see themselves as "jokes." Thus, they have low self-esteem and feel frightened, lonely, anxious, inadequate, and unimportant. Family clowns may have learning disabilities in school, or they may have difficulty paying attention in class.

Sculptures of Violent Families

Read each description of something that might happen in violent families. Use one of the following terms to identify what is happening: violence, survival roles, intermittent reinforcement, enmeshment, lack of boundaries, closed family system, enabling, consequences. Write the term on the line provided.

1. This family looks like a tiny, tight football huddle or a circle guarding some dark secret inside.

_____

_____

2. The people in this family are so tightly connected to the violent dad and his behavior that when he feels happy, they all feel happy. When he feels angry, they all feel angry. When he has a headache, they all take aspirin.

_____

_____

3. Some teens try to be perfect; some act out; some go to their room and hide; some act like clowns.

_____

_____

4. This family does everything it can to make sure its "exploding" parent doesn't slip up and have to face the consequences.

_____

_____

5. The police arrest the dad in this family for severely beating the mom.

_____

_____

6. Everyone in the family is focused on one person who uses violence when angry. Sometimes that person "explodes" or blows his or her "stack."

_____

_____

7. The mom and the child in this family are so close together, you can't tell where one ends and the other begins.

_____

_____

8. Sometimes the parent seems calm because of the teen's behavior; sometimes the parent explodes anyway.

_____

_____

Each day this week observe yourself, your family members, and your friends. Each day look for an example of one of the family patterns described today:

- violence
- the survival roles of superhero, scapegoat, lost child, or clown
- intermittent reinforcement
- enmeshment
- boundaries
- a closed family system
- enabling

Write down what you observe.

Day one

Day five

Day two

Day six

Day three

Day seven

Day four

Other comments and observations

Coping Strategies

Objectives

To help the students:

• discover 10 rules for developing coping strategies

• draw on the facts they've learned to help them cope in stressful situations

• understand that they can't fix their parents' problems, but they can take care of themselves

Session at a Glance

1. Group Rules: review if necessary—1 minute

2. Centering Exercise: "The Waterfall"— 3 minutes

3. Feelings Check-in: look at Feelings Wheel— 5 minutes

4. Basic Facts Review—6 minutes

5. Assignment Review—4 minutes

6. Mini-lecture and Discussion—8 minutes

7. Activity: discuss coping strategies and write one of your own—8 minutes

8. Basic Facts: read Basic Facts 19 and 20; discuss—2 minutes

9. Assignment—1 minute

10. Centering Exercise: repeat "The Waterfall"—3 minutes

11. Affirmation: share coping strategies— 3 minutes

12. Closing: pass a silent wish—1 minute

Preparation

• Display the posterboard copy of the group rules.

• Have posters with Basic Facts 1-18 available. (Or the List of Basic Facts, or index cards with a basic fact on each one.)

• Add the following materials to each folder:

—Handout 8A ("Rules for Relationships")

—Handout 8B ("Coping-Strategy Scenarios")

—Assignment 8.

- Have pencil, crayons or markers, and the folder ready at each student's place.

- Read through the session plan before meeting.

Background and Guidelines

One of the most difficult issues for students from at-risk families is learning to accept their inability to solve their families' problems—namely, to stop a parental divorce, a parent's chemical dependence, a parent's use of violence to express anger. Group leaders like you also face this problem. You cannot solve the students' family problems or the problems of the students themselves. Accepting this is the beginning of detachment (see Background and Guidelines for Session 7).

In this session, the students begin to own the concepts and facts they've learned in previous sessions, and begin to apply them to their lives. They will use the three Cs and the four steps in this session, as well as their problem-solving skills. You will need to draw on your understanding of codependence, detachment, and empowerment to help the students.

In this session, the students also draw on 10 simple rules for maintaining healthy relationships to help them own and apply the concepts and facts they've learned. To do this well, however, they must first detach themselves from their family problems. Because children love their parents, this is no simple task. They will need your understanding, encouragement, and reassurance that they aren't acting selfishly. They can care about others, their parents included, but they can't fix other people's problems. Many at-risk adolescents, however, really believe they can fix their parents' problems. And parents of at-risk teens frequently, and misguidedly, seek help, emotional and otherwise, from their children. Such teens need your help to see that only an adult can fix adult problems, and that

although it's okay for their parents to need help, they should get it from another adult.

Therefore, when a school counselor teaches teens to take care of themselves, the counselor is not advising selfishness. Rather, the counselor is urging self-preservation. The students need to take responsibility for handling their feelings in helpful ways. Doing so frees them to solve problems and to cope with those problems they can't solve. Remember, living in at-risk families is often difficult, frustrating, and unfair. The students will feel deeply about this situation and want to change it. They can't. They can, however, refuse to accept the responsibility for the family's problems or for their effects on the family. This frees the young people of a terrible burden and lets them use their energy to achieve personal goals.

It's important to help the students recognize that although they have no power over their parents' problems, they do have power to make things better for themselves. They can decide what they want to achieve and feel good enough about themselves to take steps to attain their goals, which will be the subject of Session 9.

The main material for this session consists of the rules for relationships. You will use these and role-playing scenarios to make sure the students understand the concepts and can apply what they have learned.

Beginning the Session

GROUP RULES

Welcome the students and begin with a quick review of the group rules. Draw attention to the poster listing the group rules. If you feel that it is necessary, call on different students to read them one at a time. Check for understanding before moving on.

CENTERING EXERCISE

Lead the students in a new centering exercise, "The Waterfall."

THE WATERFALL

Close your eyes and relax. Pretend that you're walking on a beautiful path in the mountains. You're taking a hike down the mountain. It's October, and the sky is clear and a deep shade of blue. The air is cool, but the sun is warm. The changing leaves are beautiful shades of red and orange and yellow. Look up and see the orange and yellow leaves like lace against the sky. There are also green pine trees, so imagine the green pine needles next to the orange and yellow leaves.

You keep walking down the mountain path until you come upon a waterfall, a beautiful cascading waterfall, a stream tumbling down over huge boulders. You sit on a boulder near the waterfall, and you empty your mind. You empty your mind by paying attention to the sound of the water as it rushes over the boulders and trickles down the stream. You imagine that the water is rushing over you and making you feel clean and refreshed. But you're not cold because you're drinking in the warmth of the sun.

As you sit quietly on the boulder, you see leaves floating down the stream because, remember, it's October, and the leaves are falling. The leaves are floating like tiny boats on the bubbling water. You decide to put all your worries, problems, and frustrations on the leaves and to let them all float away.

So if you're worried because *(use appropriate examples for the students in your group, such as . . .)* you don't think your boyfriend or girlfriend likes you anymore, let that worry float away on a leaf for right now. Or if you haven't gotten started on that big English paper, for right now put the English paper on a leaf and let it float away. Or if you had a fight in the hall this morning, and you're afraid you might get suspended, for right now put that worry on a leaf and let it float away. Or if you've had lots of fights with your parents lately, for right now put your anger on another leaf and watch it float away.

Put all of your worries and problems and frustrations on leaves and let them all float away for right now. When you open your eyes, you'll be able to concentrate on the work we're going to do here because all your problems have floated away. You can go back and work on those problems later.

FEELINGS CHECK-IN

Do a feelings check-in with the students. Have them take out their Feeling Wheels. Ask the group members to decide how they are feeling today. Remind the students that if they want, they can color in the section on the Feeling Wheel that describes how they're feeling today. Also remind the teens that they might have more than one feeling, since it's possible to have more than one feeling at a time. Tell the students that if they're having a feeling not named on the wheel, they can add a bubble to the outside of the wheel and name their feeling.

When the students finish, have a go-around. Begin by sharing your own feelings. Then, invite each student to share his or her feelings. Teenagers often list many feelings. For the interests of time, ask them to name the feelings they have, but then pick only two to discuss. Be sure to accept each student's feeling(s) and to affirm each student. Ask the students to return the wheels to their folders.

BASIC FACTS REVIEW

Review the basic facts learned so far. Use posters with Basic Facts 1-18, the List of Basic Facts, or index cards.

In a go-around, ask a student to read Basic Fact 1 aloud and to explain what it means. If the student has trouble explaining the fact, don't contradict or judge, simply clarify his or her explanation. Repeat the procedure for the next basic fact. This review ensures that the students understand and integrate the basic facts that have been taught. It is also easy preparation for the presentation and provides a lead-in for session material.

ASSIGNMENT REVIEW

Ask the students if they brought their assignments from last week. Remind them that they were to observe themselves, their family members, and their friends. They were to look for an example of one of the family patterns: violence, survival roles (superhero, scapegoat, lost child, clown), intermittent reinforcement, enmeshment, boundaries, a closed family system, or enabling. In a go-around, ask each student what he or she found. If students forgot to do the assignment, ask them to think about their families and friends and to see if they can recognize any of the family patterns.

Exploring the Material

MINI-LECTURE
Rules for Relationships

Remind the students that in Session 5 they learned a strategy—the anger management steps—to deal with their own anger. Have the students take Handout 8A ("Rules for Relationships") from their folders. Tell the students that these rules will help them develop strategies they can use for coping with the anger and violence of other people. Emphasize that although children can't solve a violent parent's problems, they can use a coping strategy to help themselves.

Ask a student to read Rule 1. Discuss the rule briefly. Repeat this procedure for each rule. Make sure the students understand the meaning of terms such as *I statements*, *self-talk*, and *affirmations*. Relate the rules to the basic facts the students have learned.

RULES FOR RELATIONSHIPS

1. It's always okay to ask for help.

2. You can only control your own behavior. You can't control anybody else's behavior.

3. Teenagers can't fix their parents' problems. Only parents can fix their own problems. The parents may need to ask for help, and it's okay for them to ask for help.

4. Kill-them-with-kindness sandwiches are great ways to set limits or boundaries. Example: "I'm really glad you're my boyfriend, Jack. But I'm just not going to let you hit me, shove me, or push me around. I'm just not going to let that be part of any relationship. I'm sure we can find a way to solve our disagreements without force, because I really care for you."

5. I statements are great ways to express feelings: "I feel _____ when you _____ because _____."
For example: "I feel angry when you and Mom fight all the time because I'm afraid you're going to get a divorce."

6. You can experience feelings, share them, and let them go. You can tolerate (put up with) feelings because they will pass. You can also choose to do things that make you feel better.

7. You can't control the feelings you get. However, you can look at your thinking, or self-talk, and change it from negative to positive. You can control your behavior. You can use your feelings to give you the power to make changes. You can learn to use problem-solving skills.

8. You can take care of yourself. This is self-preservation, not selfishness.

9. It's always a good idea to repeat positive affirmations for yourself.

   Example: "I am lovable and capable."

10. It's good practice to share caring, positive feelings and thoughts. Remember the three Ps: Be pleasant, positive, and polite.

Coping Strategies

Recall the three Cs: Teens don't cause, can't control, and can't change how their parents choose to express anger. Tell the students that even though children can't solve their parents' problems, they can make coping strategies to help themselves. A coping strategy is a way or plan to handle a problem you can't change or solve.

Have the students take Handout 8B ("Coping-Strategy Scenarios") from their folders. Explain that this handout provides practice in using the rules for relationships to develop coping strategies. The students can also use the basic facts and the problem-solving skills to develop strategies.

Explain that you will work through the first problem situation as a group. Read Problem Situation 1 to the students. Then have one student read the suggested coping strategies and another student read the corresponding rules. As a group, think of another coping strategy and write it on the lines provided. Have the students write the rule or rules on which the strategy is based.

Problem Situation 1:

Your parents are having a terrible fight. They are even throwing things at each other.

Coping Strategies

1. You can realize and accept that you can't make your parents stop fighting.

   It's not your job, and you wouldn't succeed anyway (Rules 2 and 3).

2. You can go to a safe place where you won't get hurt, like your bedroom (Rule 8).

3. You can listen to your favorite song to help you feel better (Rule 6).

Your Strategy

_____

_____

Use questions such as the following to discuss Problem Situation 1.

- **What are some problem situations that would cause parents to fight and throw things at each other?** (Parents might be angry about an affair or a separation, or one parent not paying child support, or one parent drinking too much, etc.)

- **Do you think children are being selfish if they won't try to solve their parents' problems?** (Look for answers showing that the students understand that it's not being selfish to take care of themselves; that while they love their parents, they can't change them; they have to work at handling their own feelings, solving their own problems, and finding strategies to cope with the problems they can't solve.)

Even if you choose not to use the above questions, make sure the discussion underscores these concepts. Affirm the students on the ways they've been putting the facts they've learned into action.

ACTIVITY

Divide the students into pairs. If a student is left out, pair up with him or her yourself. Assign each pair one of the remaining problems on Handout 8B. Explain that the pairs are to read the assigned problem and the suggested coping strategies. One student can read the strategy and the other student can read the corresponding rule or rules. If possible, the pairs should also try to write a coping strategy of their own. Direct the pairs to base their strategies on the rules for relationships and the problem-solving skills they have learned. Tell the students that you will be asking them to discuss their coping strategies with the rest of the group.

Allow a few minutes for reading and writing; then go through the problems one at a time. If the pairs have made up their own strategies, make sure that the strategies do not foster codependence and that the students can explain the rules for relationships and the problem-solving skills they used. Use the discussion questions provided below to help process each problem.

Problem Situation 2:

Your dad has been acting violent. He gave your mom a black eye and broke her arm. Your mom is crying and asking you if she should divorce your dad.

Coping Strategies

1. You can give your mom a hug and tell her you love her (Rule 10).

2. You can tell your mom that you're sorry she's having problems, but you can't tell her what to do because you love both your mom and dad. Maybe your mom should find an adult to talk to for help (Rules 3 and 4).

3. You can do something you enjoy, like listening to rock music (Rule 6), or do something that is good for you, like gymnastics (Rule 8).

4. You can talk to someone you trust if you feel worried or scared (Rules 1 and 6).

Expect some students to resist the second coping strategy. Many teenagers are their parents' confidants and will resist hearing that such a role belongs to another adult, not to them. They may resist giving up that role and will need encouragement to establish age-appropriate boundaries. Remind the students that teenagers can't solve adult problems, but that they can share feelings for their parents. Help the young people see that it is all right and healthy for them to set boundaries and to politely refuse to help their parents in cases like the one this problem describes.

DISCUSSION QUESTIONS

• **If a mom is feeling sad or angry, does the teen have to feel the same way?** (No, remember enmeshment and boundaries? Teens are separate from their parents. They have different feelings and should handle their own feelings, Rule 6. Teens can share feelings, Rule 10, with their parents, but they aren't responsible for making their parents feel better.)

Problem Situation 3:

Your mom has been very irritable since the divorce. Instead of helping you with your science fair project as she promised, she came home and drank beer. Now she's yelling that you're a lazy, worthless, good-for-nothing brat.

Coping Strategies

1. Remember your positive affirmation: "I am lovable and capable" (Rule 9). Write it on an index card and carry it in your pocket. You might write "I'm energetic, worthwhile, and a good kid."

2. If you're feeling angry, use your anger management steps (Rule 7) and talk about your angry feelings with someone you trust (Rule 1).

3. The next day, when your mom is sober, tell her how hurt you felt when she called you names because you know that you are a good person (Rule 5).

DISCUSSION QUESTIONS

• **What can teens do if their parents hurt their feelings?** (They can look at themselves and their thinking; they can choose to look at good things about themselves and to work on changing things that need changing.)

• **Should teens explode and yell if they feel angry?** (No, but they should follow the steps for anger management and put thinking between their feelings and their actions.)

• **Do teens have to figure out how to handle their anger on their own?** (No, they can ask someone they trust for help.)

• **Should teens talk to a parent about their feelings when the parent has been using alcohol or other drugs?** (No, teens should wait until a chemically dependent parent is sober before talking about how they feel.)

Make sure the students understand anger management (Basic Fact 14), positive affirmation (Rule 9), and I statements (Rule 5). Point out that the students can make positive affirmation cards (like their anger management cards) to carry with them or to post where they can see them regularly: on the refrigerator, on the bathroom mirror, on a bedpost.

Problem Situation 4:

You have a good friend who has a bad temper and is always arguing with people. You're afraid your friend will get into real trouble and get suspended from school.

Coping Strategies

1. You can remember that you can't control anybody else's behavior (Rule 2). Tell your friend how you feel in I statements (Rule 5) and how much you care (Rule 10).

2. You can stop enabling (don't cover up). Allow your friend to experience some negative consequences so he or she will have a reason to change.

3. You can keep on sharing your feelings (in I statements, Rule 5) with your friend. For example: "I feel afraid when you argue all the time because I'm afraid no one will be able to stand you" or "I felt angry when you got angry with me last week. You were putting me down."

4. You can discuss your concerns with a caring adult (Rule 1).

Problem Situation 4 is a common concern for middle and high school students. You can reinforce concepts and give the students specific steps to take if they have a friend who is acting out or using alcohol or other drugs. You can tie in Rules 2, 5, and 10 to help the students establish boundaries between their concern for their friend and their responsibility for them. Explain the second coping strategy (stop enabling) by telling the students that someone who is constantly being rescued will have no reason to change; it can be tied to the family sculpture in Session 7. *Choices & Consequences* (Schaefer, 1987) is an excellent resource to learn how to stop enabling and to make an intervention with a teenager, although it applies to teens who use alcohol or other drugs. Finally, the fourth coping strategy reinforces to students that they are not alone in their concern for a teenager who is violent.

DISCUSSION QUESTIONS

• **Can a friend make a friend stop arguing?** (No, you can't control another person's behavior—even if the person is a friend.)

• **Will you be helping a friend if you rescue, protect, or cover up for mistakes he or she makes while arguing?** (No, rescuing, protecting, or covering up for mistakes is enabling. People don't change unless they experience the consequences of their behavior.)

• **Why are I statements important to help solve a problem like this?** (They can help you give consequences in a caring way.)

• **Why is it a good idea to ask an adult for help?** (Because you don't have to solve a friend's problems all by yourself, and other people also are concerned about teens.)

After processing each problem, ask the students to place their handouts in their folders. Affirm the students on their growing ability to cope with difficult problems.

BASIC FACTS

Review the new basic facts for this session. Refer the students to the List of Basic Facts. Ask two group members to read Basic Facts 19 and 20.

19. Teens can't fix their parents' problems.

20. Teens can take good care of themselves.

Point out that the students encountered these facts in the rules for relationships. Briefly discuss each fact, checking for understanding.

ASSIGNMENT

Have the group members take Assignment 8 out of their folders. Read the directions: "Each day this week, look at how you act with your friends or family members. Each day, see if you can use one of the rules for relationships or one of the problem-solving skills. Write it down."

Wrapping Up

CENTERING EXERCISE

Settle the students and then repeat "The Waterfall" (page 169).

AFFIRMATION

Involve the group in an affirmation. Stand and join in a circle with the students, holding hands. Go around and have the students share a coping strategy they can use. Begin the affirmation yourself: "One coping strategy I can use is. . . ."

CLOSING

Remain standing in a circle with the students, holding hands, and lead the group in the closing activity. Tell the students that you're going to make a silent wish for the student on your right. Then, when you've made the wish, gently squeeze the student's hand. The student makes a silent wish for the person on his or her right, then gently squeezes that student's hand, and so on. Continue around the circle until a wish and squeeze come back to you. If necessary, the students can pass the wish in any appropriate way they choose.

Collect the folders. Fill out a copy of the Process and Progress Form (page 211) or the Progress Notes (page 213), if you are an experienced leader, as soon as possible after leading the group.

(**Note:** If you have decided to use the optional Session 10, look ahead now to make plans for the students' presentation. Check out school schedules and available audiences. Be ready to talk briefly about the presentation at the conclusion of Session 9. You will need to inform the students about the times for practicing and giving the presentation.)

Rules for Relationships

1. It's always okay to ask for help.

2. You can only control your own behavior. You can't control anybody else's behavior.

3. Teenagers can't fix their parents' problems. Only parents can fix their own problems. The parents may need to ask for help, and it's okay for them to ask for help.

4. Kill-them-with-kindness sandwiches are great ways to set limits or boundaries. Example: "I'm really glad you're my boyfriend, Jack. But I'm just not going to let you hit me, shove me, or push me around. I'm just not going to let that be part of any relationship. I'm sure we can find a way to solve our disagreements without force, because I really care for you."

5. I statements are great ways to express feelings: "I feel _____ when you _____ because _____ _____."

For example: "I feel angry when you and Mom fight all the time because I'm afraid you're going to get a divorce."

6. You can experience feelings, share them, and let them go. You can tolerate (put up with) feelings because they will pass. You can also choose to do things that make you feel better.

7. You can't control the feelings you get. However, you can look at your thinking, or self-talk, and change it from negative to positive. You can control your behavior. You can use your feelings to give you the power to make changes. You can learn to use problem-solving skills.

8. You can take care of yourself. This is self-preservation, not selfishness.

9. It's always a good idea to repeat positive affirmations for yourself.

   Example: "I am lovable and capable."

10. It's good practice to share caring, positive feelings and thoughts. Remember the three Ps: Be pleasant, positive, and polite.

COPING-STRATEGY SCENARIOS

Problem Situation 1

Your parents are having a terrible fight. They are even throwing things at each other.

Coping Strategies

1. You can realize and accept that you can't make your parents stop fighting. It's not your job, and you wouldn't succeed anyway (Rules 2 and 3).
2. You can go to a safe place where you won't get hurt, like your bedroom (Rule 8).
3. You can listen to your favorite song to help you feel better (Rule 6).

Your Strategy

_____

_____

_____

_____

_____

Problem Situation 2

Your dad has been acting violent. He gave your mom a black eye and broke her arm. Your mom is crying and asking you if she should divorce your dad.

Coping Strategies

1. You can give your mom a hug and tell her you love her (Rule 10).
2. You can tell your mom that you're sorry she's having problems, but you can't tell her what to do because you love both your mom and dad. Maybe your mom should find an adult to talk to for help (Rules 3 and 4).
3. You can do something you enjoy, like listening to rock music (Rule 6), or do something that is good for you, like gymnastics (Rule 8).
4. You can talk to someone you trust if you feel worried or scared (Rules 1 and 6).

Your Strategy

_____

_____

_____

_____

Problem Situation 3

Your mom has been very irritable since the divorce. Instead of helping you with your science fair project as she promised, she came home and drank beer. Now she's yelling at you that you're a lazy, worthless, good-for-nothing brat.

Coping Strategies

1. Remember your positive affirmation: "I am lovable and capable" (Rule 9). Write it on an index card and carry it in your pocket. Your might write "I'm energetic, worthwhile, and a good kid."
2. If you're feeling angry, use your anger management steps (Rule 7) and talk about your angry feelings with someone you trust (Rule 1).
3. The next day, when your mom is sober, tell her how hurt you felt when she called you names because you know that you are a good person (Rule 5).

Your Strategy

_____

_____

_____

Problem Situation 4

You have a good friend who has a bad temper and is always arguing with people. You're afraid your friend will get into real trouble and get suspended from school.

Coping Strategies

1. You can remember that you can't control anybody else's behavior (Rule 2). Tell your friend how you feel in I statements (Rule 5) and how much you care (Rule 10).
2. You can stop enabling (don't cover up). Allow your friend to experience some negative consequences so he or she will have a reason to change.
3. You can keep on sharing your feelings (in I statements, Rule 5) with your friend. For example: "I feel afraid when you argue all the time because I'm afraid no one will be able to stand you" or "I felt angry when you got angry with me last week. You were putting me down."
4. You can discuss your concerns with a caring adult (Rule 1).

Your Strategy

_____

_____

_____

Each day this week, look at how you act with your friends or family members. Each day, see if you can use one of the rules for relationships or one of the problem-solving skills. Write it down.

Day one

Day two

Day three

Day four

Day five

Day six

Day seven

Other comments or observations

Setting Personal Goals

Objectives

To help the students:

- discover that they need to make good choices

- set goals to take care of their bodies, feelings, minds, and choices

Session at a Glance

1. Group Rules: review if necessary—1 minute

2. Centering Exercise: "White-Water Rafting"—3 minutes

3. Feelings Check-in: look at Feelings Wheel—5 minutes

4. Basic Facts Review—7 minutes

5. Assignment Review—4 minutes

6. Mini-lecture and Discussion—5 minutes

7. Activity: draw river picture and write personal goals—12 minutes

8. Basic Facts: read Basic Fact 21; discuss—1 minute

9. Assignment—1 minute

10. Centering Exercise: repeat "White-Water Rafting"—3 minutes

11. Affirmation: share a way you can take care of yourself—2 minutes

12. Closing: pass a silent wish—1 minute

Preparation

- Display the posterboard copy of the group rules.

- Have posters with Basic Facts 1-20 available. (Or the List of Basic Facts, or index cards with a basic fact on each one.)

- Add the following materials to each folder:

    —Handout 9A ("River Picture")

    —Handout 9B ("My Personal Goals")

    —Assignment 9.

- Have pencils, crayons or markers, and the folder ready at each student's place.

- Read through the session plan before meeting.

Background and Guidelines

In this session, the students learn how to give up responsibility for their families' problems. They learn how to assume age-appropriate responsibility for themselves by setting personal goals. The students are encouraged to take good care of themselves and to make good decisions for themselves in the areas of body, mind, feelings, and choices.

As leader, you will not be recommending that the group members abandon their families, leave home, and get a job. Rather, you will encourage them to set their sights on age-appropriate responsibilities. For example, they can decide to try to get on the honor roll or decide to eat a balanced diet or decide to use problem-solving skills instead of aggressive behavior.

When you discuss goals regarding feelings, remember that teens can't control the feelings they get. However, teens can be responsible for what they do with their feelings. Teens can just wallow in feelings and be overwhelmed by them, or they can choose an appropriate coping strategy, such as talking about their feelings with someone they trust or doing something that will help them feel better. Emphasize again that although the students can't fix their families' problems, they can do things to cope with those problems.

This session has two activities. In the first one, the students step back and look at their life so far, and they imagine how they would like it to proceed. They draw a "river picture" to represent their past, present, and future. Even students who are self-conscious about their drawing ability like this exercise.

In the second activity, the students set personal goals for themselves in four areas: for their bodies, minds, feelings, and choices. Setting and sharing goals in these areas will enable the stu-dents to create the kind of future they would like. With positive feedback from you and other group members, sharing these goals helps the students assume ownership and empowers them to take the steps necessary to achieve their goals.

As the students set their goals, remind them of the principle of chunking it down. Setting small, concrete steps that are easily accomplished is a good way to start to achieve a long-term goal. For instance, someone who decides to compete in a marathon doesn't begin training by running 26 miles the first day. Rather, the person should plan a training program that starts small, running two miles a day, and slowly build up the endurance to be able to compete in a marathon. Similarly, high school students may have the goal of becoming a lawyer. As high school students, they can't apply to law school. But they can go to the library and look up the requirements for entrance into law school. They will see that a college degree is necessary. Next they can look up requirements for college entrance. Then they can make sure they are taking the appropriate courses in high school. The most basic, concrete step they can take is to get good grades in their academic classes. Toward that goal, they may decide to focus on their homework tonight instead of watching TV!

Beginning the Session

GROUP RULES

Welcome the students and begin with a quick review of the group rules. Draw attention to the poster listing the group rules. If you feel that it is necessary, call on different students to read them one at a time. Check for understanding before moving on.

CENTERING EXERCISE

Lead the students in the centering exercise "White-Water Rafting."

WHITE-WATER RAFTING

Okay, close your eyes. Imagine that you're floating down a river in a one-person boat, an inflatable kayak called a duck. You've been placed in the river by a guide, who has told you that this is a safe stretch of water. He's given you the equipment you need: a paddle, a helmet, and a life jacket, and shown you how to use them. He has told you that he will meet you a few miles down the river, and to enjoy yourself. When you first start paddling, you go around in circles, but soon you can make the kayak go in the right direction.

Right now, you're floating along in a long, calm pool of the river. No one else is around. The sky above is very clear and bright blue. The surrounding mountains are steep and green. It's a true beautiful wilderness area. You feel very safe in the calm pool, so safe that you take off your life jacket and helmet. You lie back in the kayak and put your feet up, soaking in the sunshine, and listening to the quietness. You feel very relaxed.

As you float along, you hear a noise. The sound is coming from around a bend in the river. You can't see what's around the bend. As you drift closer, the sound grows louder. It's the sound of rushing water. You begin to worry. You wonder if your guide placed you in the wrong part of the river. As the sound gets even louder, you worry more, wondering if it's a waterfall. You feel your heart beating faster and faster.

You sit up at attention. You fasten your life jacket and buckle your helmet. You grab your paddle and get yourself ready to go through whatever lies ahead. As the noise becomes even louder, you slip around the bend in the river. It's white water, all right!

You and the kayak leap into the white water. The kayak gives you a great ride around the rocks and through the rushing water. Waves break over the top of the kayak, but they don't stop you. You're feeling strong and excited. In a moment, you've passed through the rapids and you're floating gently in another of the river's calm pools.

You feel excited, and confident, and satisfied. You feel proud of yourself. You were able to get through something that was frightening because it was unknown. You got through very successfully, using the tools you'd been given and the skills you developed. You feel so good that you are sitting on top of the world! So let that excitement, pride, confidence, and satisfaction wash all over you right now.

FEELINGS CHECK-IN

Do a feelings check-in with the students. Have them take out their Feeling Wheels. Ask the group members to decide how they are feeling today. Remind the students that if they want, they can color in the section on the Feeling Wheel that describes how they're feeling today. Also remind the teens that they might have more than one feeling, since it's possible to have more than one feeling at a time. Tell the students that if they're having a feeling not named on the wheel, they can add a bubble to the outside of the wheel and name their feeling.

When the students finish, have a go-around. Begin by sharing your own feelings. Then, invite each student to share his or her feelings. Teenagers often list many feelings. For the interests of time, ask them to name the feelings they have, but then pick only two to discuss. Be sure to accept each student's feeling(s) and to affirm each student. Ask the students to return the wheels to their folders.

BASIC FACTS REVIEW

Review Basic Facts 1-20. Use the posters, the List of Basic Facts, or index cards.

In a go-around, ask a student to read Basic Fact 1 aloud and to explain what it means. If the student has trouble explaining the fact, don't contradict or judge, simply clarify the explanation. Repeat the procedure for the next basic fact. This review ensures that the students understand and integrate the basic facts that have been taught. It is also easy preparation for the presentation and provides a lead-in for session material.

ASSIGNMENT REVIEW

Ask the students to share their assignments from last week. Remind them that they were to look at how they act with family members and friends and to see if they could use the rules for relationships or the problem-solving skills. In a go-around, ask the students what they used. If students forgot to do the assignment, ask them to think about whether they used the rules or skills in the past week, or if they can think of a time when they could have used them.

Exploring the Material

MINI-LECTURE

Tell the group members that now that they have learned the three Cs—they can't cause, control, or change a parent's choice to use violence to express anger—and now that they know they can't fix a parent's problem, they are ready to learn to take care of themselves.

Explain the difference between selfishness and self-preservation. Use the example of the three people on a desert island with nothing to eat except one piece of chocolate cake. If you eat the entire piece by yourself, you are being selfish; if you take none, you are being a martyr; but if you divide the cake into thirds, and eat your share, you are practicing self-preservation.

Point out that teenagers can take care of themselves in different ways. Write *Body, Mind, Feelings,* and *Choices* on the chalkboard. Ask the students for examples for each area.

> **Body:** (eat nutritiously, exercise, get plenty of sleep)
>
> **Mind:** (read, do homework, review notes)
>
> **Feelings:** (have fun, find a friend to share your feelings with, put thinking between feelings and behavior)
>
> **Choices:** (decide not to use alcohol or other drugs, decide to follow the rules at school, decide to go to college, decide to be sexually responsible)

Point out that teenagers can set goals for taking care of their bodies, minds, feelings, and choices. Explain that goals are plans for good things

you will do for yourself. The goals might be long-term—things you hope to achieve in the distant future—or short-term, things you plan to achieve in the immediate future. Relate the process of achieving long-term goals to the principle of chunking it down. Say that long-term goals are attained by taking small, concrete steps or by achieving a series of short-term goals.

As a group, practice setting some long-term goals and short-term goals. Start with the example of an inexperienced runner. Ask the students what a long-term goal for this person might be. (To run a 26-mile marathon.) Then ask what short-term goals the runner should set to achieve the long-term goal. (Start with small distances; train every day.)

Then use the example of a high school student who wants to become a lawyer. Ask the group members to think of a series of short-term goals that the student needs to accomplish. (Obtain a college degree so you can get into law school; get good grades in high school so you can get into college; start studying tonight so you can get good grades!)

Emphasize that the same process applies to how the students handle the feeling of anger. They might have the goal to change their aggressive behavior, but it's hard to change behavior quickly. They can start by observing what they do when they get angry. Then they can look retroactively at what they could have done to make their anger work for them by using a problem-solving skill. If they practice the anger management steps regularly, even after they express anger aggressively, in two or three months, they'll start changing their behavior without even knowing it.

DISCUSSION

Lead a discussion to help the students better understand the facts—the key concepts—presented. As the group discusses, remember to go around, making sure that each student has an opportunity to add to the discussion. Encourage participation, but don't force it. Remember the group rule that allows a student to pass. Explain or clarify information where necessary to reinforce learning and correct any misconceptions. To facilitate the discussion you may use questions like the following:

- **Can teenagers fix their parents' problems?** (No.)

- **Who can teens take care of?** (Themselves.)

- **Does taking good care of yourself mean getting a job and an apartment and living on your own?** (No, it means doing things that are good for your body, mind, feelings, and choices.)

- **What are goals?** (Goals are plans for good things you will do for yourself.)

- **What does chunking it down mean?** (Chunking it down means to start to achieve a long-term goal by taking small, concrete steps that are easy to attain.)

Even if you choose not to use the suggested questions, make sure the discussion underscores these concepts.

ACTIVITY

Tell the students that two activities today will help them set personal goals.

River Picture

Have the students take Handout 9A ("River Picture") out of their folders. Explain that they will draw a river picture that can help them set personal goals. Tell them that it will be a three-part picture that shows their present, past, and future. It will include a river that will stand for, or symbolize, their present. The left bank or side of the river will stand for their past, and the right bank or side of the river will stand for their future. Tell them that they can draw the river as stormy or calm, wide or narrow, and that they can draw any objects or people or things and use any color they want to stand for their present, their past, and their future.

As an example, tell the students that one girl drew the river as very rocky and full of waves and white water because she was going through some rough times. On the bank representing her past, she drew a garden with a heavy rain falling on it because of the sad things that had happened to her. On the bank representing her future, she drew a house with trees, flowers, and a white picket fence because that's what she wanted when she got older.

Tell the students to think about what their past and present look like and to imagine what they want their future to look like. Remind them that you are not looking for artistic ability. If they don't want to draw, they can write in the names of things in their present, past, and future. Give the students time to do their drawings. When they finish, have a go-around. Ask each student to explain his or her picture to the group.

My Personal Goals

Then have the students take out Handout 9B. Read aloud the title at the top of the sheet, "My Personal Goals." Tell the students that they've drawn a picture of what they want their future to look like. Now they can set goals that will help them achieve what they want in their future. They should have goals in four areas: body, mind, feelings, and choices. People need to take care of themselves in all four areas. You may need to repeat some of the ideas the students came up with during the mini-lecture. Remind the students to chunk it down: they can reach goals that seem impossible by starting with small goals that are easy to attain. Ask them to label each goal as "ST" for short-term or "LT" for long-term.

When the students finish writing, have a go-around again. Invite each student to tell one or two goals to the group. Affirm the young people on their goal setting and on their growing willingness and ability to take good care of themselves.

BASIC FACTS

Review the new basic fact for this session. Refer the students to the List of Basic Facts. Ask a group member to read Basic Fact 21.

21. Teens need to take good care of their bodies, their minds, their feelings, and their choices.

ASSIGNMENT

Have the group members take Assignment 9 out of their folders. Read the directions: "This week, set one goal for yourself, and practice chunking it down. Write the long-term goal, and then write the small, concrete steps that will help you achieve the goal." Remind the students that it is easier to work on something if you are able to put it into words.

Wrapping Up

CENTERING EXERCISE

Settle the students and then repeat "White-Water Rafting" (page 181).

AFFIRMATION

Involve the group in an affirmation. Stand and join in a circle with the students holding hands. Go around and have the students share one goal they have for themselves and what the first step will be. Begin the affirmation yourself: "One goal I have for myself is. . . . The first step I can take is. . . ." The students may again need your help to chunk-down their goal and to decide on a small and easily obtainable first step.

CLOSING

Remain standing in a circle with the students, holding hands, and lead the group in the closing activity. Tell the students that you're going to make a silent wish for the student on your right. Then, when you've made the wish, gently squeeze the student's hand. The student makes a silent wish for the person on his or her right, then gently squeezes that student's hand, and so on. Continue around the circle until a wish and squeeze come back to you. If necessary, the students can pass the wish in any appropriate way they choose.

Collect the folders. Fill out a copy of the Process and Progress Form (page 211) or the Progress Notes (page 213), if you are an experienced leader, as soon as possible after leading the group.

(**Note:** If you have decided to use the optional Session 10, tell the students that they will be making a presentation of the material they have learned. Make arrangements to present the basic facts to a guidance counselor, to a principal or administrator, to a class in the school, or to a class in another school. Tell the students how you plan to meet in order to rehearse. A script is provided in Session 10. If possible, make plans to videotape the presentation. The students will enjoy viewing the tape in Session 11.

As alternatives to the presentation in Session 10, you might have the students present the basic facts in a bulletin board display—perhaps including artwork—or you might have the students present the basic facts in a series of broadcasts over the school's public-address system.)

River Picture

The river picture represents your life. Draw a river that symbolizes your present; the left bank symbolizes your past; the right bank symbolizes your future. You can create any kind of future for yourself that you want.

My Personal Goals

On the lines provided, write one or more goals you have for taking care of your body, mind, feelings, and choices. Indicate whether each goal is short-term (ST) or long-term (LT).

For My Body:

_____

_____

_____

_____

_____

_____

For My Mind:

_____

_____

_____

_____

_____

_____

_____

For My Feelings:

_____

_____

_____

_____

_____

_____

For My Choices:

_____

_____

_____

_____

_____

_____

This week, set one goal for yourself, and practice chunking it down. Write the long-term goal, and then write the small, concrete steps that will help you achieve the goal.

My long-term goal:

_____

_____

_____

_____

Chunking it down:
The small, concrete steps I need to take to achieve this goal:

1. _____

_____

_____

_____

_____

2. _____

_____

_____

_____

_____

3. _____

_____

_____

_____

_____

4. _____

_____

_____

_____

_____

5. _____

_____

_____

_____

_____

Group Presentation
Optional

Objectives

To help the students:

- demonstrate their understanding of the basic facts about anger management and violence prevention

- grow in self-esteem

To help the students as a group:

- share feelings of cohesiveness

- successfully complete a project

To help members of the audience:

- learn about anger management

- learn problem-solving skills to use in anger situations

- become aware of the issues that arise in a family that uses violence to express anger

- recognize that help is available for those who live in a violent family

Session at a Glance

1. Group Rules: review—1 minute

2. Centering Exercise: an exercise chosen and led by the students—3 minutes

3. Feelings Check-in: look at Feelings Wheel— 5 minutes

4. Presentation: present all the basic facts— 25 minutes

5. Audience Evaluation— 3 minutes

6. Centering Exercise: repeat the chosen exercise—3 minutes

7. Affirmation: share what you liked or appreciated about the presentation—4 minutes

8. Closing: pass a silent wish—1 minute

Preparation

- Since the structure of this session varies from that of the other sessions, you may wish to schedule two meeting times to present it. If you and the students have decided on a presentation to an audience, you can use the first time period as a rehearsal session. You can have the students practice delivering the basic facts and make any other necessary preparations. Use the second time period to conduct the actual session, allowing the students to make their presentation. Depending on your group, you may want to invite the audience only for the presentation and audience evaluation part of the session.

- Decide in advance on an appropriate audience to view the presentation. If this is the first time for such a presentation, you may wish to invite only the school principal or SAP staff. If you're an experienced leader, you may want to invite a whole grade level, a particularly effective prevention measure for middle or high school levels.

- Make sure you have suitable seating arrangements for the audience.

- If possible, videotape the students' presentation so you can play it for them in Session 11.

- Display the posterboard copy of the group rules.

- If you made a poster for each basic fact, have these available. Otherwise, have the students make them during the practice session.

- Clear a wall or bulletin board space in the meeting area where the students can post all 21 basic facts posters. Have pins or tape available.

- Have available the "Three Cs" poster (from Session 7) and the "Four Steps" poster (from Session 7) and the "Anger Management Steps" poster (from Session 5).

- Make copies of the Audience Evaluation Form (page 208) and have pens or pencils available for audience members.

- Have each student's folder ready at his or her place.

- Read through the session plan before meeting.

Background and Guidelines

This session provides guidelines for a presentation in which the students review all the basic facts, along with simple explanations, to an invited audience. Instead of having the students do a presentation, however, you might allow them to develop their own project. Such projects might include leading a schoolwide focus on violence prevention or teaching younger children about violence prevention and anger management. For instance, your group could teach younger children how to use problem-solving skills in anger situations. Creating their own project and carrying it through, although usually requiring a major commitment of time and energy, can be a major source of positive self-esteem for middle and high school students. And teaching someone else how to use the anger management steps and problem-solving skills will reinforce the learning for your group members.

If you decide to do the presentation, and you are concerned about having members of a confidential group stand up in front of an audience, rest assured that the purpose of this session is not to break confidentiality. Rather, it's to provide an effective prevention activity.

There's a lot to do for and in this session. Planning ahead, however, will make the task less daunting. The most effective way of guaranteeing the success of the students' presentation is advance planning and practice.

Arrange to have one of the teens lead the group and the audience in a centering exercise of the group's choice. The centering exercise will begin and help to conclude the session. If the students do not want to lead the exercise, plan on doing so yourself.

The students can take turns presenting the facts. In your practice session, assign basic facts to each student. During the presentation, the students will display each assigned fact on a poster, read the fact aloud, and explain it. The students then post the poster (in sequence) in the space provided in the meeting room.

After a student reads a basic fact, and explains it to the audience, you can further the discussion by asking questions of the student or of the audience. The students can also role-play different scenarios to explain selected facts. To help the presentation flow smoothly, have the students sit in a row in front of the room. Then, when you call on them to present their fact, all they need to do is stand, look at the audience, and speak slowly and distinctly. As you practice the presentation, the order and method should become clear to the teens. In order to make sure the presentation is nonthreatening to the students, tell them that you will further explain the basic fact if they don't want to.

At the conclusion of the presentation, if you have presented to students, you will ask audience members to fill out the Audience Evaluation Form. The forms will give you important feedback and can serve as a referral source for future groups. If audience members, including teachers, identify themselves as children from violent families, be ready to refer them to available help.

The overall goal of the presentation is not to showcase group members' talents or academic abilities. Rather, the goal is to reinforce learning, to allow the group members to reach out to others, to convey a sense of hope to the audience, and to assure all that help is available for students to learn good ways to deal with anger.

Beginning the Session

GROUP RULES

Welcome the students and begin with a quick review of the group rules. Draw

attention to the poster listing the group rules. If necessary, call on different students to read them one at a time. Check for understanding before moving on.

CENTERING EXERCISE

Explain to your guests that every time you meet, you begin with a centering exercise. The centering exercise teaches ways of relaxing and helps everyone get ready to work together. Then invite the designated teen to lead the exercise, for example, "Breathing Through Your Feet."

FEELINGS CHECK-IN

Do a feelings check-in with the students. Have them take out their Feeling Wheels. Ask the group members to decide how they are feeling today. Remind the students that if they want, they can color in the section on the Feeling Wheel that describes how they're feeling today. Also remind the teens that they might have more than one feeling, since it's possible to have more than one feeling at a time. Tell the students that if they're having a feeling not named on the wheel, they can add a bubble to the outside of the wheel and name their feeling.

When the students finish, have a go-around. Begin by sharing your own feelings. Then, invite each student to share his or her feelings. Teenagers often list many feelings. For the interests of time, ask them to name the feelings they have, but then pick only two to discuss. Be sure to accept each student's feeling(s) and to affirm each student. Ask the students to return the wheels to their folders.

Presentation

INTRODUCTION

Introduce the presentation using the following: "We're part of the counseling program at (*name of school*). We've been studying violence prevention and anger management, and we've learned some important ways to deal with anger. We want to share what we've learned with you."

Presenting Basic Facts 1, 2, and 3

Call on the students designated to present Basic Facts 1, 2, and 3.

1. **Violent behavior is intended to do harm. It can be emotional, to express anger, or instrumental, to attain a goal.**

2. **It is never acceptable to use violent or harmful behavior to express anger.**

3. **No matter what has influenced a person to be violent, it is his or her responsibility to choose to learn nonviolent and helpful ways to express anger.**

Have the students display a poster of each fact, read it aloud, explain it, and then post it.

Call on group and audience members to give examples of different ways people use violence to express anger. Make sure the audience hears examples of instrumental anger, such as an assassin or a soldier.

Give examples of the causes of violent behavior: having a low IQ, witnessing family violence as a child, living in poor housing in a low income area that is near illegal markets such as prostitution and drug dealing, and living in a society that glorifies violence on TV and has easy accessibility to firearms. Point out that while all of these may be sources of violence, they are not excuses. It is each person's responsibility to choose nonviolent ways to deal with anger.

Presenting Basic Facts 4 and 5

Move on to the next set of basic facts. Call on the students designated to present Basic Facts 4 and 5.

4. **Feelings aren't good or bad, or right or wrong; they just are.**

5. **Putting thinking between your feeling and your behavior enables you to choose helpful ways to express feelings.**

Have the students display a poster of each fact, read it aloud, explain it, and then post it.

Point out to the audience that all feelings are normal and that teens can't control what feelings they get; however, they certainly can control their behavior. Sometimes they need to put thinking between their feelings and behavior to make sure they express their feelings in helpful ways.

If you wish, have the students find their copies of Handout 2C ("Three Components of Emotions"). Ask them to share their examples of the three components of emotion—feeling, thinking, and behavior—and how they change due to negative or positive thinking.

Presenting Basic Facts 6, 7, and 8

Move on to the next set of basic facts. Call on the students designated to present Basic Facts 6, 7, and 8.

6. **Six ways to express anger are stuffing, withdrawing, blaming, triangling, exploding, and problem-solving.**

7. **Parents usually love their children, even when the parents are choosing to use violent or harmful ways to express their anger.**

8. **Children usually love their parents, although they may feel hate for the parents if the parents are using violent ways to express their anger.**

Have the students display a poster of each fact, read it aloud, explain it, and then post it.

If you want, have the students role-play an example of stuffing, withdrawing, blaming, triangling, and exploding. If they can't think of a scenario, give them one:

Janet and Suzanne are good friends. They make plans to go to the movies on Sunday afternoon. On Sunday, Janet calls Suzanne to say she's sick and can't go. Later, Suzanne finds out that Janet went to the movies with Natalie.

Have the students act out how Suzanne would stuff, withdraw, blame, triangle, or explode.

For Basic Facts 7 and 8, explain to the audience that if parents use violence, teens have both positive and negative feelings about them. Help the audience see that while this ambivalence may be very confusing for teens, it is also "normal" in families where parents use violence to express anger.

Presenting Basic Facts 9, 10, 11, and 12

Move on to the next set of basic facts, and call on the students designated to present Basic Facts 9, 10, 11, and 12.

9. When teens are angry about a problem they can't change, they should:

   1. Accept what they can't change.

   2. Express their anger so they can let it go.

   3. Do something good for themselves.

10. When teens are angry about a problem they can change, they should use their anger to give them the power to make changes in themselves by learning to use problem-solving skills.

11. Five good problem-solving skills to use in anger situations are *I* statements, reflective listening, kill-them-with-kindness sandwiches, apologizing, and negotiating a compromise.

12. Chunking it down is a good way to start on a long-term goal.

Have the teens display a poster of each fact, read it aloud, explain it, and then post it.

Have the students role-play the five problem-solving skills by using a scenario from Session 4. Scenario 1 is repeated here for convenience. It is a good one to use, since it teaches girls how to set limits with boyfriends.

Scenario 1

Crystal is a high school sophomore. Crystal's father is often jealous of her mother. He always wants to know where she's going and why she's late when she comes home from work. Sometimes Crystal's dad gets mad at her mother if she wears makeup or gets a new hairdo. Once, he even grabbed her and made her wash the makeup off. Sometimes Crystal's father is violent. He's pushed her mother against the wall. Sometimes her mother has bruises on her arms.

Crystal has been dating Steve, a senior, for about three months. Steve comes from a family where his father is boss. At first, Steve was nice to Crystal, but lately he's begun to be real bossy. He tells her to change her clothes if he doesn't like what she's wearing. A couple of weeks ago, he pushed her against the wall.

I statement: Crystal: "Steve, I feel angry when you tell me what to wear and push me."

Reflective listening: Crystal: "Steve, I can see that you are upset over what I'm wearing. Help me understand why you don't like it."

Kill-them-with-kindness sandwich: Crystal: "Steve, I really like you, and I'm glad we're dating. But, I'm going to decide what I'm going to wear. And I need to let you know that I don't like it when you push me. That is something I'm not going to allow anybody to do to me. So, I hope we can find another way to deal with our problems."

Apologizing: Steve: "Crystal, I was wrong to push you. I'm sorry." Stress that violence often occurs in situations where there are threats and counterthreats. An apology can often de-escalate a potentially dangerous situation.

Negotiating a compromise: Crystal: "Steve, I know that I have some clothes that are your favorites. It's important for me to decide what I'm going to wear, but I'll be glad to wear your favorites some of the time."

Explain that chunking it down means setting a long-term goal and deciding on the small, concrete steps that help you achieve the goal. In learning how to use the problem-solving skills, it helps to start by observing what you do now when angry. Then, it helps to think of which problem-solving skill you could have used in the anger situation. We would like everyone to learn how to use problem-solving skills in anger situations.

Presenting Basic Facts 13 and 14

Move on to the next set of basic facts, and call on the students designated to present Basic Facts 13 and 14.

13. The anger management steps help teens put thinking between the feeling of anger and the behavior of anger.

14. The anger management steps are:

 1. Recognize that you're angry.

 2. Accept your anger.

 3. Practice relaxation.

 4. Decide if it's a problem you can't change or a problem you can change.

 5. Think about helpful and harmful ways to express the anger.

 6. Evaluate the consequences.

 7. Choose a best way.

 8. Problem-solve or express your anger in a helpful way.

Have the students display a poster of each fact, read it aloud, explain it, and then post it.

Next, ask the students to display the poster entitled "Anger Management Steps" (from Session 5). Use a scenario from Session 5 to demonstrate how to apply the steps. Ask the students if different ways to express anger are helpful or harmful.

Presenting Basic Facts 15 and 16

Move on to the next set of basic facts, and call on the students designated to present Basic Facts 15 and 16.

15. No matter what you believe about the causes, family violence will end only if each person decides never to use violence in his or her own life.

16. To set limits against the use of force in a relationship, speak in a calm, rational way, firmly, and with conviction and determination.

Point out that there are many theories about the causes of family violence. Family violence seems to start with small, minor incidents that become more severe and more frequent. Research shows that setting firm limits that the violence will not be tolerated is the most effective way to end family violence.

Presenting Basic Facts 17 and 18

Move on to the next set of basic facts, and call on the students designated to present Basic Facts 17 and 18.

17. The three Cs are:

 1. Teens don't cause their parents to use violence to express anger.

 2. Teens can't control how their parents express anger.

 3. Teens can't change their parents' use of violence to express anger.

18. The four steps teens can take if they live in a violent family are:

 1. Find a safe place for themselves.

 2. Ask an adult for help if the parents are out of control with their violence.

 3. Learn to put thinking between their feeling and their behavior.

 4. Choose to learn nonviolent ways to express their own feelings, and learn to use problem-solving skills in anger situations.

Have the students display a poster of each fact, read it aloud, explain it, and then post it.

Tell the audience, "Teenagers often believe that their families' problems are their fault, that they've caused their parents' violent behavior: 'My parents fight because I'm always in the principal's office.' But this isn't the case. Children and teenagers are not at fault for a parent's violence. Teenagers can make their parents angry, but they can't force them to choose violence. Parents make that choice on their own. That's why it's important for all students to learn the three Cs."

Display the poster with the three Cs (from Session 7). Ask the following questions to help the students explain the three Cs.

• **How might teens think they cause a parent to use violence to express anger?** (Teens might think that a parent uses violence because they misbehave in school, don't listen to their parents, fight with their sisters and brothers, or get low grades.)

• **Can behaviors like these make a parent feel angry?** (Yes, but it's the parent's personal choice to use violence to express the anger.)

• **How might teens try to control a parent's violent behavior?** (They might tell the parents to stop fighting or tell a parent to get professional help.)

• **How might teens try to change a parent's choice to use violence?** (They might try to be perfect and get good grades in school or stay out of the parent's way and not cause any trouble.)

• **Will these actions ever change a parent's violent behavior?** (No.)

Presenting Basic Facts 19, 20, and 21

Move on to the next set of basic facts, and call on the students designated to present Basic Facts 19, 20, and 21.

19. Teens can't fix their parents' problems.

20. Teens can take good care of themselves.

21. Teens need to take good care of their bodies, their minds, their feelings, and their choices.

Have the students display a poster of each fact, read it aloud, explain it, and then post it.

Have a student explain the first problem situation on Handout 8B. ("Your parents are having a terrible fight. They are even throwing things at each other.") Then have the students read aloud or role-play one of the the coping strategies.

After discussing Basic Fact 19, move on to Basic Facts 20 and 21. Explain to the audience that teenagers can take charge of their lives. They can live good, healthy lives if they learn to make good decisions. If appropriate, the students may share some personal goals.

CONCLUDING THE PRESENTATION

Conclude the presentation by having the group stand, face the audience, and bow. Lead the audience in applause.

Wrapping Up

AUDIENCE EVALUATION

If you have presented to a class, pass out copies of the Audience Evaluation Form and pens or pencils to audience members. Encourage them to spend a moment completing the form. When the audience members finish writing, collect the forms, pens, and pencils.

CENTERING EXERCISE

Ask the student who led the centering exercise at the beginning of the session to repeat it.

AFFIRMATION

Involve the group and audience members in an affirmation. Invite everyone to stand in a circle and hold hands. Go around and have everyone share something he or she liked or appreciated about the group's presentation. Begin the affirmation yourself: "One thing I really liked about the presentation was. . . ."

CLOSING

Depending on the size of the audience, and if it seems appropriate, include the audience in the closing activity. Otherwise, do the closing after audience members leave.

Stand in a circle with the students, holding hands, and lead the group in the closing activity. Tell the students that you're going to make a silent wish for the student on your right. Then, when you've made the wish, gently squeeze the student's hand. The student makes a silent wish for the person on his or her right, then gently squeezes that student's hand, and so on. Continue around the circle until a wish and squeeze come back to you. If necessary, the students can pass the wish in any appropriate way they choose.

Collect the folders. Fill out a copy of the Process and Progress Form (page 211) or the Progress Notes (page 213), if you are an experienced leader, as soon as possible after leading the group.

Developing a Support System

Objectives

To help the students:

- review all the basic facts about violence prevention and anger management
- create a personal support system
- close out their group experience

Session at a Glance

1. Group Rules: review if necessary—1 minute
2. Centering Exercise: "The Rainbow"—3 minutes
3. Feelings Check-in: look at Feeling Wheel—4 minutes
4. Basic Facts Review (Optional: process Session 10's presentation; view videotape)—8 minutes
5. Assignment Review from Session 9—5 minutes
6. Mini-lecture and Discussion—4 minutes
7. Activity: make a list of people who can offer support—5 minutes
8. Group Evaluation—4 minutes
9. Certificates and Refreshments—7 minutes
10. Affirmation: share what you liked best about the group—3 minutes
11. Closing: pass a silent wish—1 minute

Preparation

- Display the posterboard copy of the group rules.

- Have posters with Basic Facts 1-21 available. (Or the List of Basic Facts, or index cards with a basic fact on each one.)

- If you videotaped the presentation, arrange for equipment so the students can view themselves in the presentation.

- Add the following materials to each folder:
    —Handout 11A ("My Personal Yellow Pages").

- Have pencils, crayons or markers, and the folder ready at each student's place.

- To help the students complete their personal yellow pages, make a sample yellow pages showing the people in your support system.

Have several copies of your local telephone book yellow pages available.

- Make copies of the Group Evaluation Form (page 203).

- Make copies of the Certificate of Recognition (page 204). Complete a certificate for each group member. Fill in the student's name, sign your name, and fill in the date and school. Mount each certificate on construction paper.

- Make arrangements to serve refreshments (chips and sodas, etc.) during the wrapping-up activity.

- Read through the session plan before meeting.

Background and Guidelines

This session summarizes the themes of the *Anger Management and Violence Prevention* group: education about violence prevention and anger management, putting thinking between feelings and behavior, teaching problem-solving skills to use in anger situations, correcting misconceptions, and empowerment. The students review all the basic facts, and, if they took part in Session 10, they also evaluate their group presentation.

Over the course of the group process, the students discovered that although they can't cure the violence in their families or fix family problems, they can do some crucial things to help themselves. In this session, the students realize something new: they don't have to be alone as they focus on themselves. They see that not only is it okay to ask for help, but also it's healthy and smart. Teens can ask for help to learn how to deal with their feelings, how to develop coping strategies, and how to learn new skills. Thus, although this session marks the end of their group experience, the teens see that their support system is not diminishing, but has grown and can continue to expand.

As leader, you can help the students see that the average person needs a support system of about 30 people, not just two or three. Teens need to understand that they can ask for help in many different areas of their lives, and that it's perfectly okay to have different people help in different ways at different times.

The session provides the students with a number of opportunities to share what they've gained and will remember from their group experience. But, as the students leave the group, the session does more than give them an opportunity to review. Throughout the mini-lecture, the students discover that despite all they've learned, things will happen in the future that will upset them; that's why a support system is so vital. Emphasize this important point, stressing that using their support system (their "personal yellow pages" and other sources of help) during upsetting times is a wonderful way for the young people to take good care of themselves.

Note that there is a small ceremony in which the students receive certificates for taking part in this group. Be sure to have the certificates ready for the students. Do your best to provide some refreshments. This not only helps the students feel self-worth, but also tells them that they should and can have some fun, that they should and can celebrate their learning.

Sometimes, the end of group sessions is a bittersweet time for the students. Be ready for some of this. Don't be afraid to speak and show your appreciation and feelings toward the young people.

Beginning the Session

GROUP RULES

Welcome the students and begin with a quick review of the group rules. Draw attention to the poster listing the group rules. If necessary call on different students to read them one at a time. Check for understanding before moving on.

CENTERING EXERCISE

Lead the students in a new centering exercise, "The Rainbow."

THE RAINBOW

Close your eyes and imagine you're asleep. In your sleep, you're dreaming. In your dream, you can fly. You soar way, way up into the sky, and you decide to land on a fluffy cloud. You lie back and relax on that cloud as it floats lazily across the deep blue sky. You look down and see other clouds below you. Far beneath those clouds is the world. It looks very small.

You reach deep into your pocket, and you decide to pull out all of your worries, and problems, and sadness, and frustrations. You drop them one at a time on the clouds that float below you, one worry, one sadness, one problem, or one frustration per cloud. Soon, the clouds change your worries and sadness into rain. The rain falls gently to the ground. It washes away all the dust and dirt and grime, and it helps the plants and trees to grow, and it helps make the rivers and lakes and oceans beautiful.

Eventually the rain stops, the sun comes out, and you see a beautiful rainbow. You float over on your cloud and sit on top of the rainbow. You smile to yourself because you know that you made that beautiful rainbow. You remember that before there can be a rainbow, first there must be a cloud and a storm. Without your worries and sadness, the clouds couldn't have made the rain, and there would be no beautiful rainbow now.

Because you like to have fun, you slide down the rainbow. At the bottom there is a big pot, full of happiness. You reach into the pot and fill your pockets with happiness.

Tell the students that you hope they will see their group experience as a big pot at the end of the rainbow. If they need to, in the future, you hope that they can reach into the pot and pull out what they learned with a smile.

FEELINGS CHECK-IN

Do a feelings check-in with the students. Have them take out their Feeling Wheels. Ask the group members to decide how they are feeling today. Remind the students that if they want, they can color in the section on the Feeling Wheel that describes how they're feeling today. Also remind the teens that they might have more than one feeling, since it's possible to have more than one feeling at a time. Tell the students that if they're having a feeling not named on the wheel, they can add a bubble to the outside of the wheel and name the feeling.

When the students finish, have a go-around. Begin by sharing your own feelings. Then, invite each student to share his or her feelings. Teenagers often list many feelings. For the interests of time, ask them to name the feelings they have, but then pick only two to discuss. Be sure to accept each student's feeling(s) and to affirm each student. Ask the students to return the wheels to their folders.

BASIC FACTS REVIEW

Review Basic Facts 1-21. Use posters, the List of Basic Facts, or index cards.

In a go-around, ask a student to read Basic Fact 1 aloud and to explain what it means. If the student has trouble explaining the fact, don't contradict or judge, simply clarify his or her explanation. Repeat the procedure for the next basic fact. This review ensures that the students understand and integrate the basic facts that have been taught and provides a lead-in for the session material.

Optional: If the group took part in the presentation of Session 10, take a moment to process it with the students. If you were able to videotape the presentation, show the tape now. Students generally enjoy seeing themselves on tape. Ask them what was hard and easy about the presentation, what was the most fun, and what could have made it better. Record the students' observations to use and consider when presenting Session 10 in the future.

ASSIGNMENT REVIEW

Ask the students to share their assignments from Session 9. Remind them that they were to set a goal and to practice chunking it down. They were to write the long-term goal and the small, concrete steps that will help them achieve the goal. In a go-around, ask the students about their long-term goals and the small, concrete steps. If students forgot to do the assignment, ask them to set a goal now and to determine the small, concrete steps that will help them get started.

Exploring the Material

MINI-LECTURE AND DISCUSSION

Since this is the last session, ask the group members to summarize what they've learned in group. In a go-around, ask each student to tell something he or she learned. Encourage the students to tell something not mentioned by another student.

At the conclusion of the go-around, point out that the students have learned much about violence prevention and anger management. They've learned the causes of violence, on the personal level, the family level, the social level, and the societal level. They've learned that each person has the responsibility to choose to learn nonviolent and helpful ways to deal with anger. They've learned and practiced the anger management steps and problem-solving skills. They've learned to put thinking between their feelings and their behavior, especially for the feeling of anger. They've learned about the progression of family violence and the effects on teens and families. They've learned coping strategies that teens can use in anger situations, and they've learned how to set goals for themselves.

Encourage the students to look at how they have changed. Have they set long-term goals and small, concrete goals to start with?

Tell the group members that they will continue to have problems as life goes on—that's the way life is. But they don't have to fix their problems all by themselves, or even figure out what to do all by themselves. Everyone needs a support system with many kinds of people to help in many kinds of areas. The activity today will help the students realize who is in their support system.

To help the students see the importance of asking for help, tell them the following scenario:

Scenario

Fred, a high school student, tends to have a lot of anger. His parents are divorced. He lives with his father because his mother moved out of state and doesn't have a job. His father and stepmother fight a lot, especially when she's been drinking. Fred used to hang out with his friends Chuck and Raymond; they've been friends for a long time. Lately, though, he doesn't want to see anybody or do anything. He didn't even try out for cross country this year, and he made it to state last year. He's thinking of dropping out of band, too.

Ask the students to imagine whom Fred could ask for help. He has some people in his support system already, but he's not using them.

If you wish, use the following questions to help in discussion.

1. **Who are the people in Fred's support system?** (*Family members:* his father; possibly his mother; *Friends:* Chuck and Raymond; *Teachers, coaches, clergy:* his band teacher, cross country coach)

2. **What community agencies could help Fred?** (Al-Anon; his school guidance counselor.)

3. **What could Fred do to help himself feel better?** (He could join the cross country team; he could play in band; he could spend time with his old friends, Chuck and Raymond. If he is upset with his stepmother's drinking, he could ask if there is a group at school for concerned persons; he could go to Al-Anon or Alateen.)

ACTIVITY

Show the students the yellow pages from the local telephone book. Note that the yellow pages list names and numbers of people to call for help with various problems. Tell the students they are going to make their own yellow pages. The students' personal yellow pages will contain the names and numbers of caring people they can call when they feel angry or depressed, or when they are worried about family violence. These people will form the students' support system.

Have the students take Handout 11A from their folders. Show the sample yellow pages you made prior to the session. Note that the yellow pages have space for the names of friends, family members, school personnel, community agencies, and coaches and clergy. The students might like to include your name and the names of other members of the group. Using the telephone books you brought, show the students how to locate emergency phone numbers and the numbers of local self-help or crisis agencies, such as teen hotlines, Alcoholics Anonymous, Al-Anon, and Alateen. Help them with the office numbers of school personnel. The students may have to fill in the numbers of family members and friends later.

Give the students time to complete their personal yellow pages. Then have them put their yellow pages in their folders. Tell the students they can take their folders home with them.

GROUP EVALUATION

Pass out copies of the Group Evaluation Form and ask the students to complete it. Explain to the group members that their honesty will help you make the group better for other students. Point out that they need not put their names on the form. When the students finish, collect the forms to use when you evaluate the group program.

Wrapping Up

CERTIFICATES AND REFRESHMENTS

Thank the students for their hard work, sharing, and openness by calling each forward and presenting him or her with the Certificate of Recognition. As you present the certificates, offer a personal note of thanks, mentioning something special to each student about his or her unique contribution to the group. Surprise the students with refreshments, and allow yourselves to enjoy the progress the students have made.

AFFIRMATION

Involve the group in a final affirmation. Stand and join in a circle with the students holding hands. Go around and have each student share something he or she liked or appreciated the best about being in the group. Begin the affirmation yourself: "What I liked best about being in this group is. . . ."

CLOSING

Remain standing in a circle with the students, holding hands, and lead the group in the closing activity. Tell the students that you're going to make a silent wish for the student on your right. Then, when you've made the wish, gently squeeze the student's hand. The student makes a silent wish for the person on his or her right, then gently squeezes that student's hand, and so on. Continue around the circle until a wish and squeeze come back to you. If necessary, the students can pass the wish in any appropriate way they choose.

Fill out a copy of the Process and Progress Form (page 211) or the Progress Notes (page 213), if you are an experienced leader, as soon as possible after leading the group.

My Personal Yellow Pages

Write the names and the phone numbers of anyone you would like to be in your support system. Include people you can ask for help with schoolwork and people you can talk to if you're having trouble with parents or friends. You can find the numbers of Alcoholics Anonymous, Al-Anon, Alateen, and other community agencies in the phone book yellow pages.

Friends:

_____

_____

_____

_____

Family members:

_____

_____

_____

_____

School personnel:

_____

_____

_____

_____

Community agencies:

_____

_____

_____

_____

Coaches, clergy:

_____

_____

_____

_____

Other important phone numbers:

_____

_____

_____

_____

Group Evaluation Form

1. What did you like best about this group?

_____

_____

_____

_____

2. What did you like least about this group?

_____

_____

_____

_____

3. What do you think should be done differently?

_____

_____

_____

_____

4. What would have made the group more helpful to you?

_____

_____

_____

_____

5. What do you think is the most important thing you learned from this group?

_____

_____

_____

_____

6. What is one good thing that's happened to you because you were in this group?

_____

_____

_____

_____

7. As a result of being in this group, how have you changed?

_____

_____

_____

_____

Certificate Of Recognition

This Certificate of Recognition is awarded to

_____

who has participated in an

Anger Management and Violence Prevention Group.

Congratulations!

_____
LEADER'S NAME

_____
DATE

_____
SCHOOL

Part Four

SUPPORT MATERIALS

The following list describes tools you'll need to develop and support an *Anger Management and Violence Prevention* group in your school. Unless otherwise noted, the support material appears in this section of the manual. Each of the support materials is printed in blackline master form and is suitable for copying on most photocopy machines.

Audience Evaluation Form. This form may be used to evaluate the optional presentation in Session 10. It is designed to provide important feedback regarding the presentation's effectiveness and to serve as a referral source for future groups.

Certificate of Recognition. This award or participation certificate may be photocopied and given to each group member during Session 11. (In Session 11.)

Feeling Wheel. This sheet will aid you in doing a feelings check-in with the students. Each group member will need one copy. The students will use their copy of the Feeling Wheel in Sessions 2-11. (In Session 2.)

Group Evaluation Form. This form is to be used in Session 11 by the students to evaluate their experience in the group. (In Session 11.)

Group Rules Contract. You'll need a copy of this contract for every group member. You can review the contract with prospective group members in the screening interview and then have all group members sign one in Session 1. (In Session 1.)

Handouts. Handouts in each session contain background information, scenarios, activities, and assignments. (In the individual sessions.)

List of Basic Facts. The complete List of Basic Facts is to be copied and stapled to the left inside flap of each student's folder for easy reference.

Parental Consent Letter. Once students have been referred or self-referred to a group, you should seek parental consent by sending parents a copy of a letter like the one provided here.

Process and Progress Form. This form is for you, the group leader. Make 11 copies of the form. After each session, fill out a copy of the form in order to evaluate the session and to keep timely notes on the progress of the group.

Progress Notes. This two-page form is a more condensed version of the Process and Progress Form and is suitable for the more experienced group leader. Simply copy each page and fill out the appropriate section after each group session.

Screening Interview Outline. After referrals are obtained and categorized, the students need to be interviewed individually. The Screening Interview Outline will help you get basic, necessary information about the students and their daily life. If a student seems like an appropriate referral, be sure to explain the group format and content, and show the student a copy of the Group Rules Contract. Make sure the students understand that they must attend every session and be willing to make up missed schoolwork. You might also show them a copy of the Parental Consent Letter that you will send home. If you wish, you can ask the student to take it home.

Self-referral Group Survey Form. This form can be made available to students after they've heard about the support-group program. Use the form in conjunction with a presentation at which available groups are explained to the students (see pages 15-16). When the students fill out the form, explain that if they want to be in more than one group, they should number their choices in priority. Also, make sure the students know that not everyone may be in groups right away and that groups will be offered according to need and time.

This section of the manual also includes a list of professional resources for your enrichment and names and addresses of helping agencies.

Audience Evaluation Form

1. The most interesting thing I learned from this presentation was:

_____

_____

_____

_____

_____

_____

_____

2. How much impact do you think this presentation will have on how you express your anger? (Circle one.)

NONE   SOME   MUCH

In what way?

_____

_____

_____

_____

_____

_____

If you are interested in being in an Anger Management and Violence Prevention group, please sign here. We will keep your name confidential and will contact you about your concern soon.

Name:_____

Homeroom number or teacher's name: _____

List of Basic Facts

1. Violent behavior is intended to do harm. It can be emotional, to express anger, or instrumental, to attain a goal.

2. It is never acceptable to use violent or harmful behavior to express anger.

3. No matter what has influenced a person to be violent, it is his or her responsibility to choose to learn nonviolent and helpful ways to express anger.

4. Feelings aren't good or bad, or right or wrong; they just are.

5. Putting thinking between your feeling and your behavior enables you to choose helpful ways to express feelings.

6. Six ways to express anger are stuffing, withdrawing, blaming, triangling, exploding, and problem solving.

7. Parents usually love their children, even when the parents are choosing to use violent or harmful ways to express their anger.

8. Children usually love their parents, although they may feel hate for the parents if the parents are using violent ways to express their anger.

9. When teens are angry about a problem they can't change, they should:

   1. Accept what they can't change.

   2. Express their anger so they can let it go.

   3. Do something good for themselves.

10. When teens are angry about a problem they can change, they should use their anger to give them the power to make changes in themselves by learning to use problem-solving skills.

11. Five good problem-solving skills to use in anger situations are I statements, reflective listening, kill-them-with-kindness sandwiches, apologizing, and negotiating a compromise.

12. Chunking it down is a good way to start on a long-term goal.

13. The anger management steps help teens put thinking between the feeling of anger and the behavior of anger.

14. The anger management steps are:

   1. Recognize that you're angry.

   2. Accept your anger.

   3. Practice relaxation.

   4. Decide if it's a problem you can't change or a problem you can change.

   5. Think about helpful and harmful ways to express the anger.

   6. Evaluate the consequences.

   7. Choose a best way.

   8. Problem-solve or express your anger in a helpful way.

15. No matter what you believe about the causes, family violence will end only if each person decides never to use violence in his or her own life.

16. To set limits against the use of force in a relationship, speak in a calm, rational way, firmly, and with conviction and determination.

17. The three Cs are:

   1. Teens don't **cause** their parents to use violence to express anger.

   2. Teens can't **control** how their parents express anger.

   3. Teens can't **change** their parents' use of violence to express anger.

18. The four steps teens can take if they live in a violent family are:

   1. Find a safe place for themselves.

   2. Ask an adult for help if the parents are out of control with their violence.

   3. Learn to put thinking between their feeling and their behavior.

   4. Choose to learn nonviolent ways to express their own feelings, and learn to use problem-solving skills in anger situations.

19. Teens can't fix their parents' problems.

20. Teens can take good care of themselves.

21. Teens need to take good care of their bodies, their minds, their feelings, and their choices.

Parental Consent Letter

School address
Date

Dear Parent:

The counseling staff of _____ School is happy to be offering several groups this year. One group will be for anger management and violence prevention.

In the group, we will discuss violence prevention and anger management, and we will teach students problem-solving skills they can use in anger situations. We will also address the stresses and issues for students from violent families. We will show students how to use coping strategies to deal with common stresses, how to set personal goals, and how to develop a support system.

The group will be held during the school day, one day a week, for one class period, during rotating periods, for 11 weeks. As a teaching technique, we like the students to present what they have learned in Session 10; and, as a self-esteem booster, we like to videotape the presentation. We think this group will be very beneficial in helping students cope with their stresses, and we are happy to be able to offer it.

We would like your permission for your child, _____, to participate in this group. If you do give permission, please sign the permission form below and return it to us. Please call us at _____ if you have any questions.

Sincerely,

_____

_____

- -

I give permission for my child, _____, to participate in the *Anger*

Management and Violence Prevention group to be held at _____ School.

| _____ | _____ |
| Name | Date |

Process and Progress Form

Name:_____ Session #:_____

Date:_____

Students Present:_____

_____

_____

_____

Processing the Session

1. What were the objectives of this session #: _____

_____

_____

2. How were they met?_____

_____

_____

3. What concepts must the leader understand to facilitate this session effectively?_____

_____

_____

4. What happened during the session?_____
Highs:_____

_____

Lows:_____

_____

5. What did you see as your strengths as you facilitated this session?_____

_____

_____

6. What changes would you make for next time?_____

_____

_____

Noting Progress:

_____

_____

_____

_____

_____

Progress Notes

Group:_____

Members of Group:_____

_____

Session 1:_____ Date:_____

Notes:_____

_____

_____

Session 2:_____ Date:_____

Notes:_____

_____

_____

Session 3:_____ Date:_____

Notes:_____

_____

_____

Session 4:_____ Date:_____

Notes:_____

_____

_____

Session 5:_____ Date:_____

Notes:_____

_____

_____

Session 6:_____ Date:_____

Notes:_____

_____

_____

Session 7:_____ Date:_____

Notes:_____

_____

_____

Session 8:_____ Date:_____

Notes:_____

_____

_____

Session 9:_____ Date:_____

Notes:_____

_____

_____

Session 10:_____ Date:_____

Notes:_____

_____

_____

Session 11:_____ Date:_____

Notes:_____

_____

_____

Screening Interview Outline

Group: _____

Date: _____

Name: _____

Age: _____

Date of birth: _____

Grade: _____

Do you like school? _____

What kind of grades do you get? _____

What is your behavior like in school? _____

Home address: _____

_____

_____

Phone: _____

Who lives in the house? _____

If your parents are divorced, where do they live? _____

Do you visit the divorced parent who lives somewhere else? _____

What do you do after school? _____

_____

Typical daily schedule: _____

Hobbies, sports, clubs: _____

_____

What are your strengths? _____

What are your weaknesses? _____

What do you want to do when you get older? _____

What are the stresses in your life? _____

_____

Self-referral Group Survey Form

Dear Student:

The Pupil Services Staff of _____ School is pleased to be able to offer groups to the students of _____

These groups will meet for 5 to 11 weeks, for one class period, during the school day, rotating class periods. We offer groups on many different subjects and we hope you will be interested in joining.

Please put an "X" on the group or groups you would like to join. If you are interested in more than one group, please number them in priority, with one being the highest.

_____ **Changing Families Group** *(for students from separated, divorced, or single-parent families, or from a stepfamily)*

_____ **Loss Group** *(if someone close to you has died)*

_____ **Concerned Persons Group** *(if you have concerns about someone's use of alcohol or other drugs)*

_____ **Anger Management Group** *(if you or someone close to you uses harmful ways to express anger)*

Name_____

Teacher or room number _____

We will meet with students individually before starting the groups.

_____

Guidance Counselor or School Social Worker

References And Suggested Readings

Bailey, R. H., ed. 1976. *Violence and Aggression.* New York: Time-Life Books.

Beattie, M. 1987. *Co-dependent No More.* San Francisco: Harper/Hazelden.

Black, C. 1981. *It Will Never Happen to Me.* Newport Beach, CA: ACT.

Brinegar, J. 1992. *Breaking Free from Domestic Violence.* Minneapolis: CompCare Publishers.

Cicchetti, D., and V. Carlson, eds. 1989. *Child Maltreatment: Theory and Research on the Causes and Consequences of Child Abuse and Neglect.* New York: Cambridge University Press.

Cicchetti, D., and P. W. Howes. 1991. "Developmental psychopathology in the context of the family: Illustrations from the study of child maltreatment." *Canadian Journal of Behavioral Science.* 23: 257-81.

Coleman, J. C., and L. Hendry. 1990. *The Nature of Adolescence.* New York: Routledge.

Crime in the United States, 1991: Uniform Crime Reports. Federal Bureau of Investigation, U.S. Department of Justice, Washington, D.C. 20535.

Crittenden, P. M., and M. D. S. Ainsworth. 1989. "Child maltreatment and attachment theory," in Cicchetti and Carlson, eds., *Child Maltreatment: Theory and Research on the Causes and Consequences of Child Abuse and Neglect.* New York: Cambridge University Press (pp. 432-63).

Davis, D. 1984. *Something Is Wrong at My House.* Seattle: Parenting Press.

_____. 1986. *Working with Children from Violent Homes.* Santa Cruz, CA: Network Publications, ETR Associates.

Dobash, R. E., and R. Dobash. 1979. *Violence Against Wives.* New York: Free Press.

Erikson, E. H. 1968. *Identity: Youth and Crisis.* New York: W.W. Norton.

Friel, J., and L. Friel. 1988. *Adult Children: The Secrets of Dysfunctional Families.* Deerfield Beach, FL: Health Communications.

Gabarino, J. 1989. "Troubled youth, troubled families: The dynamics of adolescent maltreatment," in Cicchetti and Carlson, eds., *Child Maltreatment. Theory and Research on the Causes and Consequences of Child Abuse and Neglect.* New York: Cambridge University Press (pp. 685-706).

Gelles, R. J., and M. A. Straus. 1988. *Intimate Violence.* New York: Simon & Schuster.

Gravitz, H. L., and J. D. Bowden. 1985. *Recovery: A Guide for Adult Children of Alcoholics.* New York: Simon & Schuster.

Jaffe, P. G., D. A. Wolfe, and S. K. Wilson. 1990. *Children of Battered Women.* Newbury Park, CA: Sage Publications.

Kalter, N. 1990. *Growing Up with Divorce.* New York: Free Press.

Kaufman, J., and E. Zigler. 1989. "The intergenerational transmission of child abuse," in Cicchetti and Carlson, eds., *Child Maltreatment: Theory and Research on the Causes and Consequences of Child Abuse and Neglect.* New York: Cambridge University Press (pp. 129-50).

Leite, E., and P. Espeland. 1987. *Different Like Me.* Minneapolis: Johnson Institute.

Lerner, H. 1985. *The Dance of Anger.* New York: Harper & Row.

Lewis, D. O., C. Mallouh, and V. Webb. 1989. "Child abuse, delinquency, and violent criminality," in Cicchetti and Carlson, eds., *Child Maltreatment: Theory and Research on the Causes and Consequences of Child Abuse and Neglect.* New York: Cambridge University Press (pp. 707-21).

McGinnis, E., and A.P. Goldstein. 1984. *Skill-streaming the Elementary School Child.* Champaign, IL: Research Press.

Moyer, K. E. 1987. *Violence and Aggression: A Physiological Perspective.* New York: Paragon House Publishers.

Neidig, P. H., and D. H. Friedman. 1984. *Spouse Abuse: A Treatment Program for Couples.* Champaign, IL: Research Press.

Reiss, A. J., and J. A. Roth, eds. 1993. *Understanding and Preventing Violence.* Washington, D.C.: National Academy Press.

Saunders, A., and B. Remsberg. 1984. *The Stress-Proof Child.* New York: Holt, Rinehart & Winston.

Schaefer, D. 1987. *Choices & Consequences.* Minneapolis: Johnson Institute.

Schmidt, T. M. 1993. *Changing Families: A Group Activities Manual for Middle and High School Students.* Minneapolis: Johnson Institute.

Schmidt, T. M., and T. Spencer. 1991. *Della the Dinosaur Talks about Violence and Anger Management.* Minneapolis: Johnson Institute.

_____. 1991. *Peter the Puppy Talks About Chemical Dependence in the Family.* Minneapolis: Johnson Institute.

_____. 1991. *Tanya Talks About Chemical Dependence in the Family.* Minneapolis: Johnson Institute.

_____. 1991. *Thomas Barker Talks About Divorce and Separation.* Minneapolis: Johnson Institute.

Stacey, W. A., and A. Shupe. 1983. *The Family Secret.* Boston: Beacon Press.

Stordeur, R. A., and R. Stille. 1989. *Ending Men's Violence Against Their Partners.* Newbury Park, CA: Sage Publications.

Wegscheider-Cruse, S. 1980. *Another Chance: Hope and Health for the Alcoholic Family.* Palo Alto, CA: Science and Behavior Books.

Weisinger, H. 1985. *Dr. Weisinger's Anger Work-Out Book.* Syracuse, NY: Evaluation Research Associates.

Wolin, S., and S. Wolin. 1993. *The Resilient Self.* New York: Villard Books.

Zevin, Jack. 1973. *Violence in America: What Is the Alternative?* Englewood Cliffs, NJ: Prentice-Hall.

Resource Materials

The following materials are available from Hazelden. To order, call toll-free (United States or Canada): 1-800-328-9000

Curricula/Books

Bell, Peter. *Growing Up Black and Proud: Preventing Alcohol and Other Drug Problems Through Building a Positive Racial Identity* (A Curriculum for African-American Youth, Grades 9-12)

DeMarco, John. *Peer Helping Skills Program for Training Peer Helpers and Peer Tutors.*

Fleming, Martin. *Conducting Support Groups for Students Affected by Chemical Dependence: A Guide for Educators and Other Professionals.*

_____. *101 Support Group Activities for Teenagers Affected by Someone Else's Alcohol/Drug Use.*

_____. *101 Support Group Activities for Teenagers at Risk for Chemical Dependence or Related Problems.*

_____. *101 Support Group Activities for Teenagers Recovering from Chemical Dependence.*

_____. *Take Charge of Your Life: What to Do When Someone In Your Family Has a Drinking or Other Drug Problem.*

Freeman, Shelley MacKay. *From Peer Pressure to Peer Support: Alcohol and Other Drug Prevention Through Group Process* (A Curriculum for Grades 7-8).

_____. *From Peer Pressure to Peer Support: Alcohol and Other Drug Prevention Through Group Process* (A Curriculum for Grades 9-10).

_____. *From Peer Pressure to Peer Support: Alcohol and Other Drug Prevention Through Group Process* (A Curriculum for Grades 11-12).

Jesse, Rosalie Cruise. *Healing the Hurt:*

Rebuilding Relationships with Your Children.

Johnson, Vernon E. *Intervention: How to Help Someone Who Doesn't Want Help.*

Lawson, Ann. *Why Kids Join Gangs.*

Leite, Evelyn, and Pamela Espeland. *Different Like Me: A Book for Teens Who Worry About Their Parents' Use of Alcohol/Drugs.*

Moe, Jerry, and Peter Ways, M.D. *Conducting Support Groups for Elementary Children K-6.*

Potter-Efron, Ron. *How to Control Your Anger (Before It Controls You).*

Remboldt, Carole. *Good Intentions, Bad Results: A Mini-program about Peer Enabling.*

Schaefer, Dick. *Choices & Consequences: What to Do When a Teenager Uses Alcohol/Drugs.*

Schmidt, Teresa. *Changing Families: A Group Activities Manual for Middle and High School Students.*

Schmidt, Teresa, and Thelma Spencer. *Building Trust, Making Friends: Four Group Activity Manuals for High-Risk Students.*

> *Della the Dinosaur Talks About Violence and Anger Management* (Grades K-6).

> *Peter the Puppy Talks About Chemical Dependence in the Family* (Grades K-6).

> *Tanya Talks About Chemical Dependence in the Family* (Grades 6-8).

> *Thomas Barker Talks About Divorce and Separation* (Grades K-6).

Wilmes, David J. *Alcohol Is a Drug, Too.*

_____. *Parenting for Prevention: A Parent Education Curriculum—Raising a Child to Say No to Alcohol and Other Drugs.*

_____. *Parenting for Prevention: How to Raise a Child to Say No to Alcohol/Drugs.*

Zarek, David, and James Sipe. *Can I Handle Alcohol/Drugs?: A Self-Assessment Guide for Youth.*

Films/Videocassettes

Another Chance to Change: A Teenager's Struggle with Relapse and Recovery. Color, 30 minutes.

Choices & Consequences: Intervention with Youth in Trouble with Alcohol/Drugs. Color, 33 minutes.

Dealing with Anger: A Violence Prevention Program for African-American Youth. Color, 52 minutes.

Different Like Me: For Teenage Children of Alcoholics. Color, 31 minutes.

Good Intentions, Bad Results: A Story About Friends Who Learn That Enabling Hurts. Color, 30 minutes.

Kids at Risk: A Four-Part Video Series for Middle School Children:

1. *Covering Up for Kevin,* Color, 18 minutes.

2. *Blaming Kitty,* Color, 17 minutes.

3. *An Attitude Adjustment for Ramie,* Color, 15 minutes.

4. *Double Bind,* Color, 15 minutes.

Land of Many Shapes. Animated, Color, 12 minutes.

A Story About Feelings. Animated, Color, 10 minutes.

Tulip Doesn't Feel Safe. Animated, Color, 12 minutes.

Twee, Fiddle and Huff. Animated, Color, 16 minutes.

Resources for Help

CENTER FOR THE PREVENTION OF SEXUAL
& DOMESTIC VIOLENCE
1914 N. 34th Street, Suite 105
Seattle, WA 98103
206-634-1903

CENTER FOR WOMEN POLICY STUDIES
2000 P. Street, N.W., Suite 508
Washington, D.C. 20036
202-872-1770

FAMILY RESEARCH INSTITUTE
University of New Hampshire
128 Horton Social Science Center
Durham, NH 03824
603-862-2761

FAMILY VIOLENCE & SEXUAL ASSAULT
INSTITUTE
1310 Clinic Drive
Tyler, TX 75701
903-595-6600

HAZELDEN
15251 Pleasant Valley Road
Center City, MN 55012
651-213-4000 or 800-328-9000
www.hazelden.org

NATIONAL CENTER ON
CHILD ABUSE AND NEGLECT
CLEARINGHOUSE ON CHILD ABUSE
AND NEGLECT INFORMATION
P.O. Box 1182
Washington, D.C. 20013-1182
703-385-7565 or 800-394-3366

NATIONAL CLEARINGHOUSE FOR
THE DEFENSE OF BATTERED WOMEN
125 S. 9th Street, Suite 302
Philadelphia, PA 19107
215-351-0010

NATIONAL COUNCIL ON CHILD
ABUSE AND FAMILY VIOLENCE
1155 Connecticut Avenue, N.W., Suite 400
Washington, D.C. 20036
202-429-6695

NATIONAL CRIMINAL JUSTICE REFERENCE
SERVICE
1600 Research Boulevard
Rockville, MD 20850
800-851-3420